The Day All
Stars Came Out

ALSO BY LEW FREEDMAN
AND FROM McFARLAND

*Hard-Luck Harvey Haddix and the
Greatest Game Ever Lost* (2009)

*Early Wynn, the Go-Go White Sox
and the 1959 World Series* (2009)

The Day All the Stars Came Out

Major League Baseball's First All-Star Game, 1933

LEW FREEDMAN

McFarland & Company, Inc., Publishers
Jefferson, North Carolina, and London

LIBRARY OF CONGRESS CATALOGUING-IN-PUBLICATION DATA

Freedman, Lew.
    The day all the stars came out : Major League baseball's
first all-star game, 1933 / Lew Freedman.
        p.   cm.
    Includes bibliographical references and index.

    ISBN 978-0-7864-4708-4
    softcover : 50# alkaline paper ∞

    1. All-Star Baseball Game — History.   I. Title.
    GV878.F74   2010
    796.357'64097309043 — dc22   2010025425

British Library cataloguing data are available

Front cover: (left to right) Babe Ruth, Lou Gehrig, young fan
Edwin Diamond and Al Simmons at the first All-Star game.

Manufactured in the United States of America

*McFarland & Company, Inc., Publishers
    Box 611, Jefferson, North Carolina 28640
    www.mcfarlandpub.com*

Table of Contents

Introduction

As soon as they heard the idea, almost everyone said, "Of course." And many said, "Why didn't I think of that?"

Arch Ward, the energetic and entrepreneurial sports editor of the *Chicago Tribune*, moved between worlds far larger than those of sports and journalism. With an imagination that saw well beyond the boundaries and horizons of either, Ward was a visionary. Just because something hadn't been done, there was no reason why it couldn't be done in the future. Just because something didn't exist didn't mean Ward's persuasiveness could not coax it into reality. His mind was fertile, brimming with ideas, and if his pen was not always as literary as the best in his game, it was convincing.

Backed by the power of the Midwest's largest and most influential newspaper, Ward's words did not sing, but they could sell. The *Chicago Tribune*, the fiefdom of Colonel Robert McCormick, with its far-flung bureaus across Europe and Asia, was a booster of its hometown. McCormick liked to flex his muscles and was proud that his product carried the nickname "World's Greatest Newspaper."

Founded in 1833, Chicago planned to celebrate its 100th birthday with a World's Fair bearing the theme "A Century of Progress Exposition." Despite the gloom of the Depression that settled upon the United States, which certainly did not spare Chicago the largest community in the Midwest was going to take note of this special occasion and throw a party of magnificent proportions.

Mayor Ed Kelly had McCormick's ear and one day whispered a wish into it. Kelly suggested that as part of this World's Fair, it would be worthwhile to develop a unique sporting event for entertainment purposes. The notion appealed to McCormick, and he conveyed the thought to Ward.

1

Ward did not scratch out lists with pencil and paper, pondering one idea and discarding it. Immediately, he concluded that the best event to fit the bill was a one-time major league all-star game pitting the finest players from the National League against the top talent in the American League.

That Ward should swiftly decide on a baseball event to shine in the spotlight of the World's Fair was not surprising. Born December 27, 1896, as Archibald Burnette Ward in the small farming community of Irwin, Illinois, he became a baseball fan at an early age. He was particularly fond of the Chicago White Sox. As a youngster Ward felt he was destined for the major leagues, but considerable doses of reality spiked that ambition. Ward never possessed an athletic build, was not a fleet runner, and could not see very well. He transferred his aspirations to becoming a sportswriter, where his big dreams were not hemmed in and his great vision overcame the handicap of poor eyesight ... and not only with wire-rim glasses.

For most scribes, entree to the games of their choice, banter with the famous athletes of the times, and the chance to focus their wit and word selection with their minds to produce gilded prose was satisfaction enough. Ward was 28 when he joined the *Tribune* as a writer. He was no Grantland Rice, no Westbrook Pegler, who would charm the reader with brilliantly crafted stories and columns. He was a man of greater ambition. He wanted to run the whole show, become the sports department chief. He achieved that goal five years later in 1930 and kept the position for a quarter of a century. By the time he gave it up he had put an indelible stamp on the sports world, leaving behind a drastically different sort of legacy than the other sports journalists of his era.

Ward never finished college because he was busy becoming the sports editor of the *Dubuque Telegraph-Herald* in Iowa. He did graduate from the hinterlands when he assumed a public relations position for the University of Notre Dame. Most of his assignment required drawing attention to football coach Knute Rockne and his Fighting Irish eleven. This was a role Rockne made easy for Ward by overseeing teams that always contended for the national championship.

Ward was a two-year PR man for the greatest college football team in the land — Notre Dame won every game during those two seasons — including the 1920 campaign that featured the death of halfback George Gipp. This was the genesis of the famous "Win one for the Gipper" line that passed into Notre Dame and sports lexicon.

The 1920s have been pronounced and summarized as "The Golden Age of Sport" in the United States. Babe Ruth became a folk hero by walloping home runs. Bobby Jones became a legend by winning golf tournaments. Red Grange became "The Galloping Ghost" for scoring touchdowns. And Arch Ward returned to the newspaper business as sports editor of the *Rockford* (Illinois) *Morning Star*. He was stationed a little more than an hour's hop from Chicago, which he regularly visited. Ward sampled the bigtime and he liked the taste. For him, it was a lure as sweet as chocolate.

When Ward gave notice to his Rockford editor that he was leaving the *Morning Star* for the bright lights shining in the City of Big Shoulders, he said, "I think I can be a big fish in a big pond."[1] He was right.

"The Golden Age of Sport" was a by-product of the Roaring Twenties. Chicago was not Broadway, but it was "the second city," and one with two major league baseball teams — Ward's favorite White Sox of the South Side and the Cubs of the North Side.

Ward began his new job in January of 1925, the year the still-looming, neo-gothic Tribune Tower that is an icon of Michigan Avenue opened. Thinking as grandly as ever, McCormick commissioned a contest in 1922 that sought proposals from architects worldwide to build a fabulous structure to house his newspaper. There were 260 entries and a New York firm won the design competition.

The *Tribune* and Ward entered a new universe together in 1925. By 1930, Ward was the sports editor, king of his corner, friend to McCormick, and empowered in 1933 to invent, create and establish an attention-getting publicity-generating, memorable sports event as a companion jewel to the World's Fair. It took little mulling and minimal brainstorming for Ward to initiate a plan. He saw clearly enough that baseball was the answer to his editor's plea. He believed baseball, as the National Pastime, would be the best representative of sport as part of a world-class presentation.

There was no cable television showing baseball games from every major league park to every corner of the country. In fact, baseball was not even televised then. Radio was a newfangled deal, not yet entrenched in the sport. Except in the cities where two big-league clubs resided (Boston, Chicago, New York, Philadelphia and St. Louis), only the privileged fans who gained entry to a World Series game ever got to see players from a different league in the flesh. Most of the knowledge about players of the day was brought forth by daily newspapers and the *Sporting News*.

An all-star game was a unique way to bring together in one place baseball's best players from both leagues for an exhibition. Ward thought he had a winner. McCormick backed the suggestion. Now all Arch Ward had to do to make it a reality was to sell his baseball extravaganza to the notoriously conservative leadership of major league baseball.

1

The First All-Stars

There was historical precedent, for there had been all-star contests of one kind or another before. For all the credit due Arch Ward as a promotional genius and for bringing the proposal of an all-star game to be played between National League and American League players to the public forefront, the idea was not *sui generis*. He was the salesman with the big mouth and the big stick in the form of the *Chicago Tribune* behind him. But he did not invent the wheel.

The mysterious death of Win Mercer is linked to the first gathering of all-stars in formal games in December 1902. George Barclay Mercer, according to the *Baseball Encyclopedia*, but also referred to as "Winifred" or "Winnie," was a right-handed pitcher born on June 20, 1874, in Chester, West Virginia, and raised in East Liverpool, Ohio. He reached the majors in 1894 with the original Washington Senators, then of the National League, and posted a 17–23 rookie mark. In a nine-year career, Mercer also represented the New York Giants, Washington in the American League, and the Detroit Tigers, and compiled a record of 132–164. His finest season featured a 25–18 mark with the Washington Nationals in 1896.

The National League was founded in 1876. The American League came into existence in 1901. The new league was the outgrowth of the Western League and shepherded to big-league status by Ban Johnson. Originally dismissed as an upstart competitor by National League officials, the American League raided rosters to establish credibility. Soon enough the "junior circuit" showed it had staying power, and peace was declared. The first World Series, between the National League's Pittsburgh Pirates and the American League's Boston franchise, forerunner of the Red Sox, was conducted in 1903.

In late 1902, after the conclusion of the regular season, groups of All-

American and All-National squads barnstormed around the country west of the Mississippi River on an exhibition tour. During that era — and for another half-century — the western-most major league team was based in St. Louis. As a treat for a baseball-mad country that in the days prior to radio and television received word about the game's biggest stars only through newspapers, the tour was designed to enrich the players in the off-season and show them off in the flesh to cities and towns in the hinterlands.

Twenty-two big leaguers signed on for a tour that would roam the West by train, eight of them accompanied by wives and children. A photograph featuring 21 of the players (pitcher Addie Joss arrived later) was snapped in Kansas City. Among those traveling were such luminaries as Jesse Tannehill, "Wee" Willie Keeler, Fielder Jones, Jake Beckley, Sam Crawford and Jack Chesbro, who in 1904 would win 41 games, the most ever recorded in a season. Win Mercer was also pictured. Around the same time the tour was hitting the rails in November, the Detroit Tigers announced that Mercer would become their manager for the 1903 season. First, however, he had other duties to fulfill as treasurer of the all-star series, and as a pitcher for the Americans.

At his best, Mercer showed evidence of being a solid, all-around player. In 1897, a year after his 25-win season, Mercer's throwing mark was 21–20. He pitched in a National League–leading 47 games that year. When Mercer wasn't pitching, he often played shortstop or third base for his club. Averaging nearly 200 at-bats a year, he compiled a lifetime batting average of .293.

The all-stars roamed the land. They traveled in a private rail car, following the sun and warmer temperatures as 1902 faded and 1903 began. There were stops in El Paso, Texas, Los Angeles, Sacramento, and San Francisco, among other locales. A story in an El Paso newspaper took note of the "gaudy costumes" worn by the players. The American League players wore "white shirts and socks with blue stars in the latter, and red coats and trousers, and the Nationals wearing uniforms of black and orange."[1] The ballplayers seemed suitably attired for Halloween.

Mercer was the custodian of the cash from the tickets sold for the exhibitions, but he was nearly taken for more than $5,000 in proceeds while in Sacramento, according to a tale reported in the *Sporting Life* in late December. It seems while the teams were playing a game at Sacramento

Park in the California state capital, a clever thief attempted to rob the ballplayers of their money by sending a messenger to the hotel with a letter asking the clerk to hand over certain envelopes in the safe. The letter was signed "Winnie Mercer," but was a forgery.

The clerk was fooled and handed over an envelope that contained railroad tickets, not cash. The bold swindler tried again 15 minutes later with a second message asking for "the other envelope" belonging to pitcher Addie Joss. The hotel worker was suspicious of these peculiar requests and upon investigation discovered that the letters were not legitimate. The headline on the report read, "Mercer's Luck: The Treasurer of the Base Ball Tourists Narrowly Escapes Being Mulcted of All the Velvet."[2]

Mercer might have been better off if the ruse had succeeded. In Los Angeles, the pitcher soon-to-turn manager found the grounds of the local race tracks to be irresistible. Convinced he was a born winner, Mercer wagered heavily on the ponies. Later, it became obvious his faith was misplaced; he had bet too heavily.

The all-stars were out West well into January, still keeping busy with their slate of exhibitions. The team was staying at the Langham Hotel, but on the night of January 11, 1903, Mercer took up residence at the Occidental Hotel in San Francisco. He registered with a false name, George Murray, and gave his hometown as Philadelphia. Mercer, notwithstanding prospects of a new leadership role in baseball with the Tigers come spring training, committed suicide in his hotel room that night or early the next day. The date of his death was declared January 12. He was 29 years old.

It was swiftly established that Mercer killed himself by asphyxiation. Mercer turned a gas jet that was hooked up to a long rubber tube up full blast, and then lay down in bed in his night clothes. Mercer covered up his head with his coat and vest, and placed the other end of the tube in his mouth. His body was discovered by a hotel watchman who smelled gas, and upon receiving no answer to his pounding on the door, broke it down.

Initial newspaper reports from the scene claimed that Mercer had been despondent and suffering from a debilitating lung ailment. One obituary noted that Mercer "got up a party" of all-star tourists for the trip that brought him to the end of his life in Northern California. It was also reported that Mercer "was considered nervous and high strung, but this aided him rather than obstructed him in his work. He was companionable and very popular both on and off the ball-field. Mercer's home was in Ohio, and he is said to have been very well off."[3]

Perhaps not as well off as generally thought by some, however. While players Addie Joss and Richard Harley, who accompanied Mercer's body across the country by train, stated that the accounts from the tour were accurate, with no shortfalls, a rumor started that receipts belonging to the teams were $2,000 shy. Some said that Mercer's plunge at the race track in Los Angeles was the likely culprit.

On January 14, the *Chicago Tribune* apparently was the first news organization to report on the possibility of the ledgers being askew and the tour finances off by $2,000. "It is said he was short $2,000 or more of the funds of the All-American and National teams of which he was treasurer. While Mercer's friends will not admit he was a defaulter he had been gambling heavily, it is said, and apparently saw no way to make the deficit good."[4]

Mercer wrote several farewell letters that he left behind in his hotel room. One stated flatly that "Winnie Mercer has taken his life." Another contained information on his finances, indicating he did not owe anyone any money. That was at odds with the belief that he had at least borrowed a certain amount of cash to play the horses.[5] A friend named Tip O'Neill was the intended recipient of one letter in which Mercer warned, "Beware of women and a game of chance."[6]

Mercer also wrote to his mother, whom he supported with monthly checks, asking her forgiveness for taking his life. "Dear mother, I must say goodbye forever," he wrote. "Say goodbye to each of my brothers and sisters."[7] Mercer had a fiancée named Martha Porter back in Liverpool, Ohio, where he grew up, and he wrote to her, as well. Before the all-stars split up, they played one final exhibition game in San Francisco, raising $1,500 to be given to Mercer's mother.

In the East, Mercer's relatives and friends took exception with some details of the investigation surrounding his death. They said he was a happy man with no reason to kill himself. His mother said Mercer never signed his letters "Winnie," and she did not believe he wrote them. "Friends who have known him from boyhood declared that he was the last man whom they would think likely to take his own life," one magazine reported. Grief-stricken and frustrated by the circumstances, Mercer's mother wired a telegram to the San Francisco chief of police professing the opinion that he probably had been murdered. Besides the strange signatures, she said, a reference to sisters in the letter addressed to her made no sense because Mercer had no sister, only five brothers. She suggested that the incident some weeks earlier in Sacramento when a mysterious embezzler sought to raid the team funds from the hotel safe might have some bearing on Mercer's demise.[8]

When Mercer was buried in Ohio in late January, hundreds of mourners went to the cemetery. If there had been any momentum for continuing the investigation looking for a murderer, it had been spiked by the revelation that Mercer purchased the rubber hose earlier in the day on which he died. The Cororner's Jury in San Francisco ruled his death a suicide on January 22.

The contents of the letter left for Mercer's fiancée had remained secret until some of the contents were printed following the funeral. "The act I am about to commit is simply terrible, but I cannot help it, dearie. I am to blame, nobody else. So I am going to face it as rigid as I have many wrong acts. Please forgive me, my dear Martha."[9] Presumably, Mercer then turned up the gas.

It was a deadly, unfortunate, depressing conclusion to a tour conceived in good cheer for the first group of American League and National League all-star players.

No one could foresee that one of the principles among the Mercer all-star tourists would be the integral figure when a fresh group of all-stars gathered in 1911 to play the closest thing to another all-star game. Once again, death and loss would be involved in the contest, though in a far different manner.

Adrian C. "Addie" Joss, the brilliant pitcher who had traveled with Mercer's teams, was at the core of the genesis of the next event. Joss, a 6' 3", 185-pound right-handed hurler, was born in Woodland, Wisconsin, the son of a cheesemaker, on April 12, 1880. He broke into the majors with the Cleveland Bronchos, as they were known before becoming the Indians, in 1902 and posted a 17–13 record. It was a promising if not magnificent start. By 1905, Joss was a 20-game winner for the first time. It was also the first of four straight 20-victory campaigns, including a career-best 27–11 season in 1905.

Over nine years, all with Cleveland, Joss collected 160 wins against 123 losses, a winning percentage of .623. He twice led the American League in earned run average, including a microscopic 1.16 ERA in 1908, and his career earned run average was a stupendous 1.89. Six times Joss completed seasons with an ERA under 2.00.

The flame throwing Joss pitched a perfect game in 1908, needing just 74 pitches to finish the nine innings in a famous 1–0 pitching duel against "Big Ed" Walsh of the Chicago White Sox. He pitched a second no-hitter in 1910. In a quirk, both of his no-hit games came against the White Sox.

In the spring of 1911, Joss fell ill and was diagnosed with tubercular meningitis. He passed away at the age of 31 on April 14. Joss had completed spring training with Cleveland and the club was headed north to start the regular season when Joss became sick. He collapsed on a field before an exhibition contest and was hospitalized overnight. He was released and promptly saw his health degenerate. Not only was Joss the mainstay of the Cleveland pitching staff, he also was very popular with his teammates. Joss's funeral was conducted in Toledo, Ohio, on April 17. Originally, American League president Ban Johnson ruled that the Cleveland team must play a regularly scheduled game rather than attend Joss's funeral. The Cleveland franchise, at this time called the Naps, withheld permission to skip the game against the Tigers and threatened suspensions and other punishments. The club rebelled and Johnson backed down. "No better man lived than Addie," said Cleveland first baseman George Stovall.[10]

Distressed over Joss's demise and wanting to do something for his family, the Nap players decided to play a special all-star game at Cleveland's home stadium, League Park, as a benefit for Joss's family. Among the star players recruited from the seven other American League teams and who committed to raising funds to help Joss's widow and family were Ty Cobb, Tris Speaker, Sam Crawford, Eddie Collins, Gabby Street, Frank "Home Run" Baker, Walter Johnson, and "Smokey" Joe Wood. Washington Senators field boss Jimmy McAleer volunteered to manage the all-stars.

"The memory of Addie Joss is sacred to everyone with whom he ever came in contact," McAleer said. "The man never wore a uniform who was a greater credit to the sport than he."[11] Johnson, one of the most dominant pitchers in baseball history, expressed his admiration for Joss. "I'll do anything they want for Addie Joss' family," he said.[12]

Among the Cleveland players were Cy Young, "Shoeless" Joe Jackson, and Nap Lajoie. The game was played on July 24, 1911, featuring the All-Stars against the Indians. There was no public address system in use, but

Herman "Germany" Schaefer of the visitors eschewed participation to announce personnel changes on a megaphone.

Some 15,270 fans attended this all-star game, and between the money taken in for tickets (some costing as little as 25 cents) and the request for additional donations, nearly $13,000 was raised. The all-stars bested Cleveland, 5–3. Cobb was forced to wear a Cleveland jersey because his Detroit uniform top was lost on its way to the park. Five players had at least two hits for the winners.

It was a quarter of a century before the Baseball Hall of Fame was established in Cooperstown, New York, and one of the rules for selection into the players' wing was 10 years of major league play. Joss died after nine seasons of competition. In 1978, the Veterans' Committee waived the barrier and voted Joss in. Some 67 years had passed since Joss died.

Although the Joss benefit game was played more than two decades before an official major league All-Star game took place, it made an impact on various minds. George Sisler, a future Hall of Famer, was an 18-year-old in attendance. He later said watching the array of stars all on one field convinced him to become a big league player.

F.C. Lane, editor of *Baseball Magazine*, took up his pen and began agitating for an all-star contest to be scheduled between the leagues. In the July 1915 issue of *Baseball Magazine*, he made his first pitch. Ferdinand Lane, born in 1885, was editor of one of the sport's early influential publications for 27 years.

A man of many interests, later in life, Lane wrote books and poems and circled the earth six times by sea. He was a member of the Polar Club, the National Geographic Society and the National Historical Society, and donated his baseball memorabilia to the Baseball Hall of Fame. Creation of an all-star game caught his fancy. In 1915, when he first wrote about it, Lane called the World Series the greatest event in sport, but said an all-star game would perform a different, notable function.

> [A]n all-star contest between two clubs of the best possible players would exert a more direct appeal onto the public. Such a contest, the real grand opera of baseball, might readily be staged in mid-season, where it would serve not only as the grand scenic display of the year, but stimulate greater interest in the pennant race.[13]

One reason an "all-star contest" would command attention and be popular, Lane argued, was the partisanship of fans that leaned towards either the American League or the National League. "Rivalry is the whole soul of sport," he wrote. "Why do not the magnates give the public a novel treat which it would be very willing to pay for, in bringing together the two teams from its hundreds of players who could give the best possible demonstrations of baseball?"[14]

Lane envisioned baseball cooperating to select experts in each major league city to vote on the best players in each league for the all-star clubs. He suggested that a week immediately after July 4 be set aside to feature a seven-game series of contests pitting the two leagues' best players against one another for bragging rights. Lane also recommended rotating between New York, Chicago and Boston, because those communities produced the best fan support. The public would be enraptured, Lane believed.

The most peculiar aspect of Lane's concept of seven games being played in a week was that regular-season games would be conducted simultaneously, with teams minus their star players. If an all-star series was approved, Lane saw winners all around. "The public would be given a unique display of baseball," he wrote. "The fortunate players would receive, of course, some form of prize money. The magnates would reap a fortune."[15]

Many, if not all, of Lane's proposals were sound. But they never made the transition from the printed page to the playing field through his efforts. They had reposed in mothballs for years and needed a fresh airing and the support of a new booster.

Certainly, Ward was aware of the merits of Lane's suggestions. Lane thought in grand fashion of permanence and a festival of all-star games. Ward had the mandate from Colonel McCormick to employ the *Chicago Tribune*'s clout to create some showcase sporting event, but as a one-time deal. Lane's plans had languished for 18 years. Now the moment was at hand for Ward to tweak, embellish, enhance, or in any way alter the original with his own scheme. He had the platform. All he had to do was win the ear and blessing of those magnates and baseball's top echelon of administrative leaders.

Yes, it was Lane's fundamental plan, but Ward was going to supply the muscle to make an abstract blueprint from a yellowing magazine into a reality.

A World-Class Sport
at a World's Fair

Chicago knew how to do the World's Fair right. The largest city in the Midwest had previous experience in bringing the world to its doorstep to entertain, inform and wow visitors by the millions. In 1893, 40 years earlier, Chicago hosted the World's Columbian Exposition. Timed to recognize the 400th anniversary of Columbus's sail to the New World, the extravaganza was a phenomenal all-around innovative, creative, scientific, show-stopping festival that left visitors gaping, smiling, disbelieving and employing all of their senses to digest the magnitude of the event.

Not only did people, the young and the old, the local, national and international ticket buyers, depart after having a flat-out good time, the Fair made its mark with many firsts that still resonate today. The Ferris wheel made its debut at the 1893 Exposition. So did Cracker Jack, Cream of Wheat, Aunt Jemima pancake mix, Juicy Fruit gum, the first U.S. postal service–produced picture postcards, and the hamburger.

In a gross miscalculation, Fair organizers rejected the inclusion of Buffalo Bill Cody's Wild West Show on the 600-acre grounds. Cody set up his usual western spectacular, with Indians, buffalo, cowboys, horses and wagons next door to the Fair and did a land office business. The Wild West Show was probably the closest thing to a sporting event even loosely connected to that Fair. Even without Buffalo Bill's help, attendance for the Fair approached 27 million.

Baseball was nearing its first quarter century as a professional sport at the time of the Columbian Exposition and the National League was 17 years past creation. The sport's popularity was well established, but its universality was still spreading. It is a reach to note tenuous connections between the 1893 Fair and baseball, but with 20-20 hindsight the stretch can at least be made. Cracker Jack, of course, became a staple of ballpark concessions that continues today. Hamburgers, too, became regular ballpark fare. Juicy Fruit gum was introduced by the same Wrigley family that owned the Cubs for decades and serves as the namesake of Wrigley Field.

In the 40 years since the Columbian Exposition, baseball had grown into a significantly larger presence on the American stage than it occupied in 1893. The claim that it was the National Pastime was routinely expressed and believed. The idea that only uneducated, no-account young men played the game for pay had been put to rest. New ballparks made of concrete and steel arose in the nation's largest cities. Teams were stable in the communities they represented. The American League was here to stay, alongside the older National League. The cast of All-Stars, led by Babe Ruth and his war club of a bat, were well-known throughout the country.

The nation had danced and partied its way through the Roaring Twenties; Ruth was a symbol of that good-time period. He had elevated the home run from a minor aspect of the game to an art form. He possessed a bigger-than-life persona and style, and it was said his ability to clout home runs great distances engendered so much popularity for baseball that the New York Yankees had to build a larger stadium to accommodate demand. Yankee Stadium opened in 1923 and was deemed "the House That Ruth Built."

By 1933, the lively ball era was well underway. Turns out the cranks — or fans — loved to watch home runs and appreciated higher-scoring games more than they did double shutouts. The waves of excitement baseball created across the United States, riding on Ruth's tails, provided every reason for Chicago officials to think that an all-star game would add luster and publicity to the Century of Progress Chicago World's Fair.

The official name of the new Chicago World's Fair was A Century of Progress Chicago International Exposition of 1933. The working theme of the Fair was to show the world the types of scientific developments and progress that had been made since Chicago's founding 100 years earlier. How this applied to baseball was not very clear, though the great Ty Cobb, in the heyday of his long Detroit Tigers career, regularly used the term "scientific game" to describe the style he played during the dead-ball era. In Cobb's mind that was the station-to-station (or base-by-base) advancement for a run, perhaps manufactured on an infield hit, stolen base, a grounder to the right side, and a sacrifice fly. All of that as opposed to a single swat of the bat producing a home run.

The 1893 Fair was held on those 600 acres, spread out on the South Side of Chicago, in the Hyde Park area. The 1933 Fair, conducted on 427 acres, was on the South Side bordering Lake Michigan, but much closer to State Street, Michigan Avenue, and the rest of the core downtown area.

Science was the stated purpose for the Fair, but organizers did not want to turn off families and emphasized that fun could be had in many ways, including at carnival-like events. A carnival was one thing, but the fun-for-all-ages theme also embraced the hard-working male head of the household, perhaps accounting for stripper Sally Rand's act being included on the program. Judy Garland sang at the Fair. Auto manufacturers, playing an increasingly larger role in the shaping of the American economy and lifestyle, displayed new models.

Although only the most optimistic of politicians would baldly make such a claim during the early planning stages, the Century of Progress Exposition was conceived to not cost taxpayers a dime. Decades later, cynicism is generally in the ear of the beholder when assessing such words. But the Fair, which attracted 48.7 million visitors, had an extended run, going months beyond the original schedule, and its original $1 million bond issue taken out in 1929 was paid off by the end of the event.

Popularity of the moment aside, just like the 1893 Exposition, there were lasting segments of the Century of Progress Exposition. This included the Fair's first-place painting, currently owned by the Polish Museum of America, and the All-Star baseball game that in some ways was an afterthought.

Mayor Ed Kelly simply thought adding a sporting event to the World's Fair lineup of activities would enhance "the nerve excitements" at the big show.[1] When summaries are prepared of Kelly's tenure as mayor, his time in politics, or his life in general, there is usually no particular mention of sports, although he did serve on a board that oversaw the construction of Soldier Field, future home of the Chicago Bears football team. Kelly had been Cook County Democratic Committee chairman and chief engineer of the Chicago Sanitary District.

On February 15, 1933, Mayor Anton Cermak was assassinated while riding in an open touring car with President-elect Franklin D. Roosevelt in Miami. Kelly ran for the vacant top city office and won. By that time, the planning for the World's Fair, begun in 1929, was essentially complete. There was little time for Kelly to alter the program at the Fair that was scheduled to start on May 27, 1933. But he suggested to the *Tribune's* Colonel McCormick that adding something with a sports flavor could be popular, and that assignment became Ward's.

This was not a particularly propitious time to be thinking of ways to spend money with grand-scale programs. When Kelly took over as mayor, the City of Chicago was $100 million in debt. While Kelly eventually performed the near-miraculous feat of wiping out that humongous debt, his trimming had not yet begun. A much greater obstacle was the financial hardship caused by the Great Depression. The United States was wallowing in the worst economic crisis of its existence. It was pure good luck for the Century of Progress that the $10 million financing bond was taken out on October 28, 1929, the day before the stock market crash that transformed American society.

By 1933, however, the full effects of the Depression were felt throughout the land. Stunningly high unemployment rates infected the populace. The stock market collapse destroyed the fortunes of businessmen and businesses. Homes were lost. Many Americans were on the edge of starvation. Banks were wiped out, taking their depositors' savings with them. Desperate men rode the rails seeking work as the unemployment rate reached 25 percent throughout the United States.

The day the bottom fell out of the stock market was termed "Black Tuesday." By March of 1933, later analysis showed the United States' economy was at its weakest point. The largest and most devastating depression of the twentieth century had reached its bleakest level. It was not the time to step forward with fresh ideas that involved any type of investment, risk, or expansion.

Yet it was into this environment that Ward inched, trying to sell a conservative audience of baseball administrators on backing a one-time all-star game to coincide with the World's Fair. Sally Rand came cheap compared to filling out the rosters of two baseball teams and luring the best professionals in the country to Chicago in the middle of the summer. Perhaps because he had the instinct of a promoter, Ward could sniff out a major idea and sense it was going to work. He was a baseball fan through and through, but something told Ward he had hit on the right concept immediately when he thought of a National League–American League All-Star game.

While Ward almost certainly was aware of F.C. Lane's articulation of the all-star idea in 1915, he did not view the concept in exactly the same manner. Lane pictured a seven-game all-star series played over a week's time in three cities. Ward envisioned a one-time "Game of the Century" played in Chicago, his town, under the umbrella auspices of his newspaper.

It was not, however, simply up to Mayor Kelly, Colonel McCormick, or World's Fair administrators to decree that there would be a baseball all-star game as part of the Century of Progress. Ward needed baseball's leadership, from Commissioner Kenesaw Mountain Landis down through the league presidents, to back him. After penning his article urging creation of an all-star series, Lane lobbied the presidents of the American and National leagues and team owners to buy into the proposal. (At the time there was no commissioner.) They turned him down.

Perhaps less motivated than Ward, who represented both the clout of his large metropolitan paper, and the specific tie-in to an event that would be the largest in the world during its run, Lane gave up pushing his plan and went on to other stories and ideas. Still, after upstart leagues went by the wayside, the explosions of new ballparks constructed, and the comfortable entrenchment of the sport in the American psyche, baseball officials had no desire to rock the boat. Things were working just fine and they didn't want to change them. If there was going to be an all-star game in the middle of the summer, there would be conflicts with scheduled regular-season games. Who needed that?

Well, Ward did, for one. He wanted to prove to McCormick that he was a can-do guy. And he wanted to prove to himself that he was not only a mere sports editor of a single newspaper, but someone whose influence transcended the written word. Ward wished to show he was a man of action who could make things happen. Yet, as much as anyone with savvy about major league baseball, he knew the administrators and owners could be intransigent. They were conservative by nature, individually and as a group. If there was one thing Ward understood, though, it was the path to the magnates' hearts lay through their wallets. Show them a way they could make money and they were likely to be a much more sympathetic audience. This was definitely a crowd of "What's in it for me?" businessmen.

Once Ward was sure that the best sporting event match with the World's Fair was a major league all-star game (and that didn't take him long), he presented the idea to his patron, McCormick. The colonel signed off on the idea. That was the easy step. Now Ward had to convince baseball's majordomos. It was already April of 1933 and time was short to implement the notion of playing a high-profile all-star game just a few months later.

Before any attempt could be made to sell team owners on their self-interest, Ward had to gain the backing of the commissioner and the presidents of the American and National leagues. He needed allies in high positions.

John Heydler was president of the National League. Elected in 1918 after previously filling in temporarily in 1909, Heydler was not going to be in office long after the first All-Star game was played. He was suffering from a heart ailment and resigned in late 1934. Heydler had been a player, umpire and league official who was even a sportswriter at one point. Heydler worked for the U.S. Bureau of Engraving for a time and supposedly recited "Casey at the Bat" to President Grover Cleveland. In 1929, decades ahead of it becoming reality, Heydler suggested that pitchers not bat and that instead an extra man be inserted into the lineup to hit, making for 10 starters. Heydler had been dead for years when the American League adopted the designated hitter rule that he imagined. Heydler would seem to be open-minded enough to hear out Ward on the proposal for an All-Star game, but Ward chose to present the plan first to American League president Will Harridge.

Harridge did not rise through baseball's ranks to his leadership position. The one-time worker for the Wabash Railroad booked train trips for sports teams and umpires. Then–American League president Ban Johnson liked Harridge's work and hired him to become AL secretary when a vacancy occurred in December 1911. In 1931, Harridge became acting American League president, and only a few months later was elected to a full three-year term. The three years expanded to 27 and he held the position until 1958.

During Harridge's time, the American League office was located on Michigan Avenue, not far from the Tribune Tower and roughly equidistant between Wrigley Field, home of the Cubs, and Comiskey Park, home of the White Sox, if a rider wished to take the red line "L" train. Well liked and admired for his gracious manner as well as his strong backbone when needed, Harridge immediately grasped the value of Ward's plan.

Ward needed a sympathizer. Ranking above Heydler and Harridge was Landis. Landis was chosen as baseball's first commissioner in 1920 after the Black Sox Scandal of 1919 came to light and eight members of the White Sox were accused of fixing the World Series against the Cincinnati Reds to benefit gamblers. A former judge, Landis was traditional in his beliefs and ironclad in his convictions. He was always more inclined to say no than yes and had one-man veto power over just about everything that happened in the sport.

Even if Harridge liked the idea, he had questions. He played devil's advocate for Ward, raising objections about the difficulty of scheduling, the risk of a rainout, and the possibility of financial loss. Fans were hard pressed to come up with even a few dollars to take in a ballgame during the Depression. The idea could flop. What if no one came? There was considerable skittishness.

But McCormick wanted to include a sporting event in the World's Fair. Ward wanted his idea to become reality. This was the biggest stage in the world to exhibit baseball. Didn't these folks understand? Ward countered the skewering of the plan with a stunning offer. If for any reason the All-Star game that was sure to become a big hit somehow lost money, the *Tribune* would cover the costs.

In one swoop, Ward had cleared the table of financial issues. He had eliminated the risk. The only problem for Ward was that he made the offer from a bargaining position of total fiction. He had not cleared his commitment to such a proposed spending of *Tribune* money with McCormick.

Ward spelled out the offer clearly. If the game was rained out or could not be played, the *Tribune* would pick up the tab. If the game was played and did not draw the anticipated number of fans to break even, the *Tribune* would make up the cost differential. It is always best to remember that in all of these discussions there was no mention that the All-Star game could become a permanent fixture on the calendar. The thinking did not expand beyond the one-time Game of the Century concept. Ward loved the sound of those grandiose words. An annual All-Star game was not the subject of debate. You couldn't have a Game of the Century every year, after all.

Ward even put his paycheck where his mouth was. When he returned to the *Tribune* and told McCormick there was interest in playing the All-

Star game but no interest in the midst of the Depression of taking a financial plunge, he informed the head of the newspaper what he had done. Ward admitted putting the full faith and confidence and good name of the *Tribune* out there to guarantee any debt. But in displaying his own utter faith that the All-Star game would be a success, Ward volunteered to surrender his salary to the cause of paying off and committed to working for free in the unlikely case the game failed.

In an era when major league clubs worked their way city to city via train, the All-Star game required careful scheduling. It had to be possible for the players selected to compete to reach Chicago in time to play. Ward did all of the research, studying both the schedules of the railroads and the baseball teams. His investigation showed that there was only one game scheduled to be played on July 6. The Fourth of July in 1933 (as well as now) was a big day in major league baseball. Every team is always in action on the holiday. However, Ward realized that many teams would be on the move right after the Independence Day games. He saw that most of the National League teams were due to train west and most of the American League teams were due to train east. Chicago was the crossroads of major league baseball rail service.

As far as Ward was concerned, all of the pieces fit together neatly. Ward met on April 20 with Harridge, who liked the grand plan. Having Harridge on his side relaxed Ward somewhat. Someone in power could help carry the torch for the game. Harridge pledged to make a presentation to American League owners at their May 9 meeting. The league presidents and the commissioner served at the pleasure of the owners, the true powers in the game.

Ward also tried to win over some National League influences. Philip K. Wrigley was the owner of the Chicago Cubs and didn't like the idea. He felt the true showcase of baseball between the American League and the National League was the World Series, and he did not want the championship tournament to be diminished. Cubs president Bill Veeck Sr. leaned towards Ward's arguments, however, and lobbied Wrigley. Wrigley didn't think much of the All-Star exhibition, but Veeck assured him such a game held in their city would promote local baseball and the Cubs were sure to be a beneficiary. Wrigley signed on.

Heydler, who presided over the eight-team coalition known as the National League, told Ward he was going to poll the eight owners about their feelings. Owners of the St. Louis Cardinals, Boston Braves and New York Giants promptly wrote back to Heydler and said they wanted no part of an all-star game. The Giants thought narrowly, worried about a schedule surrounding the July 6 date that was loaded with doubleheaders. The Cardinals' position was that no one was going to care about an exhibition game in the middle of the season and fans would pass.

The American League owners responded to Harridge's enthusiasm for the all-star game with yea votes. Ward worked the telephones, lining up influential friends of the holdout owners to persuade them to change their minds. The Boston Braves were the final holdout. According to a Ward biography, the *Tribune* sports editor may have bluffed his way into selling the contest to the Braves with a threat. The story goes that Ward telephoned the Braves and said he was prepared to announce the creation of the all-star game the next day — or report that such a game was on the verge of fruition but was being killed because of the stubbornness of the Boston franchise. "We're going to either announce that there is a game, or that we almost had one and didn't because of you," Ward said. "Now can you and the National League stand that kind of publicity?"[2] Not wishing to be viewed as obstructionist, the Braves capitulated.

With all of the owners and both league presidents backing the proposal, what could Landis say? If everyone wanted an all-star game, then so be it. Ward had his all-star game. Now all he had to do with less than two months to the scheduled event was figure out how to put it on.

At the very least Ward had pleased McCormick with approval of stage one. (Who knew how the sometimes-explosive colonel would react if the game actually did lose money?) Ward had done well clicking the tumblers into place on the lock to open the door of the safe, but he had no idea whether or not the hard part of the scheme was over or if it was just beginning. He only knew that the first major league All-Star game was going to be played in Chicago on July 6, 1933. Batter up.

And the Fans Go Crazy

After the chief honchos of major league baseball agreed to the Arch Ward plan to conduct an All-Star game in conjunction with the Century of Progress Exposition, the *Tribune* sports editor made an announcement. The newspaper and his department would oversee the process of an election to select the players for the teams. The *Tribune* would devote the manpower to produce the ballots and count them and would absorb all costs in connection with the voting.

On the surface, this may have sounded generous and magnanimous. However, the process would ensure the election of players would remain under the tight-fisted control of Ward and that the players would be chosen by readers of the *Tribune*. Given the long history of Chicago's iffy reputation of handling political elections, not everyone felt this was a great idea.

Was Ward merely being gracious in stating that his sports department would handle all of the work? Or was that aspect of the All-Star game's creation just one more way that Ward could maintain control of his baby? Or did he simply think that since the *Tribune* had initiated the proposal and guided it through to approval that the paper should reap some benefit in circulation gains?

No matter. There was an instant outcry from other sports editors about their newspapers and readers being excluded. This was now out of the hands of McCormick and Ward. Commissioner Landis intervened and ruled that other newspapers were to be included and allowed to print the ballots. Once that decree was issued, Ward solicited the participation of other papers and 55 wound up printing ballots. Still, election headquarters remained the Tribune Tower under the supervision of Ward.

With the late May approval of the game and the planned July 6 date looming, there was no time to waste in filling out the rosters and promoting the new event. Ward was an idea man, but he was truly in his element when he was on the ground generating interest in one of his ideas. That meant working the telephones, dreaming up fresh angles, and in the case of the new major league baseball All-Star game, promptly giving it a catchy label. This spectacular that baseball fans were being invited to in Ward's mind and prose immediately became "The Game of the Century."

Ward became a human teletype, churning out thousands of words about the upcoming All-Star game. Unheard of one moment, the phrase "Game of the Century" was imprinted on fans' minds virtually overnight. It was repeated so often the line became reminiscent of a jingle that won't go away. Ward wrote so much, so fast, probing for fresh angles daily and pounding the typewriter keys so furiously that it was surprising he still had fingerprints remaining by the time the game was played.

The announcement to the public that one of the grandest baseball games of all time was headed its way was made by Ward in the pages of the *Tribune* on May 19, 1933. The headline read: "Picked Stars of Big Leagues to Play July 6." A sub-head revealed the novel idea "Fans to Name Teams in Tribune Vote." Ward promptly got to the point by explaining what this unique game was all about. "It will bring together the strongest team that can be recruited from the National League against the best that can be assembled from the American League."[1]

The tie-in with the Century of Progress World's Fair was noted, as was the sponsorship of the *Tribune*. It was not clear at that moment if the game would be played at Comiskey Park or Wrigley Field, but it would definitely be held in Chicago.

Ward emphasized that "the best news of all" was that the fans would choose the starting lineups by mailing ballots to the *Tribune*.[2] Many other key details were offered. Each team would have three starting pitchers, with each one likely pitching three innings. The proceeds of the game would go to the Baseball Players' Charity organization and that everyday game prices would be charged. Whether this reflected the lack of confidence by baseball magnates that anyone would want to attend a mere exhibition or not, there was to be no price gouging at the gate. Box seats listed for $1.65, grandstand seats for $1.10, and bleachers for 55 cents.

The story played up an old baseball argument, percolating since 1901. Which league was better, the American League or the National League?

"The game in Chicago July 6," Ward wrote, "will help to clear up this controversy."[3] Previously, the only way to measure league superiority was the results of the World Series. This would be a different type of head-to-head confrontation. The All-Star game, Ward observed, would be "maximum strength against maximum strength. For years baseball fans the country over have been arguing the relative class of the two leagues."[4]

The initial article teased the baseball fan with possible lineups, pointing out that star after star would be in the same batting order. "How would you like to see Gabby Hartnett, Chuck Klein, Lefty O'Doul, Paul Waner, Pie Traynor, Bill Terry, and three or four other equally dangerous hitters in there swinging for the National League?"[5]

As it turned out, baseball fans would like that very much. Ward's instincts were correct. For all of the naysaying by nervous Nellie owners, quite a few people, as Ward and F.C. Lane surmised, were interested in seeing a "meaningless" exhibition played in the middle of the baseball campaign.

Approval was deafening. Fans shouted their huzzahs at the declaration of All-Star intent. Immediate support came from other sports editors. Ward was the man of the hour in baseball. The idea was bigger than Ward and the *Tribune*. The clamor from other newspapers to participate by printing their own ballots was like trying to hold off a tidal wave. *The Sporting News*, the weekly publication that considered itself the Bible of baseball and the last word on matters affecting the sport, unveiled a contest. The fan who wrote the best letter explaining why he made his All-Star choices would win a free trip to the game.

Of course, Ward was one step ahead of *The Sporting News*. After the basic facts about the All-Star game were announced in the *Tribune* on May 19, Ward wrote a May 20 follow-up story. This announced the creation of the newspaper's contest that revolved around the awarding of $500 in prizes. Some $250 of that was to be paid to the fan that came closest to picking the starting lineups of both teams and the starting pitchers, and the use of additional pitchers in the order they were summoned from the bullpen. Two prizes of $100 were earmarked for the voter that came closest to naming the starting lineup and starting pitcher for each league. That left $50 to be distributed at the rate of $1 each to voters that were the most accurate in selecting the entire pitching staffs for each league.

The concept of an All-Star game was so new to the populace that

Ward had to reassure fans these would be big-time rosters. "There will be no makeshift teams placed on the field," Ward wrote. "Both teams insist that only the strongest possible lineups will be employed."[6]

For good measure in this story, Ward quoted Commissioner Landis as throwing his endorsement behind the All-Star game. It seemed a day late. Ordinarily, it would have made sense for Landis to issue commentary on the developments on the day the game was announced. After all, major league baseball was his company. Perhaps this was one time when Landis lay low on purpose, allowing the owners and the league presidents to be front men and accept any blame if the proposal landed with a thud. Then he read which way the wind was blowing and threw his full support behind the plan.

"Pitting the stars of each league against one another is a very worthy undertaking," said Landis in a somewhat stilted statement. "It should enliven interest in baseball, particularly for the hot stove boys, and undoubtedly will set a new record for baseball attendance in Chicago. It is very fitting that such a game should be part of A Century of Progress program. The *Tribune* is to be congratulated for bringing it about. I heartily endorse it."[7]

Upon hearing the original response to the All-Star game idea, Ward may have been wearing a smile as wide as Lake Michigan, but he was taking no chances. A day after he broke the news that there would be such a game, his story announced broad-based support from baseball men whose reactions he had solicited. It was a shrewd move, designed to counter any backlash against the plan. Not only did Landis contribute his thoughts, but Cubs president William Veeck, Sr., White Sox manager Lou Fonseca, Washington Senators manager Joe Cronin, and Rufus C. Dawes, president of A Century of Progress Exposition, all weighed in. They wielded considerable weight and it was all tilted to one side. Essentially, their comments could be summed up as "Bravo, Arch!"

"A great idea," Fonseca said.[8]

Dawes hit upon an aspect of the game that others all mentioned. "The game will give thousands of Exposition visitors from all parts of the country an opportunity they would never get otherwise to see the greatest stars of America's most typical game in action," Dawes said.[9]

Within days Ward was reporting the stampede of other sports editors and their sections to gain the opportunity to distribute ballots in their pages. If not an actual running count announced in the *Tribune*, periodic updates informed readers how many other papers thought the All-Star game was a terrific idea. By May 22, the number of participating newspapers was up to 47, on its way to the final count of 55. The plan was to distribute 8 million ballots.

"America's response has been overwhelming," Ward wrote, saying major league baseball had nothing to fear in terms of its popularly fading.[10]

It was no surprise that newspapers representing the cities of other major league teams were in the forefront in enthusiasm, from the *Boston Herald*, *New York Daily News*, *Washington Star*, *Detroit News* and *Cleveland Plain-Dealer* to the *Pittsburgh Post-Gazette*, *Cincinnati Post*, and *St. Louis Post-Dispatch*. Perhaps more intriguing was the willingness of a large number of newspapers based in cities on the West Coast to be involved even though they were still more than two decades away from having their own clubs. Those papers included the *Los Angeles Times*, *San Francisco Chronicle*, and *Seattle Times*. Following the path blazed by the *Tribune*, many other newspapers ran contests for their own readers to guess the lineups and such, also awarding cash prizes.

The goal was to keep the fan ballots rolling in until a June 25 cutoff. Those competing in the *Tribune* contest and for the free trip to Chicago offered by *The Sporting News* had a midnight June 25 postal deadline to meet as well, and their letters for the contest could not exceed 400 words.

Ward was like an engineer constantly shoveling coal to keep the train running at high speed. He sought any angle to report that would enable him to write a daily story about the upcoming All-Star game. When the presidents of the two leagues reviewed, signed, and returned to Ward a document prepared outlining the particulars of the contest, Ward printed it in its entirety in the *Tribune*.

Only a few days after the announcement of the game's existence, Ward made his first mention of the *Tribune* printing the vote tallies while the voting was still in progress. That was just another way to keep the game in the public eye and to jump-start baseball debate. Ward teased one example from the first ballots received, writing, "It is apparent from the early returns that the keenest rivalry for positions in the big game will center around Lou Gehrig of the Yankees and Jimmie Foxx of the Athletics for first base in the American League."[11]

All of this occurred before it was decided which ballpark to play the game in. Should the host facility be the American League White Sox's Comiskey Park or the National League Cubs' Wrigley Field? The site was determined by a coin flip. At the time the commissioner's office was located in Chicago. AL president Will Harridge attended; NL president John Heydler designated Leslie O'Connor, who was Landis's secretary, to represent his interests. As Ward reported in the May 27 *Tribune* while describing the events, Harridge called heads and the coin came up heads. He also pointed out that the larger Comiskey Park had the potential to produce about $12,000 more in ticket revenue than Wrigley would in the event of a sellout. In Ward's prose, the All-Star game grew by leaps and bounds in importance with each daily report in the *Tribune*. His lead on the coin toss story read, "Comiskey Park will be the site of the game of the century. The location of the greatest attraction in baseball history, scheduled for July 6, was decided by the flip of a coin yesterday...."[12]

Ward never shied away from hyperbole when toasting his game. It was a useful sales technique for the moment, but with the passage of time the first All-Star game turned out to be nearly as important as the scribe made it out to be.

In another of his early comments on the incoming election returns, Ward noted that different areas of the country favored different personnel for the two leagues' lineups. A close race between the Cubs' Lon Warneke and the Giants' Carl Hubbell was in the making for the National League starting pitcher role.

Votes from the outlying precincts kept arriving at election central in the Tribune Tower and Ward dutifully recorded the numbers and reported the trends in the balloting. One story centered upon the fact that A's outfielder Al Simmons had received more votes than Babe Ruth. The curiosity that A's first baseman Jimmie Foxx had received votes at five different positions did not escape Ward's scrutiny, either. Foxx played long enough and dabbled sufficiently enough to appear at five spots on the diamond during his career, but he certainly did not in 1933. Fans must have worried that Foxx would lose out to Gehrig at first base and just wanted to see him somewhere on the team.

"Jimmie Foxx, most valuable player in the league last year, is considered the most versatile man in the game," wrote Ward, perhaps with a bit of tongue in cheek. "He has been placed at first base, third base, second base, catcher, and in the outfield. The fans are obviously trying to get him into the lineup because of his tremendous hitting power."[13]

Although he never hinted at his amusement in his words, Ward seemed to get a chuckle out of the subsequent debating between the leagues over the particulars of the game. Meetings were held to iron out the details and verbal battles ensued over which league should be the home team with its last at-bats, which dugout would be occupied by which team, and whether an American League or National League umpire would rule on balls and strikes from the behind the plate.

"If you think the participants are not taking it seriously," Ward wrote of the All-Star game, "you haven't sat in on conferences where details have been discussed."[14]

AL President Harridge, Ward observed dryly, seemed to conclude that when he won the coin toss to determine the locale of the game, he also won all privileges accruing to the home team. NL President Heydler came out in favor of another coin toss to determine which team got to hit in the bottom of innings. On and on it went, in essentially polite language, but with all points contested.

These bragging rights, at issue for 32 years since the American League came into being, were no small potatoes to the representatives of the majors' two leagues, Ward said. Yes, this All-Star game was an exhibition, but evidence of superiority was at stake.

"It will be more than an exhibition," Ward wrote. "It will be a contest that will give supporters of the winning club something to crow about — until the World Series, at least."[15]

As the time to play ball approached, and as the mail-in ticket purchases flooded the White Sox, it was apparent that a sellout approaching 50,000 fans at Comiskey Park was likely. There was little difficulty selling the roughly 35,000 grandstand seats or the approximately 12,500 box seats. Baseball administrators were pleased about the massive attention focused on their sport but conscious of the Great Depression afflicting so many citizens. They were happy the decision had been made early to hold ticket prices down.

On July 2, it was announced that at last the bleacher tickets, the cheapest seats at 55 cents apiece, would go on sale the next day, just three days before the contest was scheduled to be played. By now, Ward used the phrase "dream game" interchangeably with Game of the Century, perhaps just for variety. He had kept track of where ticket buyers who mailed in their payments were coming from, too, so that he was able to write in the announcement of the bleacher sales that residents of 46 of the then-48 states were coming to Chicago for the game.

"Never has there been a game like this before," he wrote,[16] just in case no one had noticed him previously mentioning that.

It had been stated that there were 2,500 Comiskey bleacher seats, but when the ticket windows were thrown open and seats went on sale, there were 2,250 available. The ducats were sold in 45 minutes, disappearing as quickly as money could change hands, and no sale of standing room tickets was contemplated.

It was a wild scene. Hopefuls lined up the night before the windows opened, camping out in the Comiskey parking lot. There also was concern about scalping, perhaps making it the second-oldest profession. Rules stated that no buyer could purchase more than four tickets. The rapid-fire sale accounted for all remaining tickets, but not all remaining prospective buyers. Hundreds of fans were turned away empty-handed, unable to score tickets.

"The last ticket to the Game of the Century has been sold," Ward wrote. "There will be no more tickets on sale before the game. That's all there is. There isn't any more."[17]

In other words, don't call me for tickets, don't call the White Sox. And definitely don't call White Sox vice president Harry Grabiner, supervisor of the ticket sale. Grabiner, reported Ward, was off to China. China? That may have been a metaphor for how scarce Grabiner intended to make himself and a joke by Ward rather than a genuinely planned vacation by Grabiner.

4

Picking the Team

The ballots poured into the Tribune Tower. Originally, it was announced that 15 players would be selected for each team before the numbers were upped to 18 per team. While the commitment was made to let the fans' opinions reign, a veto power was given to the respective league presidents, Will Harridge of the American League and John Heydler of the National.

If fans ran amok and chose someone based on popularity alone whose statistics did not warrant inclusion among the other stars, the presidents retained the power to intervene. It was much like the Founding Fathers of the United States not really having faith in the judgment of the people and putting the true authority for selecting a chief executive into the hands of the Electoral College. As it turned out, the fans took their responsibility seriously and voted according to form, rewarding the finest ballplayers.

Chicago readers filled in their recommendations for each position on the American and National league teams, clipped them out, and mailed them in. Fans throughout the country did the same, using their local newspapers. As each batch was forwarded to the *Tribune* and counted, Arch Ward dutifully provided updates.

Later, television was established and networks commandeered the airwaves with up-to-the-minute reports of precinct tallies in various states around the country as the nation selected a new president. In a simpler, more technically rudimentary time, Ward revealed the latest voting numbers. He had a monopoly on the information. Without Ward releasing the figures, baseball fans were in the dark about how the election was going. Not that Ward was secretive. He kept pumping out the vote totals, continuously stoking interest in the Game of the Century.

In one article in early June, Ward interpreted the numbers staring him in the face and proclaimed it likely that Lou Gehrig of the Yankees, Charlie Gehringer of the Tigers, Joe Cronin of the Senators and Jimmy Dykes of the Athletics would be the starting American League infield. And much like a ballgame that was a blowout, Ward assessed that Gehrig and Cronin were almost "certain starters" because "they have been given a lead in the nationwide voting which their rivals will be unable to overcome."[1]

From a viewpoint of more than three quarters of a century later, it may seem surprising that Babe Ruth, the Yankee slugger who had single handedly carried the game from the Deadball era into the lively ball era, was not the runaway leader in votes. In the 1920s, as Ruth attracted fans by the thousands to Yankee Stadium as well as to parks around the country with his home-run swing, he was clearly the most popular player in the country.

Kids loved Ruth. He posed with them in newsreels, visited sick children in hospitals, made brash promises that he would hit home runs for them, and entertained all fans with his bigger-than-life personality. When Ruth burped, it was said, much of the nation excused him.

Yet in this poll, Ruth trailed Al Simmons among outfield vote-getters. Being selected to the roster in the first All-Star game was not a lifetime achievement award. The general guidelines were to reward the players who were playing the best during the summer of 1933. Ruth was 38 years old and nearing the end of his career. Fans were beginning to wonder if the big man still had his pizzazz.

Simmons had led the American League in batting with a .390 average in 1932 and was on his way to his ninth of 11 straight seasons hitting .300 or better to start his career. He had been the gem of the Philadelphia Athletics' outfield but was in his first season with the Chicago White Sox. If anyone believed that old Athletics fans of Simmons' or new White Sox fans were stuffing the ballot box, Ward made a point to debunk the notion. "Simmons owes his leadership to the fans of no particular section," Ward wrote. "He has been slightly ahead of Ruth everywhere."[2]

Lifetime accomplishments supposedly shunted to the side or not, an All-Star game conducted with Ruth on the sidelines would have been an embarrassment to the Bambino, and an embarrassment to baseball. Ruth was older and definitely slowing, but he still slammed 34 homers that year, drove in more than 100 runs, and batted .301. Everyone who is accused of being washed up should have such a year. Ruth had accumulated more than 600 home runs in his career to that point. It wouldn't take much prodding to remind fans only in their late 20s to remember that before he came along entire teams did not hit as many four-baggers in a season as Ruth did when setting individual season records, including his mighty 60 in 1927.

When the first tallies came in and Ward revealed that Simmons was the highest vote-recipient for an American League outfield position, some alarm bells might have rung in Manhattan. Yankee manager Joe McCarthy, regarded as one of the greatest managers of all time, began lobbying for his players to be included.

"How about my man Gehrig?" McCarthy said. "You can't leave him off the American League team. He has been in there a long time, you know, hitting homers and fielding beyond reproach." McCarthy then put in a word for Ruth, discussing the likelihood of his election as if it was a foregone conclusion. "Ruth isn't getting around in the field as he once did, but he can still bust 'em and he continues to be baseball's greatest individual attraction."[3]

McCarthy was in the middle of sharing his thoughts with a *Tribune* sportswriter, presumably Ward, when Ruth stopped nearby and injected his feelings into the discussion. He wanted his opinion on the record. "I hope they count me in on it," Ruth said. "The game ought to draw a lot of people."[4]

Ruth may have been aging, but he hadn't tired of performing for throngs of fans. The bigger the crowd, the more likely the ham in Ruth was to come out. When the lights were bright, Ruth was in his element.

Regardless of the voting trends, Ward was on top of every angle. Chicago Cubs pitcher Lon Warneke built an early lead in the balloting for National League starting pitcher, but just when it appeared he might have the slot locked up sentiment began registering for the New York Giants' Carl Hubbell. It was not terribly surprising that the New York vote came in strong for Hubbell. In fact, the ratio was 4–1, as Ward reported it at the end of May. "Warneke vs. Hubbell, Chicago vs. New York," Ward wrote. "That seems to be the story of the principal contest for honors in the nationwide poll to determine the National League's outstanding players...."[5]

Ward couldn't lose. Whenever the slightest nugget of information became known about the All-Star game, it meant free publicity. If the stadium choice was announced, if the umpires were named, if one team made a move in the standings, Ward was there to trumpet it. And always, lest anyone forget it, he referred to the All-Star game as the "Game of the

Century." Sometimes he casually referenced the upcoming event as "the greatest baseball game of all time."

If Colonel McCormick had imagined a windfall of goodwill coming the *Tribune's* way when he first told Ward to invent some kind of sporting event worthy of World's Fair inclusion, he did not say. But he had to be pleased with the early response on Ward's idea. Periodically, when Ward paused for a breath, or ran a pen out of ink, the *Tribune* editorial page took its turn pumping up the volume about the game.

"A smart inspiration in the *Tribune* sporting department will give Chicago, as an incident of the Fair, the baseball game of all time," one editorial said in praise of Ward's creation. "The baseball managements could have found a million reasons why it could not be done, but found every reason why it should be. Hitters who cannot be stopped will face pitchers who cannot be hit. The man who made the invincible sword will meet the man who made the impenetrable armor. Take it any way and it is the game of the century."[6]

By then one might think that the *Tribune* had copyright rights on the phrase. The point made in the editorial, however, was well taken. Since there had never been such a galaxy of stars gathered together with the best hitters going up against the best pitchers, nobody knew what would happen. The veritable immoveable object meets the irresistible force was going to be played out before thousands in a sporting environment. No one could predict the results.

Yet regardless of Ward's label as the "Game of the Century," the All-Star contest was "only" an exhibition. It had no bearing on the league standings, it did not help determine the World Series participants, and it was not going to enrich the players one bit. Presumably, this left pride as the primary motivation for the athletes. Inevitably, a journalist asked a key question, quizzing St. Louis Cardinals second baseman Frankie Frisch if the teams would be going all out. Frisch, it should be noted, was leading the second base voting for the National League by a great margin, making him a legitimate player to ask.

The answer had to please Ward, McCormick, and the powers-that-be in the game more than any other could have. "It will be as hard-fought as any World Series contest," Frisch replied. "The class of each league will be tested for the first time and if you don't think it will be a battle royal, you will be goofy."[7]

Guardian of the game that he was, Ward took note when fan voting seemed poised to pay off for two players who were not having good years. Lefty O'Doul was running third in the National League outfield voting but was hitting just .252. "He never has been brilliant in the field, so if he doesn't improve rapidly in his hitting there seems no solid reason for giving him a place in the greatest game of all time," Ward wrote.[8]

The American League was in the same situation, Ward noted. Earl Averill was running third in the balloting among outfielders despite batting just .276 "which is hardly high enough to warrant a place among a team of all-stars."[9]

Stories like the one when McCarthy talked up Ruth, who made it clear he wanted to play, and one denigrating O'Doul's and Averill's seasons allowed Ward to influence the voting. He was like a school teacher admonishing the class when he saw voting that pushed O'Doul and Averill ahead of men he felt were more deserving. "The fans have apparently been voting on the basis of O'Doul's past accomplishments rather than on his present ability," Ward sniffed.[10]

Although it was not the publication's idea, *The Sporting News'* only constraint in its frequency of touting the All-Star event was the fact that it was a weekly and not a daily publication. As the end of June and the end of balloting approached, *The Sporting News* kept apace of the promotion. "It's Last Inning in the Big Contest for Free Trip to All-Star Game!" read a banner headline in the June 22 issue.

"By the end of this week the fans of this nation will know who will be chosen for the positions on the all-star teams to represent National and American Leagues in the Game of the Century at Chicago, July 6, in connection with the Century of Progress Exhibition."[11] Just another *Tribune* piece by Ward? Not quite. It was the lead paragraph in *The Sporting News*, showing it had bought in completely to the "Game of the Century" theme and the linkage to the World's Fair.

Voting ceased at the end of the third week in June, but mail-in ballots were accepted until June 25. Whatever the actual tally of ballots, Ward announced a rounded-off figure of 500,000. The 55 newspapers outside of Chicago, plus the *Tribune*, had printed 8 million ballots in their sports sections. *The Sporting News* had a winner of its contest. A Philadelphia motorman won the free trip to the game.

Al Simmons, "Bucketfoot," as he was nicknamed because of his peculiar stance in the batter's box, turned out to be the leading vote-getter. Simmons made a fast start and kept his lead, ending up with 346,291 votes. Whether the nudge of Ruth made any difference at all, or later voters concurred with what would seem to be prevailing sentiment that the player who had uplifted the sport on his shoulders after the distressing Black Sox Scandal belonged in the contest, Ruth rallied to total 320,518 votes. He had no reason to feel slighted.

The leading vote-getter in the National League was Philadelphia Phillies outfielder Chuck Klein, who received 342,283 votes. Ward swiftly offered an explanation of how Klein and Simmons could out-poll Ruth. "His failure to lead Simmons and Klein does not necessarily mean that he is losing his popularity," Ward assessed. "This was not a popularity contest. It was an effort to choose the strongest teams that could be recruited from the major leagues."[12]

Both O'Doul and Averill were selected, even if Ward was skeptical of their seasonal relevance. Most players who were voted high in the final totals were chosen. The presidents of the leagues thought carefully before overruling the choice of any position players. Harridge said he was "governed entirely" by the will of the fans.[13]

Heydler did not go along with the fans' support of the third-ranked pitcher, Red Lucas, of the Cincinnati Reds. Lucas, who played 15 seasons, all in the National League, and finished with a 157–135 lifetime record, missed out on his chance at immortality. Well thought of among the fans, he was in the midst of a 10–16 season.

Milking the results for maximum attention, Ward made sure that the American League and National League teams were revealed on separate days. There should have been few surprises in anyone's mind, however, since Ward had been reporting the results as they came in. Still, it was possible for there to be last-minute changes at some positions.

The great national baseball debate orchestrated by Arch Ward and the *Chicago Tribune* had finally concluded. The rosters were revealed.

American League

PITCHERS: Lefty Grove, Philadelphia Athletics; Lefty Gomez, New York Yankees; Wes Ferrell, Cleveland Indians; Oral Hildebrand, Cleveland Indians; Alvin Crowder, Washington Senators.

CATCHERS: Bill Dickey, New York Yankees; Rick Ferrell, Boston Red Sox.

FIRST BASE: Lou Gehrig, New York Yankees; Jimmie Foxx, Philadelphia Athletics.

SECOND BASE: Charlie Gehringer, Detroit Tigers; Tony Lazzeri, New York Yankees.

SHORTSTOP: Joe Cronin, Washington Senators.

THIRD BASE: Jimmy Dykes, Philadelphia Athletics.

OUTFIELD: Al Simmons, Chicago White Sox; Babe Ruth, New York Yankees; Earl Averill, Cleveland Indians; Ben Chapman, New York Yankees; Sam West, St. Louis Browns.

Simmons received the most votes among all players, but Ruth was only the fourth-highest vote-earner on the AL club. Cronin was about 8,500 votes behind Simmons, and Grove followed with 327,242 votes. There was no evidence of difficult decisions being made in the minds of the fans. Each first-place finisher at each position won by a wide margin and even most runners-up had generous margins on others receiving votes.

In what was later institutionalized by rule — and here is where Heydler did some finagling — there was at least one player on the squad from each of the eight AL teams.

National League

PITCHERS: Lon Warneke, Chicago Cubs; Carl Hubbell, New York Giants; Bill Hallahan, St. Louis Cardinals; Harold Schumacher, New York Giants.

CATCHERS: Gabby Hartnett, Chicago Cubs; Jimmy Wilson, St. Louis Cardinals.

FIRST BASE: Bill Terry, New York Giants.

SECOND BASE: Frankie Frisch, St. Louis Cardinals; Tony Cuccinello, Brooklyn Dodgers.

SHORTSTOP: Dick Bartell, Philadelphia Phillies; Woody English, Chicago Cubs.

THIRD BASE: Pie Traynor, Pittsburgh Pirates.

OUTFIELDERS: Chuck Klein, Philadelphia Phillies; Paul Waner, Pittsburgh Pirates; Pepper Martin, St. Louis Cardinals; Chick Hafey, Cincinnati Reds; Lefty O'Doul, New York Giants; Wally Berger, Boston Braves.

The first major league baseball All-Star game was held on July 6, 1933, in Comiskey Park, home of the Chicago White Sox. Players representing the American League (top) and the National League (bottom) posed for team pictures for the occasion. American League players wore their club uniforms, but the NL players wore specially made uniform tops that had "National League" lettered across the front. (Photograph courtesy National Baseball Hall of Fame.)

Warneke did out-poll Hubbell in the long run, with 312,960 votes to the screwball specialist's 299,099. The City of Big Shoulders on the Lake outdid Broadway in Ward's battle of the cities. The top finishers for starting slots at catcher, all of the infield positions, and the top three outfielders were all landslide winners; there wasn't a close contest among them. Klein was the top vote-getter for the NL, with Harnett second at 338,653 votes, and Warneke third.

Identically to the American League, each National League franchise had at least one playing representative on the roster. O'Doul was listed as a member of the Giants, but he had just been traded from the Dodgers and Heydler said the player should be counted as a Brooklyn participant. "For this particular game, O'Doul really should be considered as a Brooklyn player," the NL president said. "He was a member of the Dodgers during the period the fans of the nation were voting for their favorites."[14]

Nearing the end of his career, O'Doul batted just .284 in 1933, but only four seasons earlier he had hit .398, coming tantalizingly close to the magic .400 mark.

Surely some fan goodwill carried over from his magnificent 1929 performance. It should also be noted that although Ward acted the purist by repeatedly saying the selection of players was not a popularity contest, even Heydler mentioned that the fans were choosing "their favorites." Forevermore that matter would remain an issue when players were considered for All-Star game participation.

The Sporting News offered a place on its ballots for the fans to vote for the managers, too. Ward, considering the magnitude of his game and the box office impact, threw his clout behind two men from the start. There was sentiment, wisdom and publicity behind his leanings since no one could top Connie Mack and John McGraw for success and longevity. Mack took the AL reins and McGraw was assigned to guide the National, despite stepping down from his long-time post as manager of the Giants after the 1932 season.

Mack, nicknamed the "Tall Tactician," chose Eddie Collins, one of his former star players and an ex-manager of the White Sox, and Art Fletcher, a coach for the Yankees, as his All-Star game coaches to assist him in the dugout.

McGraw chose two contemporary managers as his coaches. He called upon Braves manager Bill McKechnie and Dodgers manager Max Carey to help him run his club in Chicago. McKechnie had been the original choice by baseball officialdom to manage the All-Stars, but fans, as well as Ward, clamored for McGraw.

The exhausting referendum was complete. The sides were chosen, their bosses in place. By that time the game was about two weeks away. Most of Arch Ward's work was done, his inventiveness rewarded by enthusiasm from all quarters, his promotional skills recognized by a sold-out event. His cheerleading had won the day. The next step was to actually play the "dream game," the "greatest baseball game of all time," the "Game of the Century."

It should be no surprise that the *Tribune*-sponsored game would also be broadcast on *Tribune*-owned WGN radio with Chicago baseball broadcaster Bob Elson at the microphone. The game was scheduled for 1:15 P.M. on July 6 and Elson was slated to come on with a pre-game show at 12:45 P.M. Just in case any fans had been on a European cruise or in Africa on safari, the *Tribune* took care to let readers know that this would be the "Game of the Century." Better yet for listeners who could not obtain tickets, Elson would provide "the outstanding baseball show of the age." The night before, Elson would host a show "to acquaint baseball fans with the principals in the big contest."[15]

Once more Ward weighed in with a slick observation. "Nobody can predict what will happen in this ballgame," he wrote. "It may be a batting orgy, or it may be a string of scoreless innings. Before the batters get a chance to study the pitcher's delivery a new moundsman with a different style will be doing the chucking. There is no precedent to guide your forecast. The greatest hitters against the most skillful pitchers, all handled by the most successful managers baseball has produced."[16]

Arch Ward's fingerprints were all over the first All-Star game. He had cleverly influenced the creation, the development, and the process of founding the event, worked to keep ticket prices low, whipsawed doubters into doing things his way, and lobbied to have the fans make the critical choices of the rosters. And now he would have to let go. Once an umpire yelled "Play ball!" the only thing Ward could do was watch like any other spectator as the game played out.

5

Getting Ready

Looking back at the massive number of words and stories produced by Arch Ward in the weeks leading up to the All-Star game of 1933, it is difficult not to smile when it is noted how many of the stories carried a "copyright *Chicago Tribune*" tag. The *Tribune* was putting its time, manpower and money on the line and wanted to make certain that other papers didn't steal Ward's words. Make no mistake, those words were the official words of the game. If Ward wasn't inventing things as he went along, he had exclusive access to the game's top administrators.

Every once in a while, the *Tribune* let some other staff writer or columnist pinch-hit for Ward. Famous columnist Westbrook Pegler jumped into the fray on June 20. Pegler was known for his sarcasm and iconoclastic nature, so he wasn't going to be a shill for the "Game of the Century" if he didn't believe in it. Having him on board in expostulating that the game's creation was a good idea added credibility.

Pegler provided his thoughts on the creation of an All-Star game in his own inimitable way. "The special ball game between selected teams of the American and National Leagues, playable in Chicago on July 6," Pegler wrote, "represents the only constructive original idea which has been introduced into the baseball industry since the invention of the recording turnstile."[1]

Pegler proceeded to denigrate the idea of doubleheaders and to dismiss night baseball, chiefly because of the likelihood of the insect world taking over under the lights. "The idea of baseball by lamplight," he wrote, "has not succeeded, the failure being largely due to the man-eating transport type mosquitoes which gnawed the patrons and poisoned them with resentment."[2] The nationally known columnist seemed smitten with the entire idea of the All-Star game, appeared surprised that it had been so enthusiastically welcomed by baseball fans all over the country, and even sounded as if he wouldn't mind the game becoming a regular fixture — and even replacing the World Series as a true test of the best players on the planet.

That was definitely not a development on anyone's agenda at the time. No one even thought there would be a second All-Star game, never mind an All-Star game that would pre-empt the world championship between the two leagues. As Ward might have said, with an intake of breath, upon reading Pegler's thoughts, "Let's get one game in first."

When Ward sold his plan for a major league All-Star game and committed the *Tribune* to paying the costs without asking his bosses, he offered to work for free in return if his idea fizzled. That was not going to be necessary, even if the top editors and publisher were going to take him up on that proposal. The energetic sports editor had done all he could to control the flow of information, to promote the game and sell tickets, and had put forth great effort to show baseball officials that their regular schedule could be manipulated with minimal disruption so the players could be shuttled to Chicago.

The one thing Ward couldn't pretend to do was control the weather. Acts of God could still interfere with the meticulously laid plans to play ball. Rain is the enemy of major league baseball, a periodic aggravation during the long season that stretches from spring, through summer, and into early fall. Rain can ruin a single day's play, but the sport adjusts, re-scheduling to fill in postponements on off-days and as part of doubleheaders.

But rain on July 6 would be disastrous. The greatest game of all time could turn out to be the greatest bust of all time. While Ward could not manipulate the weather, he could guard against its fickle nature. Using all of his art of persuasion, Ward talked major league officials into granting a rain day, re-doing the schedule not only for July 6 but July 7, as well, as a fallback date in case of rain.

Baseball officials actually referred to this plan as "giving the *Tribune* permission to keep the players in Chicago another day." Ward also contacted groundskeepers at Wrigley Field and Soldier Field, asking to borrow their tarpaulins. Comiskey Park had its own, but by bringing in extras Ward could better protect the field and even cover the grassy outfield in addition to the dirt infield. There was little more that could be done to protect the stadium's field, but Ward and the *Tribune* wanted to protect themselves, too, from financial catastrophe. So "in case of a monsoon lasting a second day, the Tribune bought a rain insurance policy."[3]

Rain insurance was probably one of the quirkier policies written in 1933. If the game could not be played because of a downpour, the *Tribune* estimated it was on the hook for about $10,000. Why take the chance? A rainout would be far more costly in other terms if the All-Star game never took place. It would be disappointment on a colossal scale given the buildup. It would be bad luck, but still embarrassing. All of the goodwill accrued by the *Tribune* might instead be twisted around to make the company a laughingstock. No, rain would not be welcome.

Choosing Connie Mack and John McGraw as the dugout leaders of the league teams was an inspiration. Mack was already the grand old man of the game. After managing for a few years in the National League before the turn of the twentieth century, Mack had become owner of the Philadelphia Athletics and appointed himself manager of that club. That gave him the most secure bench position in baseball history.

Before he was through, Mack would manage a record 53 years, retiring after the 1950 season. By 1933, Mack, who was born on December 22, 1862, as Cornelius McGillicuddy, Sr., was regarded as the most distinguished and respected individual in the sport. His teams won nine pennants. At the time of the first All-Star game, the A's had just concluded a three-year run at the top of the American League, winning the flag in 1929, 1930 and 1931.

As a player for 11 seasons, Mack was a catcher. He stood about 6'2", and because he was so slender at 150 pounds, appeared taller. A nickname Mack had when he was playing was "Slats." He batted just .245 lifetime, but was smarter about the game than he showed in the batter's box. Mack was smarter than he ever proved in school since he dropped out at age 14 to help his family. Participating in the Civil War wrecked his father's health, which limited his ability to work.

White-haired for as long as those still in the game remembered him, Mack was an icon. One of his personal traits as manager was wearing a business suit in the dugout instead of a baseball uniform. He was one of the few to ever do so and was by far the most prominent to adhere to the practice. This meant that as the man who managed the most games (7,755), winning more than 3,000 and losing more than 3,000 (all three records),

Connie Mack (left), manager of the American League, and John McGraw, (right), manager of the National League, posed jokingly holding a bat as if they were choosing up which team received last at-bats. (Photograph courtesy National Baseball Hall of Fame.)

he could not step onto the field of play to protest an umpire's call. A coach had to perform the task on his behalf.

Not just any suit sufficed for Mack, either. Early in adulthood he developed an affinity for three-piece suits and wore accompanying high collars. His attire reflected his proper personality and aversion to garishness, but he could lose control of his emotions on the field when something upset him. Depending on the season, Mack wore a derby hat or a straw hat. Considered gentlemanly and the personification of fair play, the man who remained as a big-league manager until he was 87 was called "Mr. Mack" by his players.

With the two prominent field leaders spending most of their careers in opposite leagues, there had been few occasions for them to manage against one another. The All-Star clash was going to be the fourth time they opposed each other. The previous times all occurred in World Series play, in 1905, 1911, and 1913. McGraw and the Giants won the title in 1905. Mack and the Athletics won the crown in 1911 and 1913.

McGraw was many things Mack was not. He was fiery, brash, and loud, and had the image as a man who would kick dirt in your face in order to win. It was no accident that McGraw was nicknamed "Little Napoleon" in the baseball world. He was a dictator to his New York Giants teams, but juiced up his players with exhortations and by showing them how badly he sought victory.

Although usually overshadowed by his brilliance as a manager, McGraw also had the goods as a player. His lifetime average was .334 for the Baltimore Orioles and the Giants, his 436 stolen bases indicative of his hard-nosed style of play. Passionate about baseball from an early age, McGraw was truly cast properly when he became a field boss, first with Baltimore and then with the Giants. He is acknowledged as among a handful of the greatest managers of all time and is second, behind Mack, on the all-time wins list with 2,763. When McGraw retired he was actually ahead of Mack, but Mack outlasted him. McGraw's teams won 10 pennants.

This was going to be the last possible occasion for Mack and McGraw to face one another on a baseball diamond. Baseball-savvy media people understood that. Before the game, while the fans were still streaming into Comiskey Park, a photographer posed the two men together. Mack was wearing his usual suit and straw hat. McGraw was not in uniform, but wearing his own suit and straw hat. They each grasped the handle of a baseball bat, as if choosing up sides like sandlot children for their rosters instead of them being determined by public vote. In its own way, the photograph was one of the finest pieces of memorabilia of the day's event.

After 33 years of running his own team, McGraw's health was beginning to fail and his final season in the dugout was 1932. By selecting him as manager of the first National League All-Star squad, baseball was paying tribute to the man.

There was one irony involved in McGraw being the field leader of the NL in an All-Star game against the Americans. As a younger man in charge of the Giants, McGraw had been viewed as an uncompromising opponent of the fledgling AL startup. He was outraged when the American League was deemed to be on equal footing with the more-established National League in 1903 when the first World Series was conducted pitting the Pittsburgh Pirates against the Boston Red Sox.

A year later, when McGraw's Giants won the 1904 pennant, he refused to be drawn into a battle for supremacy against Boston. He said his 106–47 team was the best in baseball and had proven it over the long season in the National League. The next season the World Series was institutionalized and no other October classic was skipped again until 1994, when a baseball strike deprived fans of a neat and appropriate ending to the campaign. Regardless of whether he had mellowed, McGraw was a willing participant in the All-Star game, though there was no question that he brought the same attitude as Frankie Frisch did to the table — it was all about winning for the National League.

The Sporting News was thrilled that Mack and McGraw would face each other as strategists once again, saying their face-off added to the already marvelous All-Star special. "Connie Mack against John McGraw!" the baseball publication opined. "That's to be the managerial hors d'œuvre for the Game of the Century. What possibilities for drama!"

Pegler was all for the notion that the teams should play for keeps, indeed remembering McGraw's initial recalcitrance to engage in World Series play and the barely civilized relations they enjoyed in the early years of the century.

"Although the two leagues are engaged in the same business, they have always maintained a formal coolness toward one another," the columnist wrote, "wherein they bear a resemblance to the Democratic and

Republican parties. Any suggestion calling for a merging of interests for the good of the industry had to come from the outside and the acceptance had to have the appearance of public-spirited acquiescence."[4]

Despite Pegler's somewhat silly suggestion that the All-Star exhibition could supplant the World Series because the players chosen for that competition would be better than the roster of any regular team, he might have been the first in 1933 to raise the issue of the game becoming a regular feature on the calendar. The thought was premature, but only until the first game was in the books. When the *Tribune* through Ward proposed the All-Star baseball game, no one knew if it would be a hit. The *Tribune* was simply lobbying for some kind of sporting event to fit in with the World's Fair. Ward was a true believer who felt the game would be a success, but he had no empirical evidence to support his faith. Baseball's chief administrators also thought the game would at least bring the sport some good publicity.

There was a subliminal fear, however, from high in the Tribune Tower to Ward's office and beyond, that the entire plan might prove to be a fiasco. Just because it was a good idea did not mean the All-Star game would be a moneymaker. Hoping fans would part with hard-earned dollars for an exhibition game was indeed taking a leap of faith in the depths of the Great Depression.

The United States' economy had been in a tailspin and failing since October of 1929. Unemployment was running at 25 percent. People were homeless. They were broke. Banks collapsed. The poor farmers in the Dust Bowl of Oklahoma and the Plains were busted by the harsh, dry weather that compounded the ills and pressures of the financial world.

Major League Baseball suffered along with every other industry in the nation. Baseball was entertainment. It was sport, a game. When the baby needed milk and the car needed gas and the family needed a roof to protect it from the elements, baseball ranked low on the list of necessities. Fans used discretionary income to buy tickets to baseball games, and discretionary income was a foreign phrase to millions of Americans in the early 1930s.

The baseball season had just concluded in the early autumn of 1929 when the stock market collapsed, sending the nation's economic system into a panic. Attendance across the two leagues encompassing 16 major league clubs was 8.5 million that season. The full effect of the Depression was not yet felt in 1930. Perhaps baseball magnates thought they were immune from the problems at large in the country because an all-time attendance mark of 10.1 million fans pushing through the turnstiles was set that season.

But that was the end of the good times. The squeeze was on. Attendance began to plummet. In 1931, major league attendance was 8.4 million, a drastic drop from the 1929 total that was actually a high-water mark for rising attendance that had begun at the start of the Roaring Twenties. It is possible team owners could delude themselves into believing the decline was a one-year aberration, but in 1932 the attendance drop was even more keenly felt. The total number of spectators fell to 6.9 million. And the season of 1933 was the worst yet, with only 6 million fans counted. That meant the number of spectators attending big league games had dwindled by 4.1 million in three years. Attendance wasn't declining, it was decaying. Business was not good.

Perhaps for the only time in professional baseball's history, players did not complain when owners cut their salaries. The average player salary was $7,500 a year in 1929, but had been reduced to an average of $6,000 in 1933. During such economic hard times it would have been unseemly for players to make a fuss. All they had to do was walk down the street from their ballparks, or step out of their apartments, to see long lines of men in fraying garments standing in line hoping for government handouts so they could feed their families. It would not do at all for baseball players, who after all were playing a game, to complain about a wage cut. It would have been the height of insensitivity and folly. The players knew they were fortunate simply to have a job.

To set a good example, Commissioner Kenesaw Mountain Landis voluntarily cut his annual salary from $65,000 to $40,000. Baseball owners tried many ways to cut corners and still put a salable product on the field. Besides slashing player salaries, more teams than ever employed player-managers. By combining two jobs into one they could save a salary. Yet little could jump-start attendance. Even die-hard fans couldn't afford to buy tickets. The St. Louis Cardinals, always one of the proudest and most prominent of National League franchises, attracted just 334,000 fans in 1933. Entire minor leagues went bankrupt and folded during the Depression.

Baseball has always prided itself as offering the least expensive tickets among the major sports Americans care about. That is still true nowadays. In the 1930s, it almost didn't matter how cheap tickets were (the best bargains were 50 cents) because people had no money at all.

In a 2008 column, veteran baseball writer Hal Bodley looked back at the Depression to examine how fans related to major league ball when they had no cash in their wallets or bank accounts. The thing that kept them going, Bodley noted, was the radio. The newfangled invention was just beginning to come into its own, and if families already had one they didn't have to buy another. They could sit by the sound box and listen to baseball game broadcasts for free. Free, no matter how you cut it, was as cheap as it was going to get to stay linked to the sport.

"During the Great Depression, baseball was a great soothing factor for the general public," Bodley wrote. "Radio was just coming in as a popular way to experience baseball during the Great Depression and it was just about the cheapest way for people to be entertained."[5]

For all of their grand thoughts about a sporting event worthy of taking its place on the stage as part of the Century of Progress Exposition, there was much reason for the *Tribune* and Ward to be skittish. Perhaps their wisest decision was holding prices down to the range of 50 cents to $1.65. And their biggest relief was not that major league baseball and its fans backed the establishment of such an All-Star game, but that enough excitement was generated to provoke them into buying nearly 50,000 tickets.

By the time the game rolled around on July 6, most fears had been assuaged. The idea of the game was accepted by baseball officials and baseball fans, and it was a sellout. No wonder Ward and the *Tribune*'s primary worry was inclement weather. They had already pulled off an upset on many fronts by molding the game into a reality. They had conjured up a big-time sporting event out of thin air and sold almost every available ticket to it when less than two months earlier no baseball game of its kind had ever existed. And the implanting of the idea, the implementing of a plan, and the selling of the seats had all occurred against the backdrop of the United States' worst economic crisis ever. That alone was an achievement worth celebrating.

6

Comiskey Park Belongs

Although the site of the first All-Star game was determined by a coin flip, Chicago and baseball were much better off with the contest being played at Comiskey Park than at Wrigley Field. Today Wrigley, built in 1914, is a beloved citadel for Cubs home games, its old green walls and ivy coating in the outfield icons representing a bygone era. Comiskey, built in 1910, was replaced by a newer facility in 1991, and subsequently lost its name and historical connections when sponsor money poured into the team resulted in a renaming in 2003 to U.S. Cellular Field.

But that is now, not then. In 1933, the circumstances were dramatically different. It was a piece of luck that the coin toss went Comiskey's way, if only because the park held nearly 50,000 fans to Wrigley's 35,000. More people could see the special game and more revenue could be raised for charity. That obvious advantage aside, it was Comiskey, not Wrigley, at the time that ranked higher in the minds of fans. For good reason.

Charles A. Comiskey, who was known as "The Old Roman," his ballpark and his White Sox were involved in several firsts. When the American League formed in 1901, Comiskey was a charter partner. The White Sox played in the first game in league history on April 24, 1901, against the Cleveland Blues, a forerunner of the Indians. Three other games were rained out that day, giving the White Sox the debut honors. The team finished 83–53 that season and won the first American League pennant.

Comiskey, who was elected to the Baseball Hall of Fame after his death in 1931, was generally well respected in the game, especially by other owners and the sport's administrators. Only his players, who considered him to be a cheapskate in paying good wages, seemed to hold a grudge against him.

"Comiskey had his critics, but few realized that he was usually two jumps ahead of everybody else," said John McGraw, set to become the first National League All-Star manager.[1]

With his franchise established, next for Comiskey came the building of the first modern baseball stadium in the American League. When Comiskey sought to build a new home for his White Sox, he investigated the latest techniques coming into vogue in the construction of stadiums. For decades, ballparks had been built with wood, which gave them an unfortunate tendency to catch on fire. In 1909, Shibe Park was built as the home of the Philadelphia Athletics. It was the first major league stadium constructed with a foundation of steel and concrete.

Comiskey recognized that was the way to go and that the future resided down that path. Comiskey had once been a fancy-footed first baseman but had graduated into the ranks of the oligarchs of the game. He was proud of his franchise and wanted to make his new ballpark a shrine worth worshipping at for fans and a building worth boasting about to his fellow owners. It was Comiskey's goal to build the shiniest, grandest baseball stadium on the face of the earth — and he succeeded.

His background as a ballplayer with the St. Louis Brown Stockings, starting in 1882, and other professional clubs long defunct, made an impression on Comiskey in terms of what the ideal ballpark would be like. When he helped found the American League and led his own team, the White Sox, he sought to make his vision a reality. At the time many major league ballparks featured goofy dimensions. Boston's Huntington Grounds ballpark, the predecessor to Fenway Park, stretched to 635 feet in center field. A batter would need a bazooka to hit a home run to that part of the stadium.

In 1908, Comiskey bought 600 acres of vacant land for $100,000 on Chicago's South Side. The parcel included 35th Street and Shields, which was the future site of the park. Comiskey wanted his stadium to be symmetrical, and when finished, the field's dimensions were 362 feet down the left- and right-field lines, with the deepest part of center measured at 420 feet.

How much construction of the park actually cost is murky. One historian pegged the price at $500,000 to $750,000 of Comiskey's personal fortune. Other estimates ran as high as $1 million. The park opened on July 1, 1910, and architectural critics liked what they saw. The park was Comiskey's pride and joy and he named it after himself. When it opened,

Comiskey liked to call the park the "baseball palace of the world." The phrase caught on in the newspapers, as well.

Although Comiskey Park was still gleaming 16 years after its opening, that did not satisfy the owner in the long run. In 1926, Comiskey poured another pile of money into stadium renovations. Once again the tally of the costs was less than precise and educated guesses ran from $600,000 to $1 million. Whichever way the counting went, it took a lot of peanuts and Cracker Jack sales to cover the spending.

This renovation created a double deck, which considerably expanded the capacity. The growing popularity of major league baseball, propelled by Babe Ruth's astonishing home runs, led to a sharp increase in attendance during the 1920s. When Yankee Stadium opened in 1923 — "The House that Ruth Built" — it could hold 50,000 fans. The White Sox had fallen on dark days after the Black Sox Scandal, when players fixed the 1919 World Series to lose to the Cincinnati Reds. Otherwise, baseball was a booming business, and Comiskey gauged that having a bigger stadium would be important. As a result, by the time of the coin flip, just seven years after being expanded and undergoing a face-lift and new coat of paint, Comiskey Park was a fully modernized stadium.

By contrast, Wrigley was showing its age. Only 19 years old, Wrigley, originally opened as Weeghman Park and then known as Cubs Park before settling on its permanent name, had been built for a different era and had yet to be upgraded. In 1937, Wrigley underwent an overhaul that included installing a new scoreboard that was state-of-the-art and the first planting of ivy on outfield walls.

While luck figured into the selection of Comiskey Park for the 1933 All-Star game, it was good fortune for all. The White Sox were not playing good enough baseball to attract enough fans to fill the stadium's seats, but they were available to be filled for a special occasion. Again by the coincidence of the coin toss, the All-Star game was slated to be played in the Chicago baseball stadium located closer to the World's Fair grounds, also on the South Side. The spruced-up building, colossal in size, also fit right in as an example of the Century of Progress theme.

The city of Chicago, the largest community in the Midwest, had grown up along the shore of Lake Michigan and on the Chicago River. Established by the state legislature in 1833, Chicago at the time had a population of just 300. Native Americans had lived along the shore for ages, and the Potawatomi Indians were the reigning tribe at the time. The first non-native resident was Jean Baptiste Pointe du Sable, a man of African and European descent who established a trading post in the 1770s. He had allegiance to neither the White Sox nor the Cubs, who were about a century shy of their 1876 beginnings. In 1833, Chicago was actually a town. A lot had happened in the century in-between.

In 1933, Chicago's image was clouded by the belief that the city was ground zero for urban lawlessness, with rum-runners and bank robbers operating without adult supervision from the local police department. Al Capone and John Dillinger were better known than many of the All-Star baseball selections. By then, Capone had suffered a career-ending injury and was trundled off to prison for income tax evasion, though half of the world thought he was still operating with impunity. Dillinger was at the height of his fame, seen by many as a Robin Hood who robbed the rich and gave to the poor, an irresistible image during the Depression. He was a year away from being gunned down in front of a Chicago theater.

To city fathers who were not corrupt, it rankled having Capone and Dillinger as front men for Chicago's reputation. A World's Fair was sup-posed to overshadow that. It was going to be proof that progress had been made since the community grew up out of a plain and overcame nearly being destroyed by a careless cow tipping over a lantern and igniting a massive conflagration in 1871. The 1893 World's Fair was supposed to put the fire in the city's rearview mirror, but undeniably some people around the world still knew little about the community other than tales from the firestorm.

With the addition of a proposed sporting event as an afterthought to the Century of Progress's agenda, the rest of the Fair not under the domain of Arch Ward proceeded to organize, add finishing flourishes, and open on May 27, 1933. The festival was underway and many oohs and ahhs were recorded when the buildings were revealed. In contrast to the White City label of 1893 at the previous Chicago World's Fair, this Fair's buildings were of many colors. The intent was to provide a Rainbow City look.

Ironically, young Judy Garland sang at the Fair six years before playing her role as Dorothy in the movie *The Wizard of Oz*, when her show-stop-ping song number was "Somewhere, Over the Rainbow." The Andrews Sisters also performed at the Fair.

As at any World's Fair, the booths touting products and countries were the core of the event. The Century of Progress Exposition adopted a motto: "Science Finds, Industry Applies, and Man Conforms." Apparently, the author had not met Babe Ruth.

Among other highlights was the arrival of the German Graf Zeppelin. The 776-foot-long air ship was sneered at by some as an unwelcome symbol of power of the extremist Adolf Hitler in Germany. Such impressions, barely formed at the time, were correct foreshadowing.

Scientifically based World's Fairs always try to show off the best of technology produced by the brains in the backgrounds of prominent companies. Ford, Lincoln and Pierce Arrow displayed cars that they hoped would become popular with the masses. There was a "Homes of Tomorrow" exhibit, featuring 12 model homes.

While these individual exhibits and the daily operations of the Fair had little to do with baseball or the All-Star game, the Fair's existence had everything to do with the existence of the diamond contest.

Many years after the game came into being, American League president Will Harridge revealed some of the behind-the-scenes discussions that earned the backing of the league owners for the exhibition. Arch Ward, Harridge said, contacted him and invited him to dinner. Harridge said he thought the sports editor was merely asking him to go out for a social visit. When the napkins were on their laps and the food was on the table, Ward revealed his true intentions behind requesting that Harridge join him for the evening's repast on that day in May. Ward laid out his entire plan for the All-Star game and Harridge was caught off-guard.

"He sprang it on me while we were having dinner together in the spring of 1933," Harridge said. "I told him I didn't think the owners would go for it because they would be laying themselves open to playing charity games for other papers, too, and there would be no end to the requests."[2]

It was not as if Harridge thought the introduction of an All-Star game was a bad idea. Quite the contrary. He liked the proposal. He just didn't think it would go over with the team owners. But he agreed with the *Chicago Tribune* emissary that the ace in the hole could be the singular tie-in with the Century of Progress World's Fair. By dessert, Harridge was on board, and when the gentlemen went separate ways that day, Harridge was committed to laying out Ward's idea to the AL owners.

Harridge seized upon the World's Fair connection as a potential tipping point. He lobbied the league's owners on that basis, that here was a really big event that could bring favorable publicity to baseball during the Depression, when attendance was hurting. The Fair argument was the clincher. "They accepted it as strictly a one-shot performance," Harridge said.[3]

Harridge, as Ward had surmised when thinking over his game plan, proved to be his most important ally. Harridge was president of the American League for 27 years, and in an era when the divisions between the two leagues were quite strong, he definitely retained a partisan outlook. Just as Frankie Frisch and John McGraw had said, if they were going to play the game, pride and passion would come to the fore and he wanted to be on the winning side.

To Harridge, winning the All-Star game, from the first one forward, became as important as winning the World Series. Those two events each year were the way to show which league was superior. In Harridge's head it was always the American League. He wanted the scoreboard to reflect his opinion.

The emotional involvement of Harridge and his National League counterpart, John Heydler, was fierce. No quarter asked and no quarter given when settling on the rules for the game. The allegiances were so strong it took Solomon-like acts to ensure that there was not the slightest hint of advantage gained by one side or the other. For that reason, when the Americans and Nationals came out to play on July 6, they used the American League ball for the first half of the game and the National League ball for the second half.

7

The Players

In 1933, there was no players union, nobody representing major league ballplayers when rules of the game were changed, when schedules were altered, when a game popped up in the middle of the summer requiring the star players' attendance in Chicago at Comiskey Park to play in an event seemingly conjured up out of nowhere.

Such a creation as the All-Star game that demanded the presence of players — even if the proceeds were going towards the players' charity — would likely take a couple of years of negotiation today. Meetings would be called, lawyers for owners and players would attend, debates would ensue, compensation would be established, travel arrangements would be hammered out, per diem expenses would be bartered. And then, if the players were in the mood, they would agree to participate in an oddity like the All-Star game, starting a year or two down the road.

There would have been no Arch Ward involved, other than perhaps penning an initial column in the *Chicago Tribune* throwing out the idea of holding an All-Star game. The newspaper would have no other role.

But when the first All-Star game was proposed, it was placed on the calendar by virtue of votes by the American League and National League owners, the approval nods of the respective league presidents, and with the all-powerful agreement of Commissioner Landis. The players? No one in officialdom asked the players if they wanted to play.

Still, no player objected to the creation of the game and no player said he would not serve if elected. There was no protest, only a feeling of being honored if selected. The Game of the Century immediately took on a special cache. It would have been unthinkable to decline to participate in favor of a vacation for a day or two, especially during the Depression when the players recognized they were lucky to have jobs at all. There would have been no percentage in angering the boss or the fans that still paid the meager salaries with ticket purchases.

Baseball was a smaller fraternity then, with 16 major league clubs. More players stuck with their first team for their entire career. The only inter-league play was the World Series. As a result, players in different leagues did not know one another as well as players do today, when they might play college ball against each other or compete in the minors before being traded around a few times. Popularity contest or not in the voting, as Ward tried to stress, there were some National League players who wanted the chance to play against the legendary Babe Ruth. Or at the least, they wanted to see him bat.

Ruth was 38 years old and while still a hitting threat for the Yankees, his grandest exploits were behind him. The country loved him, and it would have been a miscalculation of the highest order if major league baseball threw an All-Star game festival and the Bambino was on the outside looking in. In this galaxy of great baseball stars, the Babe still shone the brightest. It was fortunate for all that Ruth earned his place in the public vote.

One would think that "Wild Bill" Hallahan, the southpaw from the St. Louis Cardinals, who was one of the hurlers selected for the game, would have been happier if Ruth and his threatening bat sat this one out in New York. Instead, Hallahan made his feelings clear that he believed one of the highlights of the encounter between the leagues was having Ruth on the diamond.

"We wanted to see the Babe," Hallahan said. "Sure, he was old and had a big waistline, but that didn't make any difference. We were on the same field as Babe Ruth."[1]

There was a hint of hero worship for America's most famous athlete, even among his baseball-playing peers.

Many of the players selected to compete in the first All-Star game had enduring stature. They were famous in 1933 and they remain famous. Later, when it was created, they were elected to the National Baseball Hall of Fame in Cooperstown, New York. No one realized that anyone who was chosen to play in the first All-Star game would earn special mention for that singular achievement, regardless of what else he did in his career. Not everyone became a Hall of Famer. Hallahan was one of those lumped into that group. He was 8-2 at the All-Star break and picked a good season

Babe Ruth of the Yankees (left) was the prime attraction in the first All-Star game, which was called the "Game of the Century." Yankee teammate Lou Gehrig (center) is shown along with Al Simmons (right) of the White Sox, who was the highest vote-getter for the American League. The trio of players made the day for young fan Edwin Diamond. (Photograph courtesy National Baseball Hall of Fame.)

to get off to a fast start. That earned him his place, his one and only All-Star appearance in a 12-year career that concluded with a 102–94 lifetime mark.

Voters from throughout the nation made sure Ruth was included on the American League roster, and Ward and baseball officials were lucky there was little controversy over the final selections. Jimmie Foxx, who gained a flicker of attention early in the voting process because he was piling up the ballots at more than one position, finished second in the voting for AL first baseman and second in the voting for AL third baseman. However, even if Foxx had received all of his votes at first base, he would not have unseated Lou Gehrig at the position. His combined total, how-ever, would have given him more votes than Jimmy Dykes at third base.

A week prior to the game, American League manager Connie Mack announced his starting lineup and batting order. The A's pilot chose his own Robert Moses "Lefty" Grove, the devastating southpaw, as the starting pitcher. Grove was on his way to a 24–8 season. The rest of Mack's planned starters for the Americans were: Cleveland's Earl Averill, leading off and playing center field; Detroit's Charlie Gehringer, batting second and play-ing second base; the Yankees' Ruth hitting third and playing right field; and New York's Gehrig, batting in the cleanup spot and lodged at first base. Gehrig knocked in 139 runs that season for the Bronx Bombers, so hitting him fourth made sense.

Al Simmons, who had been jettisoned by Mack the season before and was representing the Chicago White Sox, occupied left field and fifth place in the batting order. He was followed by Washington Senators shortstop Joe Cronin in the sixth hole. Dykes, Mack's protégé but then with the White Sox, was the third baseman and hit seventh. The catcher was Bill Dickey, another Yankee, batting eighth. And in the days long before the designated hitter, Grove was batting for himself in ninth.

The voters displayed good taste and good judgment. Of the nine American League scheduled starters, Dykes was the only one not elected to the Baseball Hall of Fame in future years.

Interestingly, whether Mack was rushed into writing out his starting lineup for Ward's benefit to make news on a given day leading up to the game or not, he ended up changing his mind about a number of players. Averill only appeared in the game late as a pinch-hitter, and Mack started Simmons in center and the Yankees' Ben Chapman in left. Instead of start-ing Grove, he ended up using him in the game in relief. Another Lefty, Gomez, also of the Yankees (and another Hall of Famer), started the game, and Rick Ferrell of the Red Sox subbed for Dickey.

Maybe Mack just wanted more time to sleep on his choices, but that was substantive change. The AL batting order turned out this way: Chap-man, Gehringer, Ruth, Gehrig, Simmons, Dykes, Cronin, Ferrell and Gomez. Mack had Hall of Famers Foxx, Dickey, and Tony Lazzeri ready to come off the bench, and when he swapped Gomez for Grove and Ferrell for Dickey, he was merely switching future Hall of Famers.

John McGraw, brains of the National League outfit, countered with this lineup: third baseman Pepper Martin leading off; second baseman Frankie Frisch, hitting second; Chuck Klein, right field; Chick Hafey, left field; Bill Terry, first base; Wally Berger, center field; Dick Bartell, shortstop; Jimmy Wilson, catcher; Bill Hallahan, pitcher.

The American League had much more power. The National League had more speed on the base paths. Yet, across the board, the NL wasn't as strong. Nevertheless, by the time the game ended, the circuit was represented on the field by Hall of Famers Frisch, Klein, Paul Waner, Hafey, Terry, Pie Traynor, Carl Hubbell, and Gabby Hartnett.

The AL was the sluggers' league, but old Comiskey Park was not considered to be a hitter's park. Fifty years later, when the All-Star game returned to Comiskey for an anniversary celebration, *The Sporting News* produced a special All-Star commemorative section. Writer Dave Nightengale wrote a story that was headlined, "Comiskey: Still a Pitchers' Haven." The lead paragraph read this way: "Sometime on the night of July 6, an American League or a National League all-star batter will crush a ball. Absolutely crush it. And the ball will rise to the farthest corners of Comiskey Park, then run into a gusty freshet off of Lake Michigan and settle gently into the glove of an outfielder. And the batter will be left with little to do except curse the ghost of Big Ed Walsh."[2]

Walsh was one of the greatest pitchers of all time during his career, which occurred between 1904 and 1917, all but the final year with the White Sox. In 1908 he put together an astounding mark of 40–15, but he burned out his right arm sooner than necessary by throwing phenomenal numbers of innings. Charles Comiskey recognized that Walsh carried his ball club on his shoulders, and when the owner was designing his palace of ballparks for its 1910 inaugural, he consulted with Walsh. Naturally, Walsh urged drawing up dimensions that would favor the pitcher over the hitter. The park was renovated several years prior to the All-Star game, but still gave pitchers peace of mind and made strong hitters work twice as hard.

In 1983, despite additional modifications, Nightengale claimed Comiskey Park "is still a haven for pitchers. Just as it always has been."[3] Harkening back to the 1933 game, that meant McGraw and his charges might not have been at such a disadvantage because the ballpark's layout favored their style of play.

Leading up to the game, Mack called a team meeting at the Del Prado Hotel. He issued a pep talk to his 18 players, making it clear that the newspapers and fans might be calling this a mere exhibition game, but he considered winning the All-Star game imperative. He wanted to see the American League on top and he wanted to beat John McGraw. No one had to read between the lines to find Mack's message.

Rick Ferrell, whose pitching brother Wes was also on the American League squad, recalled that Mack summarized what his outlook would be on the bench. "Connie Mack told us," Ferrell said, "'Everyone in this room is a great player. If he weren't a great player, he wouldn't be here. We're going to play to win and I don't want anyone to be disappointed if he doesn't get in the game.'"[4]

Mack definitely played to win. Ferrell, who played the entire game, was one of the beneficiaries of the manager's approach. Even though Mack had announced Bill Dickey would start at catcher, he never got into the game because of injury.

Cronin remembered Mack's talk in much the same manner as Ferrell did. "Mr. Mack wanted to beat his old rival, John McGraw, in the worst way," Cronin said. "He told us if we went ahead he would make very few changes."[5]

McGraw never showed up at a ballpark without being 100 percent focused on victory. He showed much of his usual fire when arguing with the umpires, but in-between pitches, in the privacy of the National League dugout, to some of his players McGraw seemed worn out. This All-Star game was his last hurrah. McGraw had retired from the Giants after the 1932 season, and 10 months later this gala was going to be his last managerial moment. Barely eight months later he died from uremia poisoning.

"Playing under McGraw was a great thrill for me," said Berger, who was attached to the Boston Braves, "but it was obvious that he was ill and had lost some of his old fight."[6]

Baseball teams arrive at the ballpark well before the first pitch. Reporting time can be four hours prior to game time in the modern era. The practice was not to arrive quite so early in the 1930s, but the players certainly beat the fans to the park. Not so for the first All-Star game. When the American Leaguers showed up at Comiskey Park, they were startled to note that the seats were already full. "We were shocked to find the stands packed," noted Joe Cronin. "The fans turned out early to watch us take batting practice and we didn't disappoint 'em. Everybody was knocking the ball over the fences."[7]

Those American League sluggers got the chance to show off, and calling for batting practice hurlers to lay it in there, they walloped the ball over Comiskey's distant walls. Dickey said his team was laying into the ball with such authority it appeared they were using a special type of baseball in vogue at the time, one that was noted for its propensity to fly. "It made it look as if we were hitting against the old 97," said Dickey, referring to the Goldsmith Company's 97 ball.[8]

A month before the July 6 game took place, Cleveland Indians general manager Billy Evans offered some observations that looked both backwards and forwards. He seemed well aware that an All-Star game had been suggested before, though he perhaps lent too much credence to the idea of it being continuously on the front burner. And Evans provided a prediction indicating that the All-Star game would be better remembered than any other aspect of the World's Fair.

> ...there has been a constant clamor for such a contest. It seemed too
> big a thing to put over because of the player demand it would make
> on the various clubs during the regular season. What appeared to be
> an impossibility has been made a reality through the enterprises of
> the Tribune. It is fitting that the game is to be played during A Cen-
> tury of Progress Exposition. It will prove a spectacle in keeping with
> the other great features of the Fair. I am positive it will have wider
> appeal than any event to be held in Chicago this summer.[9]

Evans might have found some arguments from gentlemen who watched Sally Rand remove her garments during that sweltering Chicago summer, but in the long run he was more right than even he foresaw. More than 75 years later, only those conversant with history know who Sally Rand was, and recall that there was a World's Fair of some name held in Chicago way back when. The major league baseball All-Star game? Even the least interested of individuals randomly stopped while walking down the street knows that the sporting calendar offers such a game each season.

Of course, neither Ward nor Evans would have expected that because nobody had yet proposed that the All-Star game become an annual affair.

First Inning

It didn't rain. That was probably one of the most notable developments of July 6, 1933, in Chicago. As thousands waited in lines and visited
the pavilions and unusual exhibits along the shore of Lake Michigan at
the Century of Progress Exposition, the many thousand lucky ticket-hold-
ers for the Game of the Century at Comiskey Park arrived early for the
day's entertainment.

As the surprised players noted, fans showed up at the park well before
the scheduled 1:15 P.M. first pitch. The dream game promised an unprecedented showdown between the American League and National League
stars, but even batting practice featuring such a galaxy of swatters offered
enough intrigue to bring out the crowds early.

National League players wore specially made uniforms that had the
words "National League" emblazoned across the front. American League
players wore uniforms representing their own teams.

From the moment the players began taking their swings, the fans were
vocal, cheering for favorites, swooning when long balls were struck. Various
reports were made of just how many spectators were in the house that day.
Some accounts rounded off attendance to 49,000. Others noted that there
were more than 49,000 on hand. Elsewhere, it was reported that 47,595
attended. That might have been the accurate account of paid attendance,
with the higher figures including freebies for baseball officials. As had been
advertised from the start, there was no standing room; otherwise attendance would have exceeded 50,000. No matter the final count, the game
was deemed a sellout and a successful business venture before play started.

Rarely has any single game been more hyped — and that includes the
modern-era Super Bowl in pro football — and certainly no single game in
any sport had received as much attention by 1933 in an era before television,

in the early days of radio, and with newspapers the dominant medium. Players and the game's play had much to live up to in order to please the fans after the months-long campaign to create it, advertise it, and label it. Sold as the "Game of the Century," an exhibition baseball game considered a once-in-a-lifetime event better bring something special to the table.

With the sun shining, providing relief to the principals involved in organization, the event was off to a good start. With the crowd packing the stadium and reacting enthusiastically to every minor practice swish of the bat, credibility was established. As Arch Ward had previously announced in the *Chicago Tribune* after the ballots had been counted, tickets had been sold to fans from 46 of the 48 states. Assuming they had all made travel arrangements successfully, that was significant representation from the rooting public.

And if any fans retained any doubt about how much representatives of the American and National leagues wished to win, they were allayed before the first pitch. NL manager John McGraw may have retired from his three-decade stint as field boss of the New York Giants, but he had not retired his hunger for victory or shelved his old habits.

As McGraw strode onto the field, he spied an old nemesis, umpire Bill Klem. McGraw promptly shouted an insult at the ump. Showing he was not going to take any guff from "Little Napoleon," Klem yelled right back at McGraw. "You are ill-bred!" he shouted.[1] Touché.

The four umpiring slots had been divided equally, with two from each league. Klem of the National League was assigned to first base. Cy Rigler, at third, was the other NL ump. The American League was represented by Bill McGowan at second base and Bill Dineen behind the plate. With Comiskey Park as the All-Star game locale, the American League was host and gained last at-bats. When Dineen shouted, "Play ball!" that meant AL pitcher Lefty Gomez of the Yankees was the man the instructions were directed towards.

Vernon Gomez was 24, a few months shy of his 25th birthday, and was coming into his own as a top pitcher. Although he finished just 16–10 in 1933, he had already posted 21- and 24-win seasons for the Yankees, and a year later recorded a 26–5 performance. A southpaw who stood 6'2", Gomez was from Rodeo, California. Despite Gomez's precocious start, his greatest fame lay ahead of him. When the All-Star game was continued, Gomez became a seven-time selection, and after winning 189 games in a 14-year career, the player whose nickname was "Goofy," was chosen for the Baseball Hall of Fame in 1972.

As a player and later as a wildly popular after-dinner speaker at sports banquets, Gomez was considered one of the funniest players in the history of the sport. Few gained more enjoyment from his involvement with baseball, and while it was not something considered at the time, it was just as well that Gomez was named to start in the first All-Star game because he literally dined out on the fact forever. Indeed, Gomez, who was of Irish and Spanish descent, was the king of the banquet circuit, so coveted a guest because he left audiences rolling in the aisles by dessert. The fun-loving and glib Gomez married a Broadway show girl, June O'Dea, the same year as he opened the All-Star game.

Gomez was one of the players sportswriters loved to talk with because there was no predicting what he would say. The basic question of what was the secret of his success elicited this reply: "Clean living and a fast outfield," Gomez said. Also, while the phrase became a cliché, when Gomez said, "I'd rather be lucky than good," it was new.[2]

Excelling in World Series competition over the years, Gomez knew he was blessed to play on a Yankees club loaded with firepower. At his Baseball Hall of Fame induction in Cooperstown, New York, he acknowledged that. "I want to thank all my teammates who scored so many runs," he said. "Joe DiMaggio, who ran down so many of my mistakes, and Johnny Murphy, without whose relief pitching I wouldn't be here."[3]

Comedians are often self-deprecating and Gomez fit that mold. Likely one of Gomez's favorite aspects of being selected to the first All-Star team was being a teammate for a day with the A's Jimmie Foxx. It was safer that way. Foxx toting lumber to the plate always made Gomez cringe. Once, when Foxx trotted to the plate, Gomez repeatedly shook off the signs from his catcher Bill Dickey. Finally, an exasperated Dickey rose from his crouch, jogged to the mound and asked Gomez exactly what he wanted to throw to the muscular slugger. "Nothing," Gomez said. "Let's wait a while. Maybe he'll get a phone call."[4]

That was hardly Gomez's only misadventure with the massively powerful Foxx, who smashed 534 home runs in his career. Decades into retirement, Gomez was holding forth on the United States' historic achievement of putting astronaut Neil Armstrong on the moon and stumbling across unknown items on the ground. "He and all the space scientists were puzzled by an unidentifiable white object," Gomez noted. "I knew immediately what it was. That was a home-run ball hit off me in 1937 by Jimmie Foxx."[5]

It was no wonder Gomez was nicknamed "Goofy." Gomez was just 18 and being interviewed by a reporter when the moniker was bestowed upon him. When Gomez compared himself to Albert Einstein, the sportswriter asked what he had ever invented. "The revolving goldfish bowl," Gomez promptly responded. "It keeps turning so the fish can see everything in the room without swimming all the time and wearing themselves out." The reporter replied, "You're goofy." And a legend was born.[6] If any pitcher was going to be a crowd-pleaser for the All-Star game, it was a safe bet Gomez would entertain.

The game's first batter — the first hitter in All-Star history — was National League lead off man Pepper Martin. Martin, playing third base, was one of the pivotal figures on the St. Louis Cardinals' Gashouse Gang teams of the period. Born in Temple, Oklahoma, and nicknamed "The Wild Horse of the Osage," Martin's real name was Johnny Leonard. He was a spark plug, full of pepper, the type of player who could jump-start an offense.

Martin was at the top of his game in 1933. He led the National League with 122 runs scored and 26 stolen bases while batting .316. When he got on base, Martin could make pitchers twitch, wondering if he was going to steal. He sought to disrupt their rhythm and destroy their concentration. He was a late bloomer, except for some cameo appearances, doomed to the minors until he was 27. If he was in a hurry to make up for lost time, he showed it on the base paths.

Elbie Fletcher, a veteran National League first baseman, hated to see Martin coming down the line, all-out, roaring like a train engine. "He'd hit the ball and you could hear him leave home plate, stompin' and chuggin'," Fletcher said, "going down the line like his life depended on beating that ball. I used to try to get the ball and lift my foot off the base as quick as I could. He wouldn't cut you on purpose. He was just an aggressive player."[7]

As one of the ringleaders of the Gashouse Gang, Martin was periodically involved in some light-hearted moments off the field. Anyone who has watched baseball in St. Louis in the heart of the summer knows the temperature can climb to 100 degrees on the field and that the heat may be complemented by excessive humidity. On one of those 100-degree days when even fans in the bleachers incessantly fanned themselves with score-cards to stir the breeze, Martin and pitcher Dizzy Dean built a bonfire near third base between games of a double-header. Both men wrapped themselves in thick, woolen Indian blankets and cavorted by the fire. It was an astonishing sight and feat of heat endurance, as well, under the guise of being just plain silly.

McGraw had seen enough of Martin in regular-season games against his Giants to know he made an ideal leadoff hitter. Not this day, however. Martin hit a routine ground ball to Joe Cronin at short. Cronin fielded the hit cleanly, and threw to Lou Gehrig on first for the first out of the game.

Martin's teammate, Frankie Frisch, who played for McGraw for several years before being dealt to the Cardinals in 1927, was the second NL batter. He gave Gomez little grief, stroking a grounder to the Detroit Tigers' Charlie Gehringer at second. Gehringer's toss gave Gehrig his second putout. The top of the first ended when Phillies basher Chuck Klein, the right fielder, drove a line drive to Cronin at short. No runs, no hits, no threats for the National League.

Being nicknamed "Wild Bill" was not necessarily the best praise for a pitcher. It could mean that the recipient knew how to have a rowdy good time after hours, or it could mean his pitches had trouble locating the plate with radar. A 5'10" southpaw from Binghamton, New York, the unlikely starting pitcher for the National League was Bill Hallahan of the Cardinals. Not quite as big a name as many of those honored by selection to the All-Star game, after brief showings with the Cards in the 1920s Hallahan began building a resume in 1930 when he finished with a 15–9 record.

In 1931, Hallahan won a league-best 19 games. He was 12–7 in 1932, and posted a 16-win season in 1933. In 1930 and 1931, Hallahan also led the National League in strikeouts. Although he could not know at the time of the All-Star game, his best years were behind him; he would have just one more solid campaign before going into a permanent tailspin.

Alas, even in the best of times, when Hallahan threw well for the Cardinals in World Series competition, he was pretty wild on the mound. In 1930 and 1931, the same two years Hallahan led the league in strikeouts, he also led the NL in walks with 126 and 112, respectively. The man threw a lot of pitches.

Hallahan's erratic throws held him back from true stardom. Bases on

St. Louis Cardinals southpaw "Wild Bill" Hallahan got the nod as the National League starter, but he lived up to his nickname with too many walks. He also surrendered a key two-run homer to Babe Ruth and was the losing pitcher. (Photograph courtesy National Baseball Hall of Fame.)

balls are frequently a pitcher's worst enemy, and there's nothing like walking too many men to give a manager high blood pressure. Somehow, Cardinals manager Gabby Street saw past Hallahan's foibles to his good points and did not harangue him about getting the ball over the plate.

Street coached Hallahan's confidence and said, "You're going to make me a great manager."[8] Whether that was accurate or not, they did make beautiful music together.

The occasional wild thing did happen to Hallahan in addition to walking too many batters. The night before a scheduled start in 1930, Hallahan's right hand was smashed in taxi cab door. He went out the next day, and being a lefty, was able to ignore the throbbing in his opposite hand, and pitched a shutout.

Still, with rip-roaring fellas like Pepper Martin, Frankie Frisch, Dizzy and Daffy Dean, and Flint Behm, who once disappeared on a day he was supposed to pitch before turning up later that night at the team hotel saying he had been kidnapped by Brooklyn gangsters and forced to drink Prohibition booze under duress, Hallahan was hardly the wildest player off the field. By comparison, Hallahan was called "Mild Bill."[9]

Leading off for the American League was left fielder Ben Chapman. Over-shadowed by the Yankees' big guns, Chapman put together several fine seasons for the New Yorkers. In 1933, he knocked in 98 runs, batted .312, and led the league in stolen bases with 27. Two seasons earlier Chapman stole 61 bags. In a 15-year career, Chapman, who was born in Nashville, Tennessee, and lived in Alabama the rest of his life, batted .302.

Much later, in 1947, the year Jackie Robinson broke into the majors with the Brooklyn Dodgers and broke the color barrier, Chapman was managing the Philadelphia Phillies. Both at the time and later, when Robinson and more players spoke about it, Chapman was characterized as the leader of the most vicious verbal racist assaults on the black-skinned Robinson. Chapman was already known as a vociferous and argumentative player for his dust-ups with teammates, opponents and umpires. In 1933, Chapman was a key figure in a bench-clearing brawl with the Washington Senators, was accused of sucker-punching Washington pitcher Earl Whitehall, and was suspended by the league president. In 1943, Chapman was banned from baseball after he hit an umpire, though he was later reinstated.

Robinson promised Dodger general manager Branch Rickey that he would turn the other cheek when racist taunts were directed at him, and he did so. But his patience was tried more listening to Chapman's invective than any other player's or team's nasty remarks. Chapman called his insults typical bench jockeying aimed at gaining a psychological advantage on the rookie. During an era when the United States was steeped in racism, Chapman was portrayed as the chief villain in the Robinson saga of attempting to overcome discrimination. Even in his obituary, it was noted that Chapman was admonished by Commissioner A.B. "Happy" Chandler "for racist baiting of Jackie Robinson at Ebbets Field soon after Robinson broke the big leagues' color barrier."[10]

Sticking to the theme that bench jockeying was common and that he had been harassed by Northern audiences as a "Southern SOB," Chapman did not repeat his venom. Much later, what Chapman actually said was recounted in a variety of publications. Calling Chapman's comments to Robinson "filth," former Dodger traveling secretary Harold Parrott said, "Chapman mentioned everything from thick lips to the supposedly extra-thick Negro skull, which he said restricted brain growth to almost animal level when compared to white folk. He listed the repulsive diseases he said Robbie's teammates would be infected with if they touched the towels or combs he used."[11]

This was apparently just Chapman's way of speaking Southern.

Chapman resisted commenting on critiques in which commentators classified his behavior as racist for a quarter of a century, but in 1973 he spoke to *The Sporting News* and said he was unrepentant.

> What everyone said didn't upset me a great deal. After all, most of the things that people said that I and my players at Philadelphia said to Jackie were true. And I'm not ashamed of anything that happened. I wasn't then, and I'm not now. The fact of the matter is that we did nothing that we didn't do to any other rookie. Our purpose was to win, and if we could do that by getting a rookie rattled, we would. It happened to me and they pick out the thing they think will get under your skin the most.[12]

Most evidence suggests that Chapman did not have an All-Star personality. Nevertheless, he got the first at-bat for the American League in All-Star game history. Chapman grounded to third baseman Martin, who flipped the ball to Bill Terry at first for the first out.

Next up was Gehringer, who worked Hallahan for a walk and became the first base runner in All-Star history. Was Wild Bill going wild on the big stage? There was no reason for a guy who compiled a 1.36 earned run average in World Series play to get butterflies, but who knew if Hallahan's arm would be scattershot on this day?

Hallahan was the one who said everyone wanted Babe Ruth in the All-Star game and now he had a chance to face him. Gehringer stole second while the attention was on Ruth, but the big man was called out on strikes. There was Hallahan in a nutshell. He walked one batter and the next batter struck out.

Lou Gehrig, hitting fourth behind Ruth, just as he did in the everyday Yankees lineup, could not score Gehringer. Gehrig grounded to Terry, who was pulled off the base, but tossed the ball to Hallahan covering for the third out.

One inning into the Game of the Century, the scoreboard read 0–0.

9

Second Inning

Baseball never came as easily to Chick Hafey as it did for some of the other great hitters of his era. Lasik surgery was not just a snap of the fingers away. Penicillin and other wonder drugs lay in the future. Yet somehow, in 13 major league seasons, the 6', 185-pound right-side swinger compiled a .317 average.

After a long, successful stretch with the St. Louis Cardinals, including 1931 when he won the batting title with a .349 mark, Hafey was a 30-year-old outfielder with the Cincinnati Reds in 1933. His exit from St. Louis was orchestrated by his resolute belief that he deserved more money from the front office. He was asking for $15,000 a year. Instead, the Cards sold him to the perennially losing Reds, a destination considered to be one of purgatory for grumpy ballplayers at the time.

Hafey's sweet batting stroke earned him a place on the first All-Star team, and he led off the second inning for the Nationals. Lefty Gomez looked comfortable on the mound, but Hafey was never intimidated by any pitcher, and he collected a single.

In its own way, any time Hafey safely connected with a ball, it was an achievement. His eyesight was as poor as they come without needing a cane to get around, and even wearing glasses, a rarity among players in the 1930s, did not provide him with the viewing sharpness of Ted Williams, who was legendary for his eagle vision. Further eroding his eyesight were headaches and dizzy spells. Problem sinuses contributed to Hafey's poor sight. Hafey struggled through the 1926 season, including a .185 batting average in the World Series, and had sinus surgery afterwards. Hafey said he probably shouldn't have played. "One of my eyes was so bad I couldn't see across the room," he said. "That day I was groping for the ball like a man in a fog."[1] An operation to remove an abscess below one eye helped Hafey but did not eliminate his vision woes.

Trying to hit a pitched ball coming to the plate at 90 mph can be a risky proposition, and a batter needs all of his faculties to duck if necessary. Challenges picking up the ball as it swerves towards the head could result in a career-ending, if not fatal injury from a beaning. Yet Hafey was still one of the finest hitters in the sport. His other first-rate attribute was a powerful throwing arm that was regarded as one of the most potent in the pros and made base runners ratchet down their ambitions.

One of the most estimable baseball writers of the age, F.C. Lane, opined of Hafey's weakness, "In fact, how he hit at all is a mystery. What he would have done with normal sight and health at par can only be conjectured."[2]

Hafey tried glasses and wore them full-time in the field in 1929. That made him one of four players in the majors to use spectacles that season; they were lumped together as members of "the four-eyed tribe."[3]

A nine-time .300 hitter, Hafey was viewed in some quarters as the batter most likely to hit .400 — if he could only stay healthy. "Hafey seemed destined to become one of the immortals of the game," one sportswriter said.[4] By then the outfielder with the natural hitting prowess had additional health worries.

Hafey's transition from the Cardinals to the Reds did not go smoothly at the start of the 1932 season. Hafey was struck by a harsh malady that was loosely described as the flu. This flu was so debilitating, with its high fevers and capability of striking Hafey low, that he spent 21 days bed-ridden, and then retreated to the wilds of Ontario for rest and recuperation. Hafey was out of action for months, doing more fishing than batting, before returning to the Reds for 83 days and tipping the Toledoes 13 pounds under his usual weight.

In 1933, though, Hafey was back to nearly top form, en route to a .303 season and appearances in 144 games when picked for the All-Star game. His single off Gomez was an infield hit to second base and was the first spark of offense shown by the National League. Comiskey may have been an American League park, and the tilt in the stands may have favored the Americans, but it was not completely one-sided rooting for this game. Hafey's little hit generated some buzz.

The volume kicked up a bit more when the next batter stepped into

Bill Terry of the Giants was the starting first baseman for the National League in the first All-Star game. Terry was the last NL player to hit .400 when he reached .401 in 1930, and as player-manager he was chosen to lead his league's team in the 1934 All-Star contest. (Photograph courtesy National Baseball Hall of Fame.)

the box. Bill Terry, the Giants' first baseman, was more prominent than Hafey and fans of the American League knew enough to fear the bat work of "Memphis Bill." Terry would retire with a lifetime .341 average spread over 14 seasons and recorded one of the game's most memorable hitting seasons in 1930. In the year of the batter, Terry was the finest National League hitter of them all, leading the circuit with a .401 average and 254 hits. The hit total was a major league record that lasted until 2004, when Ichiro Suzuki clouted 262 hits for the Seattle Mariners.

Terry, a left-handed batter, was known for hitting for high average more than belting out home runs, but he had the capability. When he uncoiled his 6'1", 200-pound frame and connected, the ball might be launched into orbit. The first baseman had replaced his current All-Star boss John McGraw in the 1932 campaign and was in the midst of his first full season as player-manager of the Giants. It was a momentous year for Terry, who led the New Yorkers to the first of three pennants on his watch.

Actually, even before Terry came to the plate with a man on, he had influenced the happenings on the field. McGraw, not surprisingly, wanted to start Carl Hubbell, the hurler nicknamed "Meal Ticket." Hubbell had earned that reputation for steady work in McGraw's employ. But Terry was now the Giants manager and he told McGraw he didn't want Hubbell to start the All-Star game because he needed more recovery time from his regular-season job. "I thought Hub needed extra rest," Terry said. "I asked the old man not to start him."[5]

Terry made his feelings known in firmer tones than that. But then, he had always said what was on his mind, from the first time he ever met McGraw. Terry was born in Atlanta, Georgia, in 1898, but didn't play a major league game until 1923, when he was 24, and didn't play a full season until 1925. He had been busy in semi-pro ball in Memphis, Tennessee, and when McGraw thought he could sign Terry cheaply, the hard-bargaining, set-in-his-ways Terry demanded $5,000 more than McGraw planned to offer.

That was typical of the Terry-McGraw relations over their years together in New York. They argued at times and for about two years did not speak to one another. That didn't stand in the way of their success with the Giants, however. Terry hit, McGraw managed, and the Giants won, even without direct communication between the two most visible figures in uniform.

When facing Gomez in the second inning of the All-Star game, Terry did what Terry did best. He laced a base hit, a single, to left field. Hafey stopped at second base and the Nationals had the game's first threat, with men on first and second, nobody out.

That brought Wally Berger to the plate, and there was anticipation in both dugouts. This was the game's first crisis for the American League. Connie Mack was a very interested observer, wondering if Gomez could work his way out of the jam. McGraw and his club acted lively, chattering, urging Berger to take a promising situation and improve it with the start of a rally.

Berger was a local by birth, but a Westerner by upbringing. He was born in Chicago in 1905, but grew up in and around San Francisco. Berger played high school ball with fellow all-star Joe Cronin. Berger tore apart Pacific Coast League pitching on his way to the majors. In three seasons with the old Los Angeles Angels, Berger hit .365, .327, and .355. In 1929, the final year of his minor-league apprenticeship, he drove in 166 runs.

The pitching did not appear to be significantly tougher for Berger in the National League when he broke into the majors in 1930 with the Boston Braves. Not only did he bat .310 with 119 RBIs, but Berger cracked 38 homers. Although tied once, by Frank Robinson in 1956, Berger's single-season homer mark remained a rookie record for 57 years. Mark McGwire broke the record with 49 homers for the 1987 Oakland A's.

"I didn't know it was going to take so long," Berger said of McGwire's performance more than a half-century after his own attention-grabbing season. "I never thought of records. I just liked to hit."[6]

As Berger settled into his right-handed stance to face Gomez, it was a good time to muse about his enjoyment of hitting. And it was a good time for a hit. Only the outfielder didn't deliver. Instead, Berger did just about the worst thing he could have done to douse the potential big inning. He tapped a grounder to Jimmy Dykes, who stepped on third and threw to Lou Gehrig at first to complete a double play. That wiped out Hafey and Berger and left Terry on second with two outs. Big play by Gomez and his infield. The cheers this time were in support of the American League.

The circumstances were dramatically different for the next batter, shortstop Dick Bartell. Bartell represented the Phillies. For the first half of his 18-season career, Bartell was a .300-hitting shortstop. Although his

.271 average in 1933 was not one of his better years, he was coming off a .308 performance in 1932. Bartell was fully capable of knocking Terry in with a well-placed single to right field, but Gomez gave "Rowdy Richard," as Bartell was known, nothing to hit. Bartell struck out and the National League uprising fizzled.

The American League lineup was dotted with .300 hitters, and while the scheduled batch of swatters was due to face Bill Hallahan for the first time, they had studied his offerings in the first inning. First up was the All-Star team's leading vote-getter, outfielder Al Simmons. He could not handle Hallahan's best stuff and flied out to Hafey in left field. Next up was Dykes, who had started the double play. Dykes was a savvy veteran who would later try to uplift the White Sox's fortunes as manager but in 1933 was still Connie Mack's fair-haired boy.

Dykes, who broke in with the Philadelphia A's in 1918 and played 22 years in the majors, always revered Mack. They had a special rapport and Dykes considered Mack to be the wisest baseball man on the planet. Mack appreciated how Dykes paid close attention and learned the finer points of the game. He always believed Dykes would become a successful big-league manager when he finished playing.

They were definitely not clones, however. Mack's conservative street-clothes wardrobe, keeping him in the dugout and out of public view during games, said a great deal about his personality. Dykes was more outgoing. He was always prepared to dash on the field to mix it up verbally with umpires. He could be sarcastic about his players' foibles, and made the newspapermen laugh. Although Dykes had been selected as the American League's third baseman, he had been a second baseman for the first two-thirds of his career. When measured by the usual standards of second base-men his .280 batting average in 2,282 games was above average. By 1933, Dykes and Mack had parted company — with no ill will — and Dykes was a White Sox hometown guy in the All-Star game.

Dykes followed Simmons to the plate and drew a walk from Halla-han — not a surprising development given Wild Bill's resume. Shortstop Joe Cronin batted next and also walked. Two men on, one out. Could the AL take advantage in a way the NL had not been able to? It didn't look like it after catcher Rick Ferrell flied out to Chuck Klein in right field, bringing pitcher Gomez to the plate.

Gomez was not a great hitter. He had a better chance of reaching base by making Hallahan double over with laughter while throwing a pitch than by rapping a double. Gomez weighed 173 pounds and his batting average typically did not approach the level of his weight. Year in and year out, Gomez's average was in the O-fer category. He never hit a home run or a triple during his 14 seasons in the majors and he averaged less than one double per year. After one of those rare smashes that found him standing on second base with a real double, Gomez was picked off, and then was asked by his manager what happened. "How would I know?" Gomez said. "I've never been there before."[7]

Neither Hallahan nor the National League had anything to fret about when Gomez tip-toed into the batter's box, hitched up his baggy Yankees trousers and tried out his toothpick in a warm-up swing. Nor did they expect to see Gomez standing on any base at the conclusion of his at-bat. Then, staring a 0–0 tie in the eye, Gomez stuck out the bat and poked a Hallahan pitch over National League shortstop Dick Bartell's head for a single. Chugging all out, Dykes sped around third and was safe at home for a 1–0 American League lead.

It would be difficult to rate Gomez as the most surprised man in Comiskey Park because the line would be so long to determine that title holder, but he was right up there. When it came to boasting about hitting, the almost always talkative Gomez kept his mouth shut. Even reminiscing about the key hit decades later, Gomez did not feign expertise and made the occasion of batting safely sound more like an accident than anything else.

"So, you know who got the first hit in All-Star game history?" Gomez teased a reporter in 1973. "There was Ruth, Simmons, Dykes, Gehrig — the whole crowd. And guess who got the first hit in All-Star game history? You could look it up."[8] Certainly, as a trivia question Gomez might have even baseball experts guessing the right answer until closing time at the neighborhood bar, but he indeed recorded the first hit, and at an important moment.

"Don't ask me what the pitch was," Gomez added. "It could have been a fastball down the pipe. With a bat in my hands, I couldn't tell a curve from a Cuban palm ball. I do recall that only one of my eyes was closed when I swung."[9]

If Gomez, the weakest hitter in the American League lineup, brought a smile to the faces of his teammates, his flare of a single made Hallahan an unhappy camper. Gomez did all he could not to bust a gut laughing as he rested on first base and saw Cronin ahead of him on second. Hallahan's sense of humor was dented at the moment.

"I remember Hallahan looking over at me on first base with this real angry expression on his face," Gomez said. "I'm not really sure whether he was hurt or angry, or a little bit of both."[10]

It might have been a bit of both. Gomez's lifetime average was .147, and if he had come along four decades later to play for the Yankees, he might never have batted. The designated hitter was introduced to AL play in 1973. The irony is that it was first proposed by one of the administrators who helped make the All-Star game possible — National League president John Heydler — and yet his league has never embraced the concept.

Gomez figured that he was Exhibit A in arguments for introduction of the DH rule. "I don't think that many people remember that the idea of a designated hitter to bat for the pitcher was first proposed in the early 1930s (actually 1929) when I first joined the Yankees," Gomez said. "I'd like to think that it was part of my contribution to the game of baseball."[11]

Gomez did not have much time to gloat at first base. Hallahan was businesslike in dealing with the next hitter, left fielder Ben Chapman. Chapman hit a grounder to Bartell, and the shortstop made the toss to Frankie Frisch, covering second base. The play forced out Gomez and ended the inning. But the AL had a 1–0 lead.

Third Inning

Stung by Lefty Gomez's unlikely hit to fall behind, 1–0, the National League was ready for another crack at Gomez on the mound. Even trailing the American League had to give John McGraw heartburn. He knew this was going to be his final time managing a team, and even though 30 years had passed since he first developed a dislike for the upstart league, he wanted to go out a winner. McGraw had feuded with American League founder and first president Ban Johnson and transferred his irritation with Johnson to his league as a whole.

"McGraw made many enemies and kept many enemies in the National League," said another future Hall of Fame manager, Billy Southworth. "But when it came to World Series time, McGraw forgot all his animosities and feuds and was 100 percent National Leaguer. Nothing ever topped McGraw's dislike for the American League."[1]

Winning this game meant a great deal to McGraw. He knew his health was failing, though it's not clear how much he understood about his days being numbered. As a result, there was no bigger rooter for his men when one by one they came to the plate to try to reach Gomez.

Catcher Jimmy Wilson, the first scheduled batter for the NL, was a kindred spirit, the type of holler guy McGraw loved. Wilson wore his passion on his sleeve alongside any team patches from the Phillies, Cardinals, or Reds during his 18-year playing career. He was a lifelong National Leaguer.

Wilson was a career .284 hitter, but his fielding skills and knowledge of the game appealed most to McGraw. After retirement Wilson became a manager, leading the Phillies and Cubs. He was a National League man until the day he died — prematurely of a heart attack at 46.

The catcher could expound for long stretches on his baseball theories, especially about pitchers, their rest schedules, and how they took care of their arms. Of all things, Wilson developed ideas about the pitchers' angles of delivery and such by watching billiards matches. Those green felt players showed fatigue after long hours of play when the blood in their arms moved to their hands. When he realized this, Wilson snapped his fingers and decided that the pitchers' arms wearied when all the blood rushed to their hands.

"The accepted theory for breaking a pitcher of wildness is to work him plenty," Wilson said. "Managers pitch such a fellow in batting practice daily. It's the old practice makes perfect idea and with me it's the bunk. My theory is that a lot of wildness comes from tired arms. The arms are tired because they are heavy from the blood that has run down into them."[2]

Wilson was never nominated for the Nobel Prize in any scientific discipline, but baseball did come around to the idea of giving pitchers more, not less, rest. When it came to strategy, though, there was no mystery about what the National League needed when he came to bat in the third. "Just hit the ball safely, anywhere, Jimmy," was the likely advice from McGraw. He did not. Wilson hit a grounder to Dykes at third, and he easily threw the runner out at first. Putout Gehrig.

Bill Hallahan came to the plate next. He was aching for revenge on Gomez and either a walk or a hit putting him on base for the heavier hitters would advance his cause. Nothing doing. Hallahan got a good piece of a Gomez pitch but flied out to Al Simmons in center.

That brought Pepper Martin up again at the top of the order. He wanted to kick-start the National League's offense, his specialty. Martin was a hustling madman. If he tapped the ball to short, he was running all out down the first-base line trying to beat the throw. If he reached second, he might steal and slide head-first into the bag. Standing at the plate, severe concentration written on his face, Martin worked his incisors like a piston, chewing a wad of tobacco that seemed to be the size of the baseball. Even when he wasn't talking Martin was flapping his gums, pounding that chaw into a malleable lump.

Martin had the reputation of a big-game player. He excelled when the pressure was on and his Cardinals were in the World Series. He was one of the spiritual leaders of the Gashouse Gang, a good-time guy with a rollicking style who played the guitar in a Cards team band, but one who knew when it was time to take care of business.

In some ways, Martin took his cues in the game from Ty Cobb. He never hit with the flair of the Georgia Peach, but he played fiercely. It was a high priority for Gomez to keep Martin off the bases, and he dispatched the pepper pot in the best way possible. Martin hit a pop-up to Joe Cronin at short and was easily retired.

The Americans did not believe that their 1–0 lead would hold up and wanted to add a cushion. Charlie Gehringer, the Tigers' pride and one of the greatest second basemen of all time, took his turn as the lead-off man. Gehringer seven times led AL second basemen in fielding during his 19-year career and batted .320. Gehringer's bat contained serious pop and as a player he did everything well. In 1929, "The Mechanical Man," as he was sometimes called because of his near-perfection in several facets of the game, led the American League in games played, runs, hits, doubles, triples, stolen bases and fielding, while compiling a .339 average. It was the sort of all-around showing that could turn opposing pitchers' knees to jelly. A few years after this All-Star game, Gehringer recorded a 60-double season, and another year he won a batting title with a .371 average.

The longer Gehringer played, the more admirers he accumulated. Frank Navin, who owned the Tigers from 1908 to 1935, admitted that Gehringer was his favorite player. "He's everything a ballplayer should be," Navin said. "He has all the virtues and none of the faults. I don't think there has ever been another player just like him, meaning Charlie's equal as a hitter and fielder and deportment on and off the field was so near perfect."[3]

Gehringer was not flashy, and that nickname "Mechanical Man" was only one of a handful that illustrated both his talent and his quiet demeanor. He was also called "The Robot of the Infield" and "The Silent Man." For the time being, Lefty Gomez was counting on Gehringer as a teammate, but most of the year they were foes. Gomez had many one-on-one confrontations with Gehringer in Yankees-Tigers games, and he said while the guy never said much, he was always on base. When someone else criticized Gehringer for being colorless, Gomez replied, "Yeah, he's in a rut. He hits .350 on opening day and keeps hitting .350 the rest of the season."[4]

At the moment Gehringer was officially 0-for-0 in All-Star play because he had walked in the first inning. Now up for a second shot at Hallahan, Gehringer remained 0-for-0, and kept his on-base percentage at 1.000 because he walked again. Wild Bill's plague of wildness was sneaking up on him. Babe Ruth was due up next. Was this the window of opportunity?

The American League batboy for the All-Star game was a Comiskey Park regular. John McBride lived with his family four blocks from the White Sox's home and he started doing various errands for the Comiskey family owners. Louis J. Comiskey, Charles' son, took an interest in McBride. The youth said he was frequently asked to go to a store to buy cigarettes for all the players. Louis Comiskey gave him $8 for the $4.50 purchase and the remainder was his tip.

In 1929, McBride became the home-team batboy, a job he kept until 1934, and one that positioned him to work the Game of the Century. "I was as excited as anyone about the prospect of being part of the show with all those great players," McBride reminisced 50 years later.[5]

McBride started work at 9:00 A.M. that day for the 1:15 P.M. first pitch. His chores involved doing some of the little things to make the locker room feel homey for the players. He taped their names over their lockers and made sure that each player had a stool in front of his locker. When the players arrived from the other American League teams, McBride, with some help, identified their bats so that in the heat of the game it would be easy for a player to grab one. Strips with the players' initials were taped to the handles. McBride said it was easy to tell which bats belonged to Ruth because they were the biggest and heaviest.

Like the first-arriving players, McBride was surprised to see how many fans had come to Comiskey long before the game's start. The crowd was unusual in other ways. He could identify various luminaries. McBride spotted Mayor Ed Kelly in a private box and he saw Commissioner Kenesaw Mountain Landis when he came in. Landis had a fine box seat near the screen behind the plate.

McBride noted that the atmosphere in the park differed from a regular season game. The mood was lively, more festive. He was more excited, and he had been around big-league players for four seasons at that point. But so were the players themselves, he recalled. "The players felt the excitement," McBride said. "There was a sort of holiday spirit throughout the park."[6]

In a bit of foreshadowing, when Ruth first stepped out of the dugout onto the field, fans cheered loudly. And when he stepped into the batter's box to take batting practice and began powdering the ball into the distant stands, they roared.

Once the game began, McBride had a set routine, as well. The American League squad occupied the dugout on the third-base side of Comiskey Park and McBride stayed out of the way of the players, coaches and managers while the action was taking place. He positioned himself at the extreme right side of the dugout. When the National League was batting, McBride made chit-chat with the AL players who were not on the field. He also busied himself watching Connie Mack run the team. Mack was known for carrying a rolled-up scorecard around the dugout. He regularly waved it to urge his outfielders to move around, depending upon the batter.

When the American League was at bat, McBride was on the field, ready to chase down foul balls behind home plate or help re-supply the home plate umpire with new balls. He remained next to the on-deck hitter. In the third inning, when it was Ruth's turn to hit, Lou Gehrig was in the on-deck circle. McBride was next to Gehrig when Ruth stepped in against Hallahan for the second time that day.

Ruth was the star of stars in the first All-Star game. He was nearing the end of a spectacular 22-year career that had begun with the Boston Red Sox in 1914. He was already a legend. Most overlooked was Ruth's brilliance as a left-handed pitcher who won 94 games and excelled in the World Series. Although he was showing signs of becoming the first true home-run threat to put up large totals, the Red Sox famously and cataclysmically traded Ruth to the New York Yankees after the 1919 season.

The dead-ball era of baseball was about to end and Ruth was poised to generate the greatest period of excitement the game had ever known since professionals first took a buck to play in 1869. Clearly, the Red Sox did not know what they had, but they should have. In 1918, the year the Red Sox won their last World Series for 86 years, Ruth took on a much more mixed role of pitching and playing the field on off-days. He appeared in 95 games and batted .300 while leading the American League in homers for the first of 12 times with 11.

The next season, in 1919, Ruth's last in Boston, he hit a then-record 29 homers with 114 RBIs and a .322 batting average. Ruth was already a phenomenon, an almost unstoppable weapon. Yet the Red Sox still dealt the Bambino to the Yanks. When he exploded in 1920 with 54 homers, baseball's new dawn began. The lively ball was now part of the game, and soon enough Ruth was hitting 59 homers in a season, then 60. Everyone was hitting home runs, but no one brought such panache, such power, such style to the task as Ruth. Wherever the Yankees played, fans went wild for the Babe. In New York, the demand for tickets was unprecedented. Yankee Stadium was constructed and opened in 1923 to accommodate the fans clamoring for a glimpse of Ruth.

When the world fawned over Ruth, he inhaled the adulation like an elixir. He was the ultimate party boy, carousing, drinking, and eating to excess at all hours of the night. When he ate too many hot dogs at one sitting, he suffered "the belly ache heard around the world." Once the possessor of the somewhat svelte figure of an athlete, that belly grew and grew. He was impish and charming, benevolent to children, dashing in a fur coat, and friendly to everyone. The public loved Ruth.

Teammates joked about rooming with Ruth's suitcase because he was never in the hotel room. He winked at film-makers of newsreels, flirted with all the gals, and hit home runs that tantalized astronomers for the distances they traveled. He was too good, too much, too out of control, and the only ones who cared about it were his managers and team officials. When Ruth was making $80,000 a year during the Depression, a writer asked how it felt to be making more than President Herbert Hoover. Ruth replied that he had had a better year. It was indisputably the truth.

For all that was reported about Ruth's playful and playboy nature, much of his behavior remained a secret from his family, withheld as gossip by friendly sportswriters. It was a different era. If there was a "That's just the Babe" attitude towards the slugger, there was no attempt to embarrass him.

Long after Ruth died, veteran sportswriter Fred Lieb took the liberty of recalling a couple of incidents involving Ruth that never made it into the newspapers. They smacked of burlesque in their outrageousness, though they carried a whiff of violent threat, too.

Following a Yankees' exhibition game in Shreveport, Louisiana, in 1921, the team's departing train paused in Baton Rouge to take on coal or water, as Lieb remembered. "Suddenly, the door of one of the cars opened and a puffing, scary-eyed Ruth came rushing into the car," Lieb wrote. "Some five feet behind him came a frantic woman. She wielded a knife and had its blade aimed at the fleeing Ruth. Ruth, running as fast as he ever did on the bases, ran back out on the platform, the length of the train, and jumped on the train as the engineer was pulling out."[7]

Lieb, an eyewitness, could only guess that it was a matter of unrequited love. No one asked Ruth about the apparently tense relationship. On another occasion that same season, a particularly risky one for Ruth one might surmise, on a road trip to Detroit Ruth was seen sprinting out the door of a hotel with an angry man brandishing a pistol in full-speed-ahead pursuit. To elude the man, Ruth hailed a taxi, jumped in, and yelled, "Anywhere!" to the driver. As the driver accelerated, Ruth slipped out the far door and ducked down in traffic before hiding out in a store across the street. The red-faced, gun-wielding pursuer followed the taxi cab. What was it about? Lieb didn't know and didn't ask. It would have been news if the beloved Ruth had been shot, but other than that, Lieb felt, probably nobody would have cared about Ruth's personal business.[8]

In an era such as today with round-the-clock media and no athlete's business being considered personal anymore, Ruth's image likely would have been different. But any time he came to bat in the All-Star game, the applause was warm, the cheering was loud, and the fans hoped to see just one thing to satisfy them — a home run that required the Lewis and Clark Expedition to locate.

In the first inning, Hallahan had the upper hand, whiffing Ruth on a called strike. Hallahan was the one who expressly said everyone wanted to see Ruth in the game. So far, from his perch on the mound, the view had been OK. There was nothing more satisfying for a pitcher than watching the Bambino — who had smacked 670 careers homers by then — being baffled by your best stuff. This was round two.

Hallahan checked on Gehringer on first. Perhaps he was worried about his control after walking the Detroit star twice. Perhaps he grew overconfident because he had nailed the Babe in the opening frame. But Hallahan, who periodically had serious difficulty controlling the direction of his pitches, still seemed careful. He had two strikes on Ruth when he served up a fat one. Ruth drew back his huge bat and swung. The sound of bat hitting ball was a percussive one. The ball soared towards right field. When it finally came down, deep in the seats, Ruth was trotting around the bases behind Gehringer, the author of a two-run homer. Comiskey fans went wild. This is what they came to see. The Babe always knew how to rise to the occasion. He set out on his familiar home-run trot. At this stage of his career, Ruth didn't run all out very often. He took short, mincing steps as he rounded the bases.

McBride was closer than any non-participant when Ruth swung, and when he connected the batboy knew the score. "I knew it was gone," he said. "I raced to home plate with my heart pounding and was waiting long before Babe arrived. When Babe got there, I shook his hand and said, 'Nice going, Babe.' He said, 'Thanks, kid.'"[9]

As the decibel level increased in Comiskey, Lou Gehrig, who had barely reacted to Ruth crossing the plate, stepped up to hit. Hallahan had little to offer, walking "The Iron Horse," who was well into his consecutive games playing streak in 1933. That was Hallahan's fourth walk. The National League trailed, and there were still no outs in the third. McGraw had seen enough. Hallahan was sent to the showers and the Cubs' Lon Warneke came on in relief.

The stalwart right-hander had led the National League in 1932 with 22 victories and was on his way to an 18-win season in 1933. Warneke had led the fan voting for pitchers and by rights should have been the starter. McGraw chose Hallahan instead, but now needed Warneke to bail him out. The strategy proved sound. Al Simmons was up. He flicked a grounder to Dick Bartell at short. Bartell scooped the ball up, threw to Frankie Frisch covering second, who threw it on to first to Bill Terry. The NL had a double play.

Jimmy Dykes was the next batter and he singled to left field. But Joe Cronin could do nothing against Warneke. He flied out to center to end the inning. After three innings, the American League led, 3–0, thanks to Babe Ruth.

11

Fourth Inning

Lefty Gomez had tamed the National League hitters and even dented his opponent with a timely swing of the bat, but manager Connie Mack decided that three innings was all he would ask from Gomez's arm. To start the fourth, Mack inserted Alvin Crowder, whose nickname was "General." The moniker did not attach itself to Crowder because he made those approaching him salute, but because he had the same last name as World War I General Enoch Crowder, who oversaw the Selective Service Act, i.e., the draft.

Crowder the pitcher was pretty much in command on the mound. He won a career-high 26 games for the Washington Senators in 1932, and during the All-Star game year of '33 Crowder finished with 24 victories. Crowder also had a fine 1926 for the St. Louis Browns when he posted a 21–5 record.

A right-hander who stood just 5'10" and weighed 170 pounds, Crowder had surprisingly good throwing speed for his size, but when his fastball began to desert him around the time of the All-Star game, he began relying on guile to get men out. Crowder was a latecomer to professional baseball. Growing up in North Carolina, Crowder worked in a tobacco factory and then joined the army. His service featured a colorful itinerary, including being stationed in Siberia, first in Vladivostok and then on the shore of Lake Baikal, the largest lake in the world. "They have real winters in Siberia," said Crowder, who said he experienced temperatures of minus-60 Fahrenheit.[1]

While in the army Crowder traveled through Manchuria and Japan and spent time in the Philippines. That's where he worked hard on his game and improved enough to turn professional when he was discharged back in the United States. His baseball incentive overseas was fueled by a desire to avoid latrine duty by competing for the post team.

Crowder's date of birth was listed as January 11, 1901, in some publications, but was set at January 11, 1899, in the *Baseball Encyclopedia*. Since
he did not see his first major league action until 1926, it is possible Crowder
tried to shave a couple of years off his true age when seeking a baseball
job. When *The Sporting News* carried his obituary in 1972, his age was
given as 73.

Besides his military ties, in an era when practically only soldiers and
sailors gave into their artistic impulses, Crowder was heavily tattooed. He
was apparently "The Illustrated Man" of his time, a walking piece of art
in the dugout. "The gentleman's collection of chest murals, shoulder
marines and forearm still lifes would make an important contribution to
the Metropolitan Art Museum," wrote one sportswriter, who added that
Crowder was "a human picture gallery."[2]

Crowder did not distract hitters with his colorful tattoos, but he got
the job done. First up against Crowder was second baseman Frankie Frisch.
Like his teammate Pepper Martin, Frisch was a manager's delight for firing
up rallies. Manager John McGraw knew well what Frisch could do since
he had played eight seasons for him with the Giants, once producing 223
hits in a season.

An article in a national magazine, written by famous journalist
Quentin Reynolds, made it clear McGraw had a soft spot for Frisch because
of the man's hustle and desire on the field. "Frisch is my boy," McGraw
said.[3] It was suggested in some quarters that McGraw, who raised Frisch
from a rookie in 1919, had made him in his own image, feisty and heady.

If Frisch was the second coming of McGraw, just like a son to him,
McGraw proved that the number one thing in his life was the pursuit of
victory. He traded Frisch to the Cardinals for Rogers Hornsby and a
pitcher. But he wasn't going to waste Frisch's talents now that he had him
a second time around, even for just a day. Frisch got good wood on the
ball and tattooed it on a line to center where Al Simmons speared the shot.

The second batter stepping into the box for the National League in
the fourth inning was Philadelphia outfielder Chuck Klein. At that point
in his career Klein was one of the most feared hitters in the game. He was
on an incredible season-after-season tear, in the so-called zone, for five
years. By 1933, he was completing his fifth straight season with at least
200 hits, including a spectacular high of 250 in 1930. During this skein
Klein won two batting titles, scored more than 150 runs in a season twice,

cracked many as 59 doubles, and drove in 170 runs once. He led the National League in homers four times.

Klein, who ended up batting .320 lifetime and being elected to the Baseball Hall of Fame, was not a batter to mess around with. A wise occupant of the mound knew to be very cautious throwing to Klein. Crowder was, and he retired Klein on another grounder. The hit bounced to Lou Gehrig at first, and he fielded it and then stepped on the bag. Chick Hafey gave it a try next, but he popped up to Jimmy Dykes at third. No problems for Crowder. Promote him to five-star general. After four times up, the National League had collected two hits and no runs.

NL hurler Lon Warneke had taken over for Bill Hallahan in the third after it appeared Wild Bill might walk in a run or two if he wasn't relieved. Now Warneke started his first inning from scratch.

Although Warneke was a singer who dressed in Western garb at times, his "The Arkansas Hummingbird" nickname stemmed from his baseball career. Arkansas was Warneke's home and he threw the ball with such a rushed motion that a sportswriter thought he was moving as quickly as a hummingbird. As a right-hander Warneke offered a change from Hallahan's southpaw deliveries, something McGraw hoped would bother the American League batters.

There was minimal quoting of players in advance of big games in the newspaper world in the 1930s. There were more newspapers, but no television stations, fewer radio stations, and no Internet. Most reporting on games was play-by-play, but periodically, especially before the Game of the Century, members of the media sought out players for their thoughts. Warneke had made a radio appearance before the game and while he revealed nothing of note, he did provide a quote on what he would do if he played. "I'll be out there bearin' down all I can," Warneke said.[4] Presumably he did so in all games, so it was not exactly sizzling news being imparted, but at least fans could hear the pitcher's voice.

Regarded as a superb fielder, the 6'2", 185-pound Warneke was toiling in the minors when the Chicago Cubs spotted him and paid $100 to a minor-league club to obtain his rights. Warneke was just 21 when he made his major league debut with a single game in 1930. In a 15-year career he won 20 or more games three times.

Warneke brought a lot of passion to the mound when he pitched. He threw hard and carried to work the arrogance of a first-rate starter who believed he could get every hitter out every time. If he didn't win a ballgame he sometimes remained in an angry mood. In 1932, when he won 22 games, Warneke blew up after one disappointing pitching performance, smashing his teammates' straw hats in the clubhouse. Less than two weeks prior to the All-Star game, Warneke suffered a 2–1 defeat to the Boston Braves. He felt the outcome should have gone the other way and when he returned to the visitors' locker room, he grabbed a bat and smashed the water heater. The Braves billed the Cubs $25 for a replacement unit.

Hitting for the American League to lead off the bottom of the fourth inning was Boston Red Sox catcher Rick Ferrell, whose brother Wes was also selected for the All-Star team. The scheduled AL catcher was the Yankees' Bill Dickey, but he was ruled out of participating the day before the game. Dickey had suffered a torn muscle in his right leg above the knee. He tried treating it for a few days, but when he couldn't play for his regular club on July 5, it was decided he would not travel to the All-Star game. Dickey, Mack's first choice as catcher, was blocking the plate against a stolen base in a game against the Senators when injured. With Dickey sidelined, Ferrell joined the starting lineup.

Another man might have been saddened missing out on the Game of the Century and being part of an inaugural event that blossomed into something permanent and special on the baseball calendar. But Dickey said years later he was philosophical about being hurt for the first All-Star game. "I wasn't disappointed about not playing," Dickey said. "Being chosen was the big thing."[5]

Ferrell grew up in North Carolina, one of six baseball-playing brothers. Wes was the only other one to reach the majors, and he won 20 or more games five times for the Cleveland Indians and the Red Sox. His career was cut short by arm woes and his image was besmirched by his violent temper.

Rick Ferrell was regarded as a genius of a receiver, a tremendous fielder who called a smart game. But he always was open to learning more and chose to sit by Mack during the All-Star game when his side was at bat to see what the so-called master did. Eventually, Ferrell, who was selected to the Baseball Hall of Fame in 1984, became a long-time front office executive with the Detroit Tigers.

Wes Ferrell, in his last season with the Indians, had as much bench time as Mack. He did not get into the game in relief and said he was not surprised after the manager's pep talk at the Del Prado Hotel suggested if things were going the American League's way he was not going to change much. Wes Ferrell did observe how energetic Mack, a former catcher, was at age 70 and how he kept his brother Rick close at hand for instructions.

"What surprised me, he wanted his catcher sitting next to him every play," said Wes Ferrell. "He kept a scorecard the whole game, moving up and down the dugout in civilian clothes."[6]

Given his tantrums when things didn't go his way and destroyed his chances of winning a game, Warneke was McGraw's kind of guy. The boss felt more warmly towards his pitcher when Warneke made Ferrell fly to Chuck Klein in right field. Crowder came to the plate and he posed no threat, grounding out second to first, Frisch to Bill Terry.

That brought up Ben Chapman, the American League leadoff man. Chapman was an interesting case. The Alabaman who became infamous later in life for taunting Jackie Robinson with racist invective was another hard-nosed player, representative of an era when many players came from the Deep South, had minimal schooling, and needed the game to raise themselves from poverty.

Chapman's playing career was overshadowed by the avalanche of publicity he received when managing the Phillies and the incident with Robinson took place, and also by the company he kept with the Yankees. Chapman played on New York pennant-winning teams with Babe Ruth, Lou Gehrig, and Joe DiMaggio. There were only so many accolades passed around per team in the newspapers, so it was difficult to obtain attention when playing with those guys.

However, when Chapman was first making his mark in the Yanks' lineup, manager Joe McCarthy predicted he would be a star. "He has everything that goes to make the grand ballplayer," McCarthy said, "youth, perfect health, and physique, ambition and eagerness, speed and judgment, style and genius. If he doesn't reach the top, he will have only himself to blame."[7]

Not knowing when to keep his mouth shut harmed Chapman's career and legacy in more ways than one. By the time he came across Robinson, he had already been labeled a temperamental player who got into scraps with teammates. As part of his how-not-to-make-friends-and-influence-people routine, Chapman once ripped Ruth to his face for being overrated. "If you were paid as much as you were worth, you'd be making less than

I am," he told the Bambino.[8] Not everyone in the New York clubhouse loved the Babe, but the odds were that more liked the slugger — and recognized his importance to the team — than liked Chapman. And certainly Ruth had more clout with the franchise.

Chapman was not only chosen to play in the first All-Star game in 1933, but he represented the Yankees in 1934 and 1935, too. Despite his exemplary on-field performances, New York traded him in 1936 to Washington, where Chapman made a fourth All-Star team.

Chapman was not going to beat teams with his home-run prowess, but he was a dangerous hitter. He excelled at getting on base and he hit for average. Warneke was well aware of Chapman's traits. Unlike Hallahan, however, Warneke was not unusually wild and he took care with his pitches around the plate. He fooled Chapman, got him to nibble, and the left fielder could manage no more than a routine grounder to Pepper Martin at third. Martin made the easy throw to Terry at first and the Nationals were out of the inning.

Warneke had done his job by keeping the door shut on the American League offense. With the score 3–0, a comeback was well within reach for McGraw's bunch.

At that point, unlike in future All-Star games, Mack and McGraw had made few adjustments. Playing to win did not mean making sure everyone got a taste of the action. After four innings complete, the starting lineups were intact. Only the starting pitchers had been replaced — Hallahan, no doubt in McGraw's mind, out of necessity, and Gomez for no obvious reason.

......
12
......

Fifth Inning

It was a comfort to American League shortstop Joe Cronin that Alvin Crowder was on the mound. Not only had Cronin seen what Crowder could do when he was right, but he was a teammate. Both men played for the Washington Senators, and to Cronin that meant something. The strangest thing about the Game of the Century to the 26-year-old infielder who had begun life in San Francisco was that he had been thrown together with all of these other guys just for a day.

This special group of AL All-Star players were comrades, united in the common effort to defeat the National League. But since April they had been foes, enemies seeking the same prize that wasn't big enough to be shared. Tomorrow they would be opponents again. For 24 hours they were pals.

"It was a great honor to be chosen to play with people like Babe Ruth, Lou Gehrig, Jimmie Foxx and Tony Lazzeri, but it was a little bit strange, too," Cronin recalled. "Your teammates were guys you battled hard against during the season. You hated them one day and were playing together the next."[1]

The mindset of the players, Cronin remembered, was to make a good impression on the National League guys that were known primarily by reputation. If you hadn't been in the World Series practically every year like the Yankees, the only times you saw the NL guys was in spring training. The All-Star game counted more than that. Cronin said the festive scene, full house, and belief that the game was a one-time thing did not make him nervous. He just wanted to show well. In the first inning, between two grounders and a line drive, he was involved in all three National League outs. "When I came to the bench," Cronin said, "Connie Mack said, 'They're trying you out, kid.'"[2]

Cronin, who ended up playing in six more All-Star games, fielded well the entire game. In a 20-year career, primarily with the Senators and Red Sox, Cronin, who became a player-manager, batted .301 and was eventually chosen for the Baseball Hall of Fame. It was not only his exploits in the field that recommended him, either. Before he left the sport he ascended to American League president.

Good fielding helped the AL stars in the dream game. It was first sacker Lou Gehrig's turn to stay busy in the top of the fifth. Bill Terry led off and hit a grounder to Charlie Gehringer at second, who grabbed the ball and tossed it to Gehrig for the first out. Wally Berger batted next, and with Crowder keeping his pitches low, also hit a grounder. This one bounced to Cronin, who threw to Gehrig at first without incident for the second out.

By 1933, the 6', 200-pound left-handed swinger was well on his way to becoming the greatest first baseman of all time. Although he broke into the big leagues in 1923 when he was 20, fresh off the Ivy League campus of Columbia University in New York, Gehrig did not become the New York Yankee regular first baseman until 1925. More than 100 years after his birth and many decades after his death, Gehrig remains one of the icons of the sport, his origins and demise as a player both the stuff of legend.

On June 1, 1925, Gehrig entered a Yankees game as a pinch-hitter. It was an innocuous substitution by manager Miller Huggins. The next day, regular Yankee starting first baseman Wally Pipp complained of a minor injury. Since Pipp was slumping anyway, Huggins gave him the day off and inserted Gehrig into the starting lineup. The move was designed to be temporary. But Gehrig acquitted himself so well that Huggins gave him the job permanently. Pipp evolved into the answer to a trivia question. Gehrig evolved into a superstar.

For the next 15 seasons, every time the Yankees played a game, Gehrig was at first base. He ended up playing in 2,130 consecutive games, easily the record and one most baseball fans thought would never be broken. Eventually, it was, by Baltimore Orioles Hall of Fame shortstop Cal Ripken Jr. At the height of his powers, Gehrig, regarded as the quiet man of the Yankee roster, formed the sport's most devastating one-two hitting punch with Babe Ruth.

Gehrig was chosen for the first eight All-Star games, and when he retired he had accumulated 493 home runs, 1,995 runs batted in, and an average of .340. Yankee managers employed Gehrig in the fourth spot, or cleanup, in their batting orders, usually reserved for the most feared slugger. In this case, he was slotted one position behind Ruth. The thinking went that pitchers would have to throw honestly to Ruth because they wouldn't want to walk him and face Gehrig. Time after time, opposing pitchers did provide Ruth with bases on balls, and he reposed on base, waiting for Gehrig to strike. Gehrig made those hurlers pay for putting Ruth on ahead of him.

Off the field, Ruth, whose middle name might as well have been "flamboyance," and Gehrig, whose middle name might as well have been "homebody," were yin and yang. There were times during their careers when they quietly feuded, but by the time Ruth retired and Gehrig became ill in the late 1930s, they had patched things up.

"I never knew a fellow who lived a cleaner life," Ruth said of Gehrig, hinting of one way in which the two men differed by nature. "He was a clean living boy, a good baseball player, a great hustler. He was just a grand guy."[3]

Ruth wasn't simply uttering a platitude when he said Gehrig was a clean liver. Gehrig was more choirboy than playboy. He came under the influence of his mother and wife much more than Ruth. When he did hire a press agent, the irrepressible Christy Walsh, and opportunities to perform in Hollywood opened up, Gehrig was very conservative about roles he might be interested in. "This stuff's all right, but no lipstick," he said when being primped for an audition. "And I won't go for that Tarzan stuff, either."[4] Apparently, Gehrig was neither a Ruth nor a Johnny Weissmuller.

Gehrig had a clear sense of self. That meant he knew he was not a swinger or a bright lights person off the field, and he recognized that Ruth always would be, in his own mind and in the view of others.

"Let's face it," Gehrig said, "I'm not a headline guy. I always knew that as long as I was following the Babe to the plate I could have gone up there and stood on my head. No one would have noticed the difference. When the Babe was through swinging, whether he hit one or fanned, nobody paid any attention to the next hitter. They were all talking about what the Babe had done."[5]

That may have been a bit of an exaggeration since baseball people always recognized Gehrig's worth, but there were elements of truth to the generalization. Even in the first All-Star game, while Gehrig was quietly going about doing his job, Ruth hit the two-run homer that left people buzzing.

Gehrig offended no one, came to work every day, worked hard while he was on the job, and was so good that everyone in the sport knew it, whether his personality was tame or not. He earned respect from everyone who saw him play.

"Gehrig never learned that a ballplayer couldn't be good every day," said long-time catcher Hank Gowdy.[6]

Regardless of whether he dabbled with Hollywood or not, baseball was always going to be Gehrig's primary source of income. It was at the root of his identity. He was definitely more likely to win the Most Valuable Player award than an Academy Award.

There were two outs and Crowder didn't appear to have broken a sweat in handling the National League's top batsmen. The third batter up was shortstop Dick Bartell. Bartell's reputation was built around his solid glove and his durability — he played in nearly every game, but in his early years in the majors he regularly hit over .300 for the Pittsburgh Pirates. Now with the Phillies, his average remained respectable for a middle infielder, but he was only a lukewarm threat.

When Bartell got a small piece of a Crowder pitch and hit it high but foul down the first-base line, he looked like dead meat. Gehrig drifted across the foul line, keeping his eye on the ball's flight. But when it came down, Gehrig dropped it, giving Bartell new life.

That was one thing a pitcher did not like to see happen to benefit Bartell. He was scrappy, rarely made mistakes, and usually took advantage of second chances. He was another classic John McGraw type, always playing with fire in his belly and hollering to rouse his teammates. When covering second base he held his ground against hard-sliding runners and his legs were decorated with a series of scars where cuts from sharp spikes had healed.

Some opponents compared Bartell's hard-nosed style with the ultimate, never-give-an-inch ballplayer, Ty Cobb, and labeled Bartell "dirty" or "rowdy." He protested, saying that's not what he was about and that his critics were mistaking his will to win with negative play. "The price of victory is extra effort," Bartell said. "To win you must put forth that added ounce of endeavor."[7]

Bartell was born in Chicago in 1907 and grew up in a middle-class family. His father was an accountant who had been a good semi-pro base-ball player who once made an unassisted triple play in a game. Bartell was not raised in the Midwest, however. Soon after he was born, his family moved to California. It was there he gained his real introduction to the National Pastime.

Bartell broke into the majors in 1927 and played 18 years, collecting 2,165 hits, before becoming a coach and then a minor-league manager. But his image was established early. He routinely got into arguments with umpires and always made his feelings known when his emotions bubbled up. Well into his career, Bartell made his American League debut with the Detroit Tigers. He felt he was greeted inhospitably by St. Louis Browns right-hander Slick Coffman, and the result was the most satisfying base hit of his career.

"I thought he was going to hit me in the ear," said Bartell of being forced to duck a Coffman offering. "When I got up, I was furious and I never wanted to hit more than I did then. I got a two-bagger on the next pitch and I still grin every time I recall it."[8]

After escaping the certainty of making an easy out on Gehrig's muff, Bartell put some pep into his warm-up swings. Crowder, who was cruising, felt he still had the upper hand and his delivery proved it. Once again, Bartell got a small piece of it. Once again the ball shot high in the sky down the first-base line, and once again it was in foul ground. Gehrig stepped across the bag into foul territory, where history did not repeat itself. This time Gehrig closed his glove on the ball for the third out.

The Game of the Century was half over. Unlike football and basket-ball where regularly scheduled halftimes bring out entertainment such as marching bands, normally the only acknowledgement of a halfway point in baseball is likely to be watching groundskeepers drag the infield to smooth the dirt.

By pre-arrangement for this special game, however, there were some changes in the offing. Through the top of the fifth inning, the American League ball was in use. For the remainder of the game the National League ball would be in play. The four umpires also switched assignments. Bill Klem moved behind the plate in place of Bill Dineen. Would it make any difference in the calls having an American League arbiter or a National League umpire behind the dish? There had been no controversy over balls and strikes — and none followed.

Lon Warneke still represented the NL on the mound. Unlike Bill Hallahan, he was stingy with free passes and the walk was no longer an easy way on base. The American League was happy with its 3–0 lead, content to watch pitchers Lefty Gomez and General Crowder handcuff the best the NL had to offer. But the home team was on the prowl for more runs, too.

Second baseman Charlie Gehringer led off the bottom of the fifth inning and was retired on a fly ball to Wally Berger in center field. Babe Ruth was up next, and proving he did not care if pitchers were throwing an American League ball, a National League ball, or a beach ball, he singled off Warneke to center. Gehrig came to the plate hoping to do what he did so many times a year in the regular season — drive home his Yankee teammate Ruth. He could not do so this time, with Gehrig striking out.

That brought AL center fielder Al Simmons into the batter's box. Simmons had led all players nominated for the All-Star game in votes received but had not yet distinguished himself that day at Comiskey Park. With Ruth on first, it lined up as a good time to smash the ball somewhere safely in the spacious stadium. That was something Simmons had proven he was very good at since reaching the majors with the Philadelphia A's in 1924.

Simmons was born into a family of Polish heritage in Milwaukee in 1902 as Aloys Syzmanski and his name was Americanized to better fit in with baseball teammates. Box score typists were forever thankful. From the moment he broke into the big time, the righty-swinging Simmons was an exceptional hitter. He drove in 100 or more runs his first 11 years — still a record — and in his second season he gathered 253 hits en route to a .387 average. He hit even higher, .390, in 1931. But after the A's recent scorched earth run of pennants, Connie Mack began economizing and shipped Simmons to the White Sox. For this All-Star game, Simmons was playing under his old boss in his new home park.

Simmons never hit as well in spacious Comiskey as he had in tiny Shibe Park, but he remained a dangerous hitter. Simmons and Mack got off to a slow start. When still a local semi-pro player with a train-load of confidence, Simmons wrote a letter to the famous Mack asking to accompany the A's to spring training. He politely said that if given a try, he felt he could make the team. "If you take me South with you, I am sure I can make good," Simmons wrote in part.[9]

Al Simmons (left) was in his first year with the White Sox and playing in his home park when he kidded around with hard-hitting slugger Chuck Klein of the Phillies before the All-Star game encounter that was supposed to be only a one-time event. No one pushed harder for the establishment of the game than *Chicago Tribune* sports editor Arch Ward, who was credited with the idea to start it. (Photograph courtesy National Baseball Hall of Fame.)

Mack could have ignored the entreaty altogether, but he didn't. However, he turned down the chance to evaluate Simmons for free. "I appreciate your interest in my team and me," Mack replied, "but it is impossible for me to give you a tryout this season. I receive about 1,000 similar requests each year."[10] If Mack wrote back to each aspirant, then bully for him, but not having any awareness of Simmons' skills cost him.

Not long after, in 1922, Simmons was tearing the cover off the ball for the minor league Milwaukee Brewers. A former Mackman, Harry Davis, was in the audience on a day when Simmons cracked a home run, triple and single. Davis took note. Another year of Simmons simmering in Shreveport, Louisiana, was all it took to virtually wipe out Mack's bank account. Mack spent $50,000 to acquire the future star he could have had at no cost for a simple look-see.

Simmons got results despite a batting stance that was ridiculed as certain to hold him back. As a young major leaguer, he earned the nickname "Bucketfoot," for, as it was said, putting his right foot in the bucket, or behind him. This was not a compliment but an observation that his stance was hopeless. Standing in the batter's box, Simmons pointed his left foot down the left-field line when he swung. This supposed disadvantage never handicapped him, though. Simmons did things his way and his unabashed success quieted all critics. To Mack's credit, he did not try to alter Simmons' style because he had learned enough about the player's natural hitting ability. Simmons always admired Mack for the manager choosing to let the hitter be himself.

The 5'11", 190-pound Simmons expressed fondness for Mack, but he did not have nice things to say about opposing pitchers, whom he lumped together as public enemy number one. "I hate all pitchers," Simmons said. "Hits are my bread and butter. They're trying to take the bread and butter out of my mouth. I hate them."[11]

In 1931, Mack signed Simmons to a three-year, $100,000 contract. He did not begrudge him the bucks after repeated years of success and his aid in leading the A's to multiple pennants. However, the Great Depression intervened and Philadelphia's attendance plummeted. Mack could no longer afford Simmons' deal. After the 1932 season, Mack began shedding payroll, and that led to shipping Simmons to the White Sox. Without such drastic action — Mack sold other players, too — the Tall Tactician feared his business would sink into bankruptcy, as so many others did during the awful economic times.

Warneke worked the count to 0–2 on Simmons. That is a pitcher's count, and the common strategy is to waste a pitch, throw it low or high, inside or outside, wherever the batter's best-known weakness lay. Warneke's attempt to fool Simmons didn't work. Instead, Simmons lashed a single to left field. That advanced the Babe to second. There were two men on and two men out. The fans at Comiskey came to life, rooting for the American League men to add another run.

Jimmy Dykes came to the plate. After his playing career, Dykes would become the long-time manager of the White Sox, brought in to piece together a fresh, winning team to make the fans forget the disgrace of the

Black Sox Scandal and the years of terrible teams that represented the city in the following years. He was a genial fellow, prone to making jokes, and popular with newspapermen and Chicagoans. He wanted to make some noise now, make his mark with a run-scoring hit. But he couldn't do it.

Dykes swung at a Warneke pitch, and hit it directly to Bartell at short. Bartell vacuumed the ball, made the flip to Frankie Frisch covering second, and Simmons was out on a force play to end the inning. No hero's welcome for Dykes this time up.

·····
13
·····

Sixth Inning

For five complete innings the American League had dominated the National League in the Game of the Century. For frustrated NL manager John McGraw, it wasn't even the Game of the Week. His hired hands, allegedly the cream of the crop in the senior circuit, were barely clouting loud fouls off the American League moundsmen.

The fiercely competitive McGraw did not like the situation. His men had to do better. Mulling a change of lineup, McGraw chose to send up a pinch-hitter to lead off the top of the sixth. Jimmy Wilson was a renowned fielder, but he was no Babe Ruth at bat.

McGraw's eyes roamed the bench. Who might jump-start a National League rally? He settled on Lefty O'Doul. O'Doul, a left-handed swinger representing the Brooklyn Dodgers in the big game, was nearing the end of a short but very productive career. He had batted .398 in 1929, and when he retired after the 1934 season, O'Doul's lifetime hitting mark would be .349.

The slashing, line-drive hitter was 31 before he became a major league regular, and he had a most nontraditional education in the game. O'Doul was a San Francisco boy who grew to a sturdy 6', 180 pounds, and was equally enthralled with the Pacific Coast League as the majors. Although he was aware of baseball as a youth and was an active participant, he was just another kid on the block until he reached junior high school.

O'Doul's seventh-grade teacher was Rosie Stultz, a baseball fanatic — and coach. She taught him the finer points of the sport. "It's probably the strangest story in baseball," O'Doul said. "A woman actually taught me to play the game. Sure, I had always played some ball since I learned to walk, but it was Miss Stultz who taught me the essential fundamentals of the game. She taught me to pitch, field and hit."[1]

Although O'Doul was a late bloomer in making it to the majors, he turned in some spectacular performances, once gathering 254 hits in a season. He also managed to hit more than 30 home runs in a season while striking out just 19 times. The man could control his bat. When you can hit like that, people pay attention to everything you do, even your quirks. O'Doul, who had green eyes, was Irish in every sense of the word. He wore green suits like a leprechaun. When he ran out of green suits, he wore green pants, green hats and green socks.

After a goodwill baseball tour of Japan in 1931, O'Doul returned to the Asian country to instigate a more sophisticated level of play. While this gesture was appreciated, the efforts to make Japanese baseball big league were shelved by a minor interruption known as World War II. Between Pearl Harbor in 1941 and Hiroshima in 1945, O'Doul's baseball involvement in Japan was placed on hold. However, after peace was declared, O'Doul brought a team of Pacific League All-Stars to Japan and resumed his work in building the Japanese game. General Douglas MacArthur proclaimed that O'Doul's 1949 ability to smooth over differences between occupying U.S. troops and embittered Japanese citizens was "the greatest piece of diplomacy ever."[2]

O'Doul's selection to the first All-Star team was tinged with a bit of controversy. He went 0-for-27 to start the 1933 season and he was traded from Brooklyn to the New York Giants just prior to the game. When O'Doul retired just a year later, he returned to the West Coast and managed the San Francisco Seals for 17 years. That, however, was in the future and McGraw wanted results in the present.

O'Doul wanted to do something dramatic, but he could not. Instead, he grounded to the American League's Charlie Gehringer at second, who fielded the ball and threw O'Doul out at first. McGraw's strategy fizzled. While McGraw subbed out Wilson, he allowed pitcher Lon Warneke to hit for himself. Unexpectedly, Warneke cracked a triple off AL hurler Crowder.

At last the National League was threatening. Next up was Pepper Martin. These were the types of situations Martin excelled at, but this time he hit a routine ground ball to Jimmy Dykes at third. Dykes threw to Lou Gehrig covering first for the first out, but he was unable to hold the runner and Warneke scored. That made the score American League 3, National League 1.

The bases were empty but the NL players felt better about things. Frankie Frisch, "The Fordham Flash," was due up at the plate. The man known as "McGraw's boy," was no longer a Giant but a St. Louis Cardinal, a ringleader of the Gashouse Gang. The trading of Frisch hurt McGraw, but he believed in the move. Giants fans, too, lamented Frisch going over to the enemy. The famous poet, Ogden Nash, wrote about Frisch's transfer:

> F is for Fordham
> And Frankie and Frisch;
> I wish he were back
> With the Giants, I wish.[3]

Whether it was for league pride, as a favor to McGraw, or just to rekindle days of yesteryear, Frisch stepped up to the plate against Crowder with mayhem on his mind. Then he promptly slugged a solo home run to pull the National League within one run, 3–2. The ball sailed deep out of play to the right-field side. Things were cooking for the NL. Could they erase the deficit in one shot? McGraw and the others had to be thinking maybe so after Chuck Klein singled to left-center.

There were two men out, one man on, in a one-run game for Chick Hafey when he came to the plate. This might be a turning point. NL fans had high hopes. But Hafey couldn't hit anything solid. Instead, he hit a grounder to Dykes, who fired the ball to Gehrig for the third out. Nevertheless, it was a one-run job with three innings to play. The Americans were no longer looking invincible.

After making few changes in the lineup — certainly many fewer than baseball fans are used to seeing in the modern All-Star game — McGraw and Connie Mack on the American League side indulged in a little chess playing. With Wilson out of the game following O'Doul's pinch-hitting duties, McGraw inserted Chicago Cub Gabby Hartnett at catcher for the bottom of the sixth.

Hartnett's given name was Charles Leo, but he earned his nickname by being a chatty, or gabby, guy. During his playing days, Hartnett was sometimes called the sport's "noisiest" catcher. Hartnett was a say-hey player for his teammates, constantly keeping them apprised of the outs and count. He talked to hitters in the batter's box and kept up a running conversation with umpires, kindly informing them if they had missed a pitch thrown by a compatriot that he was sure should have been a strike.

Born in 1900, Hartnett was a player for pay in his home state of Rhode Island by the time he was 17. He was following in his father's catcher's mask, so to speak, since his dad was also a catcher. Talking on the field came naturally to Hartnett because it was simply an extension of his natural personality. He talked everywhere he went. He would have been ill-suited for silent movies because he never shut up. Hartnett even talked with fans after games. "By the time friends let him get to the showers after a game the water is usually cold," one sportswriter observed. "And when he walks the streets of Chicago, boys in such large numbers flock around him that he requires a police escort."[4]

Hartnett's gabby nature and willingness to banter with anyone in earshot or sight, once got him into hot water. One infamous spectator at a Cubs game was gangster Al Capone. Capone was seated in a box at Wrigley Field and Hartnett autographed a ball for Capone's son. Photographers leaped into action as Hartnett brandished a pen and the picture produced widespread publicity. Non-plussed, National League president John Heydler felt this besmirched baseball's good name, but he groped for an appropriate response. The fact was that Capone was a free man, not under indictment, and while everyone knew he was a kingpin of organized crime, he had escaped prosecution. Heydler issued a decree banning ballplayers from speaking to any fans in the stands under penalty of a fine.

Hartnett protested his innocence in the sense that his signing of the ball for Capone's son was an innocent act, not an indication that he was in cahoots with Capone in any nefarious business. "I'll do that for any kid," Hartnett said of the favor for the boy.[5]

Good-natured was also an accurate description of Hartnett. Not only did he talk a lot, his discussions were more likely to be characterized by laughter than philosophy. When the Cubs were on the road, he said, he preferred to sleep all day after breakfast in his hotel room to make up for lost sleep on the train. But when he was home in Chicago, he was a man about town, taking in live vaudeville shows whenever and wherever he could squeeze them in. "No musical comedies, nor dramas for me," he said. "I've got to have a variety. Give me an acrobatic act, some trained seals, a flock of dancers, a couple of good singers, a jazz orchestra, and a couple of smart wise-crackers and I'll say it's a good show."[6]

Given his love of the live shows and his regular exercise of his vocal cords, it probably was no surprise that Hartnett decided to give show business a try once in the offseason. He gathered a few teammates and they went on the vaudeville circuit in Chicago, singing their hearts out. They were paid $1,000 a week to do so.

Hartnett had a second nickname besides Gabby. The Irishman was also called "Old Tomato Face." His ruddy complexion prompted that moniker, not having tomatoes heaved at him while on stage.

Although Hartnett didn't earn the start in the Game of the Century, McGraw knew he was in good hands with Hartnett behind the plate. He was regarded as the best fielding catcher of the first half century of the 1900s. "If I had that guy to pitch to all the time," said Dizzy Dean after joining the Cubs from the Cardinals, "I'd never lose me a game."[7]

The hullabaloo over being seen with Capone was only a temporary glitch in Hartnett's career. At the time of the All-Star game he was in the middle of a 20-year career as a backstop, all but one of them with the Cubs, and in his best years was a .300 hitter. He later managed the Cubs.

Hartnett's appearance in the National League lineup did not immediately improve his club's luck. The first batter up for the Americans in the bottom of the sixth was shortstop Joe Cronin. Cronin struck a single to center. Trying to increase the AL lead, Mack ordered Rick Ferrell to bunt Cronin over to second. Ferrell's attempt at a sacrifice was successful. He placed a delicate bunt down the first-base line. While Cronin steamed into second safely, NL first sacker Bill Terry charged the ball, picked it up, and threw to Frisch covering first. Ferrell was out, but Cronin was in scoring position.

Alvin Crowder was due up, but Mack called the pitcher back to the dugout and informed him he was finished for the day. Crowder had completed three innings in workmanlike fashion. He allowed just two hits, but also two runs. Mack wanted to extend the Americans' one-run lead and called upon Cleveland's Earl Averill to pinch-hit.

The lefty-hitting outfielder was called "The Earl of Snohomish" for his ties to western Washington, where he grew up. Averill was one of the steadiest hitters in the American League in the early 1930s, clearing the .300 mark by some distance in average, topping 30 home runs each season, and driving in as many as 143 runs in 1931. He was also a durable player, almost never missing a game with injury, and he six times led the AL in games played.

Averill had traveled a long way in a decade. He grew up poor on a farm after his father died when the boy was just 18 months old, and he had to walk two miles to school. But Averill became the darling of the locals in Snohomish, where sawmills and lumber were king and ballplayers represented the town on weekends during the summers. Averill emerged as the best of the best from his neighborhood, batting .480 in 1923. The fans wanted to honor Averill. Rather than simply give him a trophy to rest on the mantle, the faithful took up a collection to pay his expenses to spring training in California with Seattle of the Pacific Coast League the next year. Manager Howard Ness extolled Averill's talents and virtues by saying, "I doubt that the great Ty Cobb, Tris Speaker, or Babe Ruth came anywhere near that mark even when they were in the bush leagues." Averill, he argued, deserved a chance to prove himself on a larger stage. The fans anted up and made Averill's trip to California possible.

Alas, he was a dismal failure. Players ridiculed him, made jokes at his expense, and the team sent him home with the ringing description that he was a loser who could not play the game. "The world looked mighty blue after that," Averill said.[8]

It would not have been surprising if the young man had forsaken baseball right then. Humiliated by the experience, Averill refused to return to Snohomish. He wandered up the Pacific Coast seeking baseball employment wherever he stopped. Finally, Averill hooked on with a team in Bellingham, Washington. He bounced between a few minor league clubs and showed his stuff. In 1928, after one of several years of posting high averages, the Indians spent $50,000 to secure his rights from the San Francisco Seals.

Averill stood just over 5' 9" and weighed 172 pounds, so he was not a hugely impressive physical specimen. And in the late 1920s, $50,000 was a large sum of money to spend on an untried ballplayer. Reacting to the sight of the comparatively slight Averill, Indians owner Alva Bradley questioned judgment of his general manager Billy Evans. "You paid all that money for a midget," Bradley said.[9]

Appearances aside, it turned out to be a wise investment, and Averill's original backers at home in Washington were thrilled. "Maybe you think the boys who paid my expenses to train with the Seattle club didn't get a kick out of that," Averill said.[10] A year later he was a full-time starter for Cleveland, and being chosen for the first All-Star game provided additional vindication. Averill was still improving, too. He hit a career-best .378 in 1936.

Not every moment in the bigs was perfect for Averill. On an off-day picnic with family and teammates in 1936, Averill was involved in an ill-advised joke. He tossed a firecracker, but when it didn't go off, he picked it up again. Oops. It went off that time and exploded in his hands. More than a half-century later he could point to some markings on his hand and indicate those were souvenir scars. Although Averill recounted the event in light-hearted fashion many years later, it was a serious matter at the time. "It looked bad," said teammate Mel Harder, who was present and drove Averill to the hospital. "There was a lot of blood."[11] The firecracker had torn flesh off the fingers and palm of Averill's right hand and burned his forehead and chest. The injuries sidelined Averill for six weeks.

Another time, during a game, Averill turned around to talk to an umpire. While he was yappily engaged, a runner stole second. That was memorable, but the consequences were less severe. For those who watched Averill hit, however, it was his prowess with the bat that made an impression. The lively ball era predated Averill by barely a decade, yet he was a proficient home-run hitter, amassing 238 in his career, with three seasons of 30 or more. When Averill hit the ball, it stayed hit. "When he hit the ball, it looked like a golf ball (disappearing in the distance)," Harder said. "He'd hit them in any park. League Park (in Cleveland) wasn't that easy for homers because of the 40-foot wall."[12]

Averill could always hit, and when he stepped into the batter's box as a pinch-hitter at Comiskey Park, he knew that's what he was being asked to do. Averill came through, slapping a single to center field. Ferrell's sacrifice bunt paid off, too, as Cronin came around to score. Connie Mack was on a hot streak. Everything he suggested came up roses. Figuring the National League would not expect another bunt, Mack called for Chapman to bunt. Chapman sent the ball spinning towards third base, and while Averill dashed to second safely, Chapman's perfect placement won him first base clean.

The American League had runners on first and second with one out and the heart of the order scheduled to follow. The prospect for blowing the game open was realistic. Charlie Gehringer was up. The Tigers' second baseman eyed Warneke carefully. When he swung, he lofted a fly down the right-field line. The ball floated into foul territory. Chuck Klein drifted over and stabbed the ball for the out, but it was not a totally worthless swat. Averill tagged up and went into third.

The American League still had a man in scoring position and two men on for Babe Ruth. The Yankee slugger had already delivered the key blow of the game with his third-inning home run. That made the fans happy. Now he sought to make the fans delirious and perhaps clinch the game for his team. Well aware of the stakes and the circumstances, Warneke tried to avoid making the mistake that had killed Wild Bill Hallahan.

Although no one talked in such terms in 1933, Warneke had no desire to be linked with Babe Ruth's name as the answer to an All-Star lore question. Ruth's legend was fat enough, from lifting the Yankees to pennant and World Series championships to his called shot home run against the Cubs in 1932. He already had his glory this day, too. No one could blame Warneke for preferring to remain anonymous at the other end of an offering to Ruth. As usual, though, Ruth was not shy about taking his cuts. He came to the plate, surveyed the situation, virtually salivated, and thought a second home run would be just dandy.

Not this time, Babe, one could almost hear Warneke muttering. Good pitches, smart pitches, came Ruth's way. And in the end, the mighty Babe struck out. That punctuated the sixth inning, but the AL gained another run and led 4–2. Time was running a little bit short as the game entered the seventh inning, yet there was still plenty of baseball to be played. In a sport where a single swing could change momentum and alter the picture hurriedly, a two-run deficit was nothing to fear.

······

14

······

Seventh Inning

Connie Mack knew just the pitcher he wanted throwing against the National League to preserve his club's hard-won lead after he had pinch-hit for Alvin Crowder. Robert Moses Grove was practically never referred to by his given name; everyone in baseball knew him simply as "Lefty." Perhaps they were alter-egos. Mr. Grove was nice to children, giving them baseball equipment and encouraging their pursuit of the sport that had defined his life. Lefty Grove was something else. He was cantankerous, grumpier than the similarly named one of Walt Disney's seven dwarfs, so despised losing that he berated his own fielders for making errors.

Seeking to tie the record of 17 straight victories, Grove threw a world-class tantrum when a back-up outfielder named Jimmy Moore botched a fly ball, costing him a 1–0 defeat. At game's conclusion, Grove stomped off the mound, marched to the A's team clubhouse and destroyed it in full view of his teammates. He threw benches and ripped lockers out of the wall. Then he performed a bizarre striptease, ripping up his uniform as he took it off. For good measure, he tore his glove to shreds. Yet Grove did not yell at Moore. He focused his anger on the missing starter, Al Simmons, who took the day off to handle personal business and was out of town. "If that miserable so-and-so had been here," Grove shouted, "we would have won the game. I'll never forgive him."[1]

It was not difficult to get on Grove's bad side. A misjudgment at second base, a poor throw, a booted ground ball, earned snarls, snipes or possibly even physical accosting. Grove was never the most popular man in his own locker room, never mind amongst opponents who didn't possess the eyesight to see his fast one coming, either over the plate for a strike or at their heads if he was in a foul mood and wanted to protect the plate.

Although it was likely that Grove grew up in Maryland with such a sour personality, being exiled to the minors until he was 25 despite a record of 100–36 surely did not help his disposition. Ultimately, Grove finished 300–140 in the majors, with a sterling .680 winning percentage. Being held back by Baltimore Oriole Jack Dunn, who controlled Grove's rights, certainly cost Grove a faster start to his career totals. "I should have been up at least three years earlier," Grove later reflected. "I could have won 400 games."[2]

Grove even gave his kindly Philadelphia A's manager Mack heartburn. If Grove felt slighted or if his body felt slightly out of kilter, he might inform Mack that he was feeling sick or come up with other reasons why he couldn't take his turn in the rotation. However, when Grove was right, he was fabulous, one of the greatest pitchers of all time. In 1931, Grove produced one of the finest pitching seasons in history, finishing 31–4 with a 2.06 earned run average.

An eight-time 20-game winner, Grove led the American League in strikeouts seven times and in earned run average nine times. He was as stingy as they come. Although it was not apparent at the time, Grove was in his final season with the A's before being transferred to the Red Sox. At 24–8, the 1933 campaign was also his last true dominating season.

Mack had originally planned to start Grove against the National League, but he now found a critical moment to use him. The opposition had seen little of Grove's repertoire, and if ever there was a man who could be a likely candidate to blank the NL, Grove was the choice. In theory, this was a brilliant stroke, but you could never tell with Grove. If he was unhappy about being passed over for the start, he might not bear down. Pride might push him to overpower the foes.

The first batter up against Grove was first baseman Bill Terry. Terry had never faced a pitcher he couldn't hit. He had supreme confidence and the statistics to back up his attitude. Terry promptly singled to left to put the lead runner on. Was this going to be one of those rare days when Grove just didn't have it? National League center fielder Wally Berger was about to test that theory. This was a critical at-bat. A Berger hit would put Grove in trouble with two men on and nobody out. Yet a routine grounder could clear the bases if the Americans could pull off a double play. Berger hit the needed grounder, but it was not easy to handle. Joe Cronin grabbed the ball at shortstop and flipped it to Charlie Gehringer covering second for the force out on Terry. But Berger beat the throw to first.

Sensing that this was the time to strike, manager John McGraw went to his bench and called upon Pirates third baseman Pie Traynor to pinch-hit for Dick Bartell. Of all the Pittsburgh greats throughout franchise history, Traynor was likely the least colorful and the quietest, but he brought his flavorful childhood nickname to the big leagues. The story went that young Traynor was a habitué of a grocery store in Somerville, Massachusetts, that was run by a priest and specialized in selling pie. He sought out a taste of the delicacy so often that the proprietor called him "Pieface." That was shortened over time. Ironically, also over time Traynor lost his taste for pie.

As a pro player, Traynor basically did his job at a high level for 17 seasons but made no fuss in establishing a greatness that included a .320 lifetime batting average. He was at least as well known for his slick fielding, and during his years running the Giants, McGraw, his temporary manager, had seen more than enough of Traynor's wizardry manning third base. Traynor, he said, was "the best. I've never seen anything like him. I'll bet he ruined more base hits for my club than any other two infielders in the game."[3] McGraw was not the only one who felt this way. A phrase grew up around Traynor's magic with the glove and propensity to rob batters of hits describing a commonly seen scenario. A batter was said to have "doubled down the third base line, but Traynor threw him out."[4]

The right-handed-hitting Traynor, whose given name

Pittsburgh Pirate great Pie Traynor was selected for the National League All-Star team in 1933 but only saw action as a pinch-hitter in the seventh inning. Traynor was also chosen for the 1934 team. He is shown here while managing the Pirates. (Photograph courtesy National Baseball Hall of Fame.)

when born in Massachusetts was Harold Joseph, stood 6' tall and weighed 170 pounds in his prime. He was not a slugger, only once reaching double figures in home runs in a season, but he was a clutch batter who seven times drove in more than 100 runs in a campaign. That was the type of hitter — and type of production — McGraw needed at the moment to keep the threat alive against Grove. Traynor versus Grove; it was a rare showdown between two Hall of Famers destined to spend their entire careers in opposite leagues. Traynor got the best of this confrontation. He slapped a double to center, but did not place it just so and the slow-running Berger could not score from first. He held up at third.

Still, this was a big chance for the National League. Men on second and third with one out offered an appealing circumstance for the next batter. Cubs catcher Gabby Hartnett had a chance to be a hero, a chance to tie the game, even take the lead with a home run, or at the least score one run and keep the rally going. No doubt muttering and growling on the mound over his predicament, Grove bore down. One could almost hear Grove grumble, saying something akin to "That's enough, boys." The competitor in Grove came to the forefront and his fastball picked up speed. Either that or Hartnett's usually sharp eye failed him. Hartnett struck out. Grove was not out of danger, but the pressure was eased somewhat.

NL pitcher Lon Warneke was scheduled to hit, but McGraw was not going to let that happen with a star-studded cast sitting around on the bench. McGraw's next strategic move in his attempt to save the day was to insert Cubs shortstop Woody English as a pinch-hitter for his teammate Warneke. This was the game's pivotal moment. The American League had controlled play since getting on the scoreboard. The National League had been trying to fight back. This was the best opportunity McGraw's crew had to eliminate its two-run deficit.

English was a superb fielder who had a knack for reaching base and could hit in crucial moments when called upon. In 1930 he batted .335 and scored 152 runs, the happy beneficiary of a two-way partnership with Hack Wilson, who was on his way to setting the all-time record for RBIs that season. English held up his part of the bargain by getting on base, and Wilson routinely drove him in.

When he was young, the Newark, Ohio, prospect was mired in the minors and in danger of being released following a season when he could muster only a .234 batting average. Normally that labels a young player a bust, but English got another chance a year later when his Toledo team brought in a new manager. It was an early sign that Casey Stengel might know how to handle players. Every morning, English and Stengel met at the ballpark. They endured the stench in the air from a nearby tobacco factory to work on English's hitting and the efforts paid huge dividends. "I went up 100 points under Casey," English said.[5]

The manager of the Louisville club took notice and when Joe McCarthy took over the Cubs he urged management to purchase English's contract. That's how the shortstop ended up in Chicago at a time when the Cubs won National League pennants every three years, in 1929, 1932, and 1935, during his decade-long stay. That put English on the field in the 1932 World Series against the New York Yankees, the event when Babe Ruth reportedly hit his "called shot" home run. For the rest of his life, however, English disputed that Ruth had named his tune. Ruth had signaled the first and second strike calls to the rowdy Cubs dugout, English said, but then just waved in the general direction of center field, not pointed to the spot where he was positive he would hit a home run. "Ruth did not call his shot," English insisted.[6]

When English ruminated over the Game of the Century — which he often did since it was his only appearance in a 12-year career that concluded with the Brooklyn Dodgers — he remembered best McGraw pulling out all of the stops to win, the trademark of the feisty manager's long career. In this game, English recalled, McGraw was at his big-mouth best, loudly directing protests at umpire Bill Klem, his old adversary. "There were three or four close plays at first base," English said, "and Klem called them all in favor of the American League. McGraw was a pretty good umpire baiter, and he started in on Klem, called him everything that was unprintable. Klem took it for a while, and after four-and-a-half innings he came to our dugout on the first-base side. I thought, 'Here it goes.' I figured he was going to run McGraw out of the game. But he just came into our dugout to put on the umpire's equipment to work home plate the rest of the game. He never said a word to McGraw."[7]

Maybe Klem held his temper in check in recognition that this was a one-time event of huge stature and that no one would appreciate the manager of the National League being ejected. And maybe he remembered that it was only an exhibition game. Perhaps McGraw, on the other hand, thought that he might get away with more than usual because it was known this was his final game and that indeed there would be a hullabaloo if he was dumped from the Game of the Century. McGraw, as usual, was going after every inch of advantage he could plot. Klem was apparently, as befits an umpire, being more judicial.

English set up in his stance, but Grove made short work of him. English got decent wood on the ball, before his fly ball carried to center field and nestled into Al Simmons' glove for the third out. End of threat. End of inning.

While English remained in the game for the National League in the bottom of the seventh, the biggest change in the NL roster was on the mound. Replacing Warneke was Carl Hubbell, the stalwart Giants hurler who was just bursting onto the national scene with his finest year since his debut in 1928. The southpaw who baffled hitters with his screwball was en route to a 23-win season that would see him named NL Most Valuable Player, the first of two such awards he garnered. Soon enough Hubbell would enjoy the nickname "King Carl" for his ability to dominate batters as he compiled a lifetime record of nearly 100 victories over the .500 mark. Hubbell, of course, was used to McGraw issuing orders. He knew what was expected and he could deliver.

Hubbell was born in Carthage, Missouri, in 1903 and grew up on a farm in Oklahoma. In his heyday he produced five consecutive 20-win seasons. Success did not come immediately, though. Hubbell had his struggles in the minors, and even in his early seasons with the Giants he was still improving. It was McGraw that took Hubbell aside for a pep talk and urged him to rely as heavily as possible on the screwball — or backwards curve as some called it — because it was his best pitch. The advice took.

Hubbell had been ticketed to start the Game of the Century for the National League. Loyalty and familiarity with the star twirler influenced McGraw to pick Hubbell as his man. However, fate intervened a few days before the game. On July 2, before 50,000 fans at the Polo Grounds, in an epic confrontation with the Cardinals, New York won, 1–0. Hubbell went the distance in an 18-inning game, throwing in essence a double shutout. He scattered just six hits and didn't walk a man while striking out 12. The game took more than four hours to play. "I thought it would never end," Hubbell said much later.[8] The taxing effort was recorded too close to the scheduled All-Star event for Hubbell to start and be counted on to pitch his best.

The first batter to face Hubbell in the first All-Star game was Lou Gehrig. Gehrig always hated swinging against Hubbell because he could never tell what that screwball was going to do. Once, when Gehrig was on an airplane with famed journalist Quentin Reynolds, the craft ran into some turbulence, dove, and then steered to the right before resuming its normal course. "That's what Hubbell's screwball is like," Gehrig said. "You never know when it's coming and when it does come, you can't do anything about it."[9]

For once, Gehrig stood his ground against the boggling screwball and drew a walk from Hubbell. Having the lead man on did nothing for McGraw's digestive tract. Al Simmons was next up and the situation was tailor-made for the leading vote-recipient in the fan balloting to make some noise with his bat. But he couldn't do it. Simmons got only flimsy wood on a Hubbell offering, hitting a grounder to Pepper Martin at third. Martin made the play and threw to Frankie Frisch at second for the force out on Gehrig. Simmons beat the throw to first.

Jimmy Dykes strode to the plate. Dykes had a father-son relationship with Connie Mack. Once known primarily as a good fielder who couldn't wield a big enough stick, Dykes improved to become a lifetime .280 hitter under Mack's tutelage. He became an indispensable player whose true worth was not measured in numbers. When he was managing the Tigers, Ty Cobb supposedly offered $80,000 to Mack for Dykes' contract but was rebuffed. Although he was an all-star at third base, Dykes ended up playing all four infield positions for Mack during his career.

Observers used to marvel at the strength of Dykes' throwing arm. When asked about it Dykes said he always had the power, but while growing up threw something year-round. In the summer, it was baseballs; in the winter it was snowballs. And he said he never got a sore arm.

Dykes loved playing for Mack and loved the manager. He wanted to shine for him in this game, and he was not at all taken aback by Hubbell's screwball. Dykes bided his time, timed his swing, and stroked a single to left field. Simmons huffed into second safely and the American League quickly developed a threat. Once again the chance presented itself to pad the lead as shortstop Joe Cronin came to the plate.

Cronin was in his prime in 1933, gradually approaching the halfway point in what would be a 20-year career split mostly between the Washington Senators and the Boston Red Sox. Cronin had hit a robust .346 in

1930 and preserved a lifetime .301 average. A feisty player who later made an impact in a long career as a baseball administrator in the Red Sox's organization and ultimately as president of the American League, Cronin twice led the AL in fielding.

Appearing in the inaugural All-Star game was just one milestone in Cronin's career that took place in 1933. He had been installed as player-manager of the Senators at the ripe young age of 27, and led the team to a 99-victory campaign and the American League pennant to boot. Newspaper reporters took to calling him "the boy pilot" and "boy manager." In some ways, Cronin was at the peak of his fame in 1933, so much so that he was offered a post-season vaudeville contract that called for 10 weeks of performing at $3,500 per, or a total of $35,000. That was truly big money during the Depression, especially given that it wasn't even the man's primary career. Yet Cronin apparently knew his limitations off the field and turned down the easy money. "I'm a ballplayer," he said.[10]

If Cronin had chosen to go on stage, he could have broadened his usual audience of rapt sportswriters. Soon after the 1933 World Series he told a story about his early days in the minors with Kansas City. His average was stuck on .241 and Cronin feared being released after being sent down by the Pittsburgh Pirates following two seasons worth of bench-warming in Pennsylvania. Instead, when summoned to the team's offices, he was addressed by scout Joe Engel. Engel had been reviewing another player when he was struck by Cronin's natural ability. It would have to have been reading the invisible because that day Cronin's swings were futile. He made four outs and fans were screaming for him to be benched. Engel read between the lines and told Cronin he was taking him to Washington.

Engel told Cronin to "doll up. You know, we might call upon the president." The president Engel had in mind was Clark Griffith of the Senators, not Calvin Coolidge of the White House, but the teasing went over well. Engel had a propensity for wearing loud suits, so when he talked about the more conservative Cronin "dolling up" he meant dressing colorfully enough to shame a peacock. Engel was slipping into a plaid suit when he made the comment, considered things for a moment, then handed it to Cronin. The suit fit, and when the duo reached D.C. Cronin put on his bright outfit once more. So taken with the unlikely sight of himself in such garb before leaving for the Senators' offices, Cronin posed before mirrors in the hotel lobby. Suddenly, he heard a shrill female voice yelling, "Joe Engel! How dare you return to the city without coming home!" Cronin spun around, providing a full facial view to a woman who must have thought there was only one such suit of its kind on earth. "Oh, pardon me," the lady said to Cronin. "You see, I mistook you for my husband."[11] Right suit, wrong guy.

Cronin was wearing a Washington Senators suit when he took a few practice swings to warm up before hitting against Hubbell. It did him little good. Cronin lofted a soft pop-up into the air in foul territory east of first base that Bill Terry grabbed for the out. Two down. Rick Ferrell took his turn next and grounded to Frisch at second, who made the easy throw to Terry to retire the side. The National League and Hubbell were out of trouble, but McGraw's players were running out of time to gain the lead.

······

15

······

Eighth Inning

The game now belonged to Lefty Grove. If he seemed vulnerable in his first inning of work, there were no hints of him being hittable in the eighth inning. Grove was Grove at his best, mastering the best National League hitters as they marched to the plate and took their chances.

Yet for a moment or two the National Leaguers created hope of a rally once more. Pepper Martin was first up. The Cardinals' third baseman had played flawlessly in the field, but burned to bring his team back from its 4–2 deficit.

Martin, whose given name was John Leonard, was awarded his nickname of Pepper by the president of the Cardinals' minor league outfit in Fort Smith, Arkansas, in 1925 because he brought spice to the playing field. This was one occasion where he truly wished to spice up the action. Martin had a talent for getting on base and wanted to practice that at this moment. He also stole bases in the clutch. In the 1931 World Series he swiped five bases in six tries against Hall of Fame catcher Mickey Cochrane.

Martin was a good man to have at the plate in these circumstances. It was easy to picture him stroking a single and then advancing to scoring position with a steal. Martin had the fire in his belly that manager John McGraw loved to see. Later, when he was a minor league manager, Martin was suspended and fined for choking an umpire. He was more than a decade into his managing and coaching career in 1956, while working with the Chicago Cubs, when he acknowledged having mellowed a bit. "I have never hurt anyone intentionally," Martin said. "I always played hard, but never dirty or viciously. There was a time when if I was insulted, or had just taken too much, I simply would double up my fists and start swinging. But now I have learned to walk away."[1]

At the least in this at-bat, Martin sought to hurt Grove's earned run average. But the southpaw had the upper hand and whiffed Martin with a fast one that froze the hitter and caught him looking. One out. This is what made Grove effective — dashing the hopes and aspirations of other men with big toothpicks in their hands.

Whether they liked Grove or not, whether they were put off by his terrible temper or not, the players on opposing teams who tried to reach base against Grove admired his ability. "When planes take off from a ship, people say they catapult," said Yankee shortstop Frank Crossetti in an intriguing comparison in 1932. "That is what his (Grove's) fastball did halfway to the plate. He threw just plain fastballs. He didn't need anything else."[2]

Grove was born in Maryland in 1900 and the one thing he learned early in his life was that he was going to have to scrap for anything he got. His father was a coal miner and Grove determined young that he was not going to follow that career path. When Grove was 16 his mining brother sprained an ankle and Grove was called upon to fill in so the family wouldn't lose the income. Two weeks underground was enough to convince Lefty that the only dirt he wished to rub off his hands would be that from a baseball diamond.

Most of the time Grove was so poor he could not afford to practice throwing with a real hard ball. He either threw rocks to limber up his arm, or he and his friends rolled up some wool socks and covered them with black tape to use as a substitute baseball. Perhaps this Spartan upbringing contributed to Grove's perpetual dark mood in adulthood. Maybe he was simply protecting what he had earned and feared someone would take away from him if he lost on the field.

"They used to say that I was mean in those days," Grove reflected after retirement, "but I had a reason. Everybody was mean to me. It was rough on a kid trying to make it in baseball in those days. I was with the Baltimore club (in the minors) for two weeks before anyone spoke to me."[3]

And yes, Grove admitted, growing up in the harsh coal country did have something to do with his interaction with teammates and other players in the majors. He was shy and distrustful. "I was suspicious of everybody," Grove said. "And I guess I was scared of the big cities. My attitude was the best defense I could muster. I figured that if I scared people away, they wouldn't bother me."[4] No telling what a psychiatrist would have made out of that belated confession.

Connie Mack recognized Grove's talent and realized Grove's temper might backfire and cost him in crucial moments. Mack worked Grove shrewdly. He did not order him about but handled him gently, hoping his messages would penetrate Grove's stubbornness and hold his anger in check. Sometimes it worked, sometimes it didn't. Mack admonished Grove to take hold of his temper. He hoped his pitcher would harness and channel this energy towards getting batters out, not imploding.

Traveling in a separate but parallel universe, Satchel Paige, the most prominent African American pitcher in the Negro leagues, catalogued a list of reasons to support his amazing longevity pitching at the top of his game. Widely circulated and often re-published, the most famous among Paige's rules for clean living and baseball success was, "Don't look back, something might be gaining on you." Lesser known was that Grove wrote down his own rules for success. They read:

1) Attend to business;
2) Eat regularly, get at least eight hours of sleep — especially from 10 P.M. to 2 A.M., when sleep is soundest — and observe moderate habits.
3) Don't "Know it all" — give the other fellow credit for a little knowledge.[5]

It's not clear if the frequently stuffy Grove practiced this last adage as well as preached it.

There was apparently nothing on Grove's good-behavior traits list that precluded throwing tantrums. He could be as obstinate and unreasonable as a two-year-old stomping around the living room screeching and crying. During a June 1930 game, Grove was called upon in relief for the A's against the Cleveland Indians. He pitched six fine innings before surrendering a two-run homer and being tagged with the loss. Years later, then-teammate Jimmy Dykes recalled the post-game Grove. This time the frustration went beyond ranting. "He was so mad, he didn't talk to anyone," Dykes said. "He got in his Pierce Arrow and drove to his home in Lonaconing, Maryland. He didn't show up at the park for three days."[6]

There is little to suggest that Grove learned to control his outbursts while playing. He was no different with the Red Sox than he was with the A's. If a fielder made a game-costing error behind him, Grove might go berserk. In a 1936 Boston game shortstop Joe Cronin made an error that decided the result, giving Grove what he believed to be was an undeserved loss. Unlike other teammates, Cronin was player-manager and had some-where to hide. "We all started fleeing for the clubhouse," said second base-man Ski Melillo, "and leading the way was Cronin. He knew what was coming."[7]

When the teams departed the field, Cronin sprinted for his office and locked the door. As Sox teammates looked on in amazement, Grove seemed prepared to wield a battering ram against the door. "Cronin raced into his little cubby-hole office and locked the door, but nobody was going to stop Lefty. There was some wire netting around the top of Cronin's office and Grove pulled up a bench, climbed on it and started shouting at Cronin, calling him all kinds of things. I'll tell you, that Lefty was a terror."[8]

As the first All-Star game was playing out, with Grove on the mound doing his duty for Mack, neither man knew that within months the ace of the A's would be gone from Philadelphia, traded to Boston. For all of the manager's tolerance and appreciation of Grove's skill, Mack was hurting for cash during the Depression. Grove, who would post a .750 winning percentage, was making his career-high salary of $28,000 in 1933. How-ever, at the end of the season, Mack told his famous pitcher that he had to take a large salary cut because finances were tight. Grove asked to be traded.

Mack showed he wasn't bluffing or lying about his team's financial bind. At the winter meetings, which were held not far from Comiskey Park at the Chicago Parker House Hotel, Mack peddled Grove to the Red Sox for $125,000. In July, though, with the results of the Game of the Century riding on Grove's whippet arm, the two men were still a team.

With Martin disposed of, Frankie Frisch stepped to the plate. He didn't connect solidly with a Grove offering but got just enough wood on the ball to place it awkwardly out of Gehrig's reach at first base. The ball did not leave the infield, but Frisch out-ran the ball and recorded an infield single. There was one man on and one man out. Again, this was simply a case of a player doing what he did best, bringing one of his strengths to bear on the game at a critical moment.

Could the National League take advantage of Frisch's speed and chop that tantalizingly small lead? Could the NL batters reach the gritty Grove? Chuck Klein seemed like a good possibility to swat a Grove fastball high and deep enough to tie the game. In 1933, Klein was at the end of an astonishing five-year hitting run for the Phillies. Between 1929 and the conclusion of the 1933 season, "The Hoosier Hammer" (who naturally was from Indiana) posted more than 40 homers twice and never drove in fewer than 120 runs, with his high reaching 170 in 1930. "His 1930 season with the Phillies is remembered as one of the most remarkable in big league history," a Hall of Fame comment notes.[9]

Klein five times reached 200 or more hits, with a low of 200 and a high of 250. Klein was the MVP of the National League in 1932 and won the Triple Crown, leading the circuit in homers, RBIs and batting average in 1933. This was his time. This was the guy McGraw wanted to see at the plate.

But as is well known to baseball buffs, even the greatest of hitters fail to bat safely much more often than three times out of 10, and this was one of those off-times for Klein. Klein could not advance the runner while flying out to Al Simmons in center. Two outs and it was Chick Hafey's turn to bat. Desperation might have been too strong a word for what the National League bench was feeling, but there had to be attention paid to the dwindling number of opportunities the team was scheduled to receive. There were two outs in the eighth and a man on base. Somebody had to move the runner along or else the National League would be down to its final three outs.

Fans at Comiskey were enjoying the show. They were loud advocates for the American League club. Perhaps they were not as warmly received as the hometown White Sox would have been, but the White Sox's league was in favor, and the spectators liked what they were seeing. The game was not a slugfest, but the caliber of players coming to bat, one after the other, the style of the players holding down their positions in the field, all made for theatre to remember. Was it truly the Game of the Century? Maybe, maybe not, but it might well have been the Baseball Event of the Century. No one was running down to the box office to ask for his money back, in any case.

To some extent, the game was in the hands of the bespectacled Chick Hafey, who followed Klein to the plate. He was determined not to let Frisch wither on first base. Time for some fireworks, if he could only solve Grove. So beset by illnesses and physical woes affecting his eyesight that he never played more than 144 games in season — and that only once, in 1933 — Hafey was in full recovery mode by the all-star game.

Hafey grew up in a baseball-playing family. He had three older brothers who played the sport, one of whom pitched for Portland in the Pacific Coast League. Hafey had not reached that exalted league and was occupying himself in a San Francisco winter league when spotted by the Cardinals and invited to spring training in 1923. He was paid merely train fare to travel across the country to Bradenton, Florida, but the deal was worth it for both parties. A year later Hafey made his major league debut for St. Louis.

When Hafey was bartered to Cincinnati in 1932, his new manager, Dan Howley, was thrilled. But Hafey was healthy enough to play in just 83 games and the Reds finished 60–94. Howley lamented the loss of Hafey and its cost to his club. "In my opinion, he's the greatest player in the league," said Howley, who was fired after that season. "He's a great outfielder with the best arm in the business, a good man on the bases and a smart ballplayer. And he's a wonderful, natural hitter."[10]

Hafey waggled his bat, staring out at Grove. Lefty reared back, kicked his foot high and delivered one of his prime fastballs. There was a loud crack as Hafey connected. The ball soared beyond the infield, deep into right field, where Yankee giant Babe Ruth patrolled. The suspense lasted a few seconds, long enough for the crowd to shout with surprise, long enough for fans to wonder if this was it, the big, needed bash for the National League.

Of the 48,000 or so souls who had bought their way into Comiskey Park for the Game of the Century, many had never seen Babe Ruth in action. To them he was as appropriate an exhibited item at the Century of Progress as any other booth touting a new invention or a country's natural delights. Granted, he was not the Ruth of yore, but he was Ruth and still "Ruthian" in most minds.

Ruth stood 6'2" and the *Baseball Encyclopedia* lists his playing weight as 215 pounds. He was probably a bit lighter when he broke in with the Boston Red Sox in 1914 and a bit heavier when he jogged around the bases for his 714th and final home run with the Boston Braves in 1935. He was athletic enough to win 94 games as a left-handed pitcher and virtually invented slugging. Most newsreels in existence portray the Babe as a roly-poly dude in his waning years, running the bases in tight little steps. The films just don't exist that show the more athletic version, when he could run the bases smartly and field his position as well as most.

There was considerable tut-tutting as Ruth aged since he most likely had lost a step due to his raucous lifestyle. Neither Ruth nor any of his contemporaries were any more aware of the benefits of weight training than they were knowledgeable about rocket ships to the moon. By all accounts, Ruth stretched the boundaries of good sense in abusing his body with wine, women and song, rich food and cigars. Surely years of long nights and partying hard took a toll. But even as late as 1933, a full 20 seasons after he broke into the majors, it was at the pitcher's own risk if he chose to treat Ruth with anything less than the greatest of respect. Just what he was still able to do in the field was open to question in some minds, however. The designated hitter role would not be created for four more decades, so Ruth played the field if he played at all.

Ruth was like a moth drawn to the bright outdoor lights. If there was a spotlight shining, Ruth found his way to it. If the stage was big, Ruth took it over. In this game, he had slugged a two-run homer, the critical blow of the contest. He had drawn the wrong kind of attention to himself in poorly playing Lon Warneke's fly that went for a triple. Now the game might be on the line and the ball was coming to him. Hafey got a good chunk of horsehide and he put Ruth on the run to the deep right-field wall.

Ruth raced to the wall and reached its base as the ball arrived. The ball was coming in high and he had to jump. Ruth made the required leap, as high as he could go at age 38. He flung his glove, reached with his right hand, and speared the shot in the webbing, just shy of bouncing away for an extra-base hit and just short of clearing the wall for a home run. Some accounts say Ruth's hand was actually over the wall. The momentum of the run and the catch thrust Ruth against the wall, hitting back first. The Bambino, who did so much damage to opponents with his bat, drove a stake into the heart of the National League players with his leather glove.

Talkative as he always was, Ruth had praised Lefty Gomez for his performance early in the game and promised him some runs. He delivered on that pledge. By all accounts, Ruth was embarrassed by his goof in the field in the sixth. He made up for it with the stab in right in the eighth that recorded the third out for the NL and spiked a budding comeback. The National League still had one more chance, but Ruth's play took the steam out of one more game effort to put runs on the board. Afterwards, McGraw noted how important Ruth's play was. "Babe Ruth checked our rally when he went to the wall to grab Hafey's long fly," McGraw said. "I

thought sure it was going to be a home run. You have to give Ruth credit.
He was marvelous. That old boy certainly came through when they needed
him."[11]

In the bottom of the ninth, Pirates star Paul Waner trotted out to
play right field for the National League. Although not known for his sentiment, McGraw might have installed Waner in the game just to give him
a taste of the special occasion. Or with the removal of Klein, he might
have been thinking the slugger had his chance and hadn't made anything
of it that day. Surely it would be difficult to brand the move a white flag
surrender. It would have been against every fiber in McGraw's body to
think that way. And if Waner was to come to the plate later on, nobody
was going to claim he was chopped liver.

Waner remains one of the best players in Pittsburgh history. During
his 20-year career, begun in 1926 and almost all of it spent with the Pirates,
he batted .333. He accumulated 200 or more hits eight times on his way
to a career total of 3,152. Waner was joined in the Pirates' outfield in 1927
by his younger brother Lloyd and together the scappy hitters drove pitchers
crazy. Paul, the elder, was known as "Big Poison," and Lloyd was known
as "Little Poison," as in pick your poison for pitchers. Paul Waner hit over
.300 14 times and three times led the National League in hitting. The
irony was that neither of the Waner brothers as big. Paul stood a shade
under 5'9" and weighed 153 pounds.

While attending college for two years in Oklahoma as a young man,
Waner considered becoming a teacher. Instead, he became a remarkable
hitter, and for years following retirement, a batting instructor (using those
teaching skills) for the Milwaukee Braves, St. Louis Cardinals and Philadelphia Phillies. As great as he was for as long as he was, it sometimes seemed
that nothing topped Waner's second year when he shocked the world by
batting .380 with 237 hits. He talked about being in the equivalent of a
zone long before the phrase was used. "I just couldn't do anything wrong
that season," Waner said. "It was only necessary for me to poke my bat at
the ball and hits would explode to all fields. It surely was fun. I was hitting
right-handers and southpaws with equal ease."[12]

Although the All-Star game came along when Waner was years into
his career, this brief appearance in the field was not his only selection. He
played in four of the first five All-Star games, but for all of his talent with
the bat, he could never get a hit in the exhibition contests. He joked later

Paul Waner was another Pirate Hall of Famer selected for the 1933 game whose only action came as a pinch-hitter. Waner was chosen to represent the National League for three additional All-Star games. (Photograph courtesy National Baseball Hall of Fame.)

in life that the American League players must have thought he was a lousy hitter.

Meanwhile, Connie Mack had to be feeling pretty good about the way things were unfolding. To display his continuing confidence in Grove, Mack left him in to bat for himself and lead off the American League half of the eighth. Grove did little with the opportunity, hitting a grounder to Terry at first base. Terry easily put Grove out unassisted. Carl Hubbell was humming along, facing no difficulties with the Americans.

Next up was Ben Chapman and it was a cruise control at-bat for the screwball artist. Hubbell struck out Chapman for the second out of the inning. That brought up Charlie Gehringer. This was Gehringer's fifth time up. He had played the entire game. He walked twice, but he did not bat safely. The American League was ahead, but that lead could disappear quickly. No one had scored since the bottom of the sixth. Pitching ruled. Gehringer swung and he had good reason to think this time he had pummeled the ball for a hit. The shot was hard enough but well within Wally Berger's reach in center. The American League went down in order and the Game of the Century was one inning — a half-inning, actually — from completion, if the National League could not muster at least two runs.

16

Ninth Inning

This was it. Last at-bats. Last chance for the National League. John McGraw's team's batting turns had been characterized by a series of almosts in the late innings. One batter would reach safely and then be erased. Another batter would reach safely and not advance. From the American League standpoint, they had been a series of brushfires to contend with, but none had raged out of control.

Lefty Gomez had been superb in his three innings of work. "General" Crowder had been workmanlike. And now Lefty Grove was trying to wrap up a third inning of shutout ball. As he had promised in his hotel meeting with the Americans, Connie Mack played to win and in his mind that meant sticking with the men who got him the lead. He made few substitutions, especially compared to latter-day All-Star games when ballplayers were shuttled in and out of lineups like free substitution on a football field.

Mack's starting lineup was intact headed into the ninth. Only Earl Averill had pinch-hit. Jimmie Foxx, the powerful slugger who had received hundreds of thousands of votes to appear in the starting lineup at various positions, had not moved his butt from a seat on the bench. Mack had spaced his pitchers out, working them for three innings apiece, and he had Cleveland's Wes Ferrell and Oral Hildebrand in reserve in case Grove was injured or unexpectedly shelled by the Nationals.

On the other side of the field, McGraw was down to his final maneuvering. He still had the Giants' Hal Schumacher available to throw, but unless his team produced some fireworks at the plate the Nationals would not take the field again. Schumacher merely represented insurance. Carl Hubbell was still in charge on the mound and did not seem to be faltering. More importantly for McGraw was whom he might be able to use as a pinch-hitter in order to generate runs. There was just one batsman remaining on the bench — Brooklyn's Tony Cuccinello. McGraw essentially had to stick with the lineup as it was and hope the scheduled hitters could solve Grove.

Before the inning began, Mack did a little bit of shuffling for defensive purposes. He moved Ben Chapman from left field to right field. He shifted Al Simmons from center field to left field, and he inserted Sam West in center field. The odd defender out was the man who might have won the game for the American League with his fielding. Babe Ruth took a seat. The aging Babe had done his job in all-star form. He clubbed a two-run homer and made a spectacular catch. He had proven to be the star of stars, as so many hoped. Comiskey Park fans lapped up the Bambino's performance, providing rousing cheers for his efforts. He played for the enemy Yankees, but for one day at least he was a friend and was accorded warm treatment. Besides, it was those Cubs fans on the North Side who held the grudge against Ruth for that blasted called-shot homer the year before, not Pale Hose fans.

Sam West was far from the most accomplished player who took the field in the first All-Star game that day, but he was a solid outfielder when he could stay healthy. West was a left-handed-hitting and throwing Texan who spent 16 seasons in the majors, most of them with the Washington Senators, the team he broke in with in 1927. He batted .300 or better 10 times and finished with a lifetime average of .299. West was not a power hitter but possessed excellent speed and bat control. He collected 10 or more triples in a season five times and drove in his share of runs. More significantly, considering his use for defensive reasons, he twice led the American League in fielding.

Over time, West actually earned the compliment of being called the best center fielder in the league, a reputation that influenced Mack's last-minute usage of him in the close game. West's biggest problem was staying in one piece for entire seasons. He suffered a broken leg, a fractured elbow, the effects of a beaning, and a damaged shoulder that inhibited his throwing. He might have been tapped for early ads for duct tape. Or perhaps West could have hired the immortal Walter Johnson as a personal press agent. Johnson, winner of 416 games, was a teammate with Washington during the pitcher's final season and the outfielder's first one, and then managed the burgeoning star. Johnson glimpsed West's potential in between trips to the emergency ward.

"West is the best young outfielder in the American League," Johnson said in 1929. "There'd be a lot more talk about this young player around the circuit if we were up in the race. Veteran performers who see him in action frequently come to me and tell me he is a brilliant prospect who will make his name in the game before many more seasons."[1]

The 1929 season under Johnson was not a good one for either the Senators or West, who dipped to a .267 average. Johnson considered that a temporary condition and was proven correct. "West is not hitting as he should," Johnson said, "but he will get his eye peeled and then the boys will be asking all about him."[2] West raised his average 51 points, to .328, the next season and was rightfully considered a young star by the time the Game of the Century rolled around.

Earlier in 1933, West recorded one of his finest accomplishments, an effort that produced the type of publicity that may have gained sentiment in the public vote for the Game of the Century. In an April game against the White Sox, West went six-for-six at the plate. That was part of an eight-for-eight hitting streak. West's hitting exploits aside, Mack did not want to contemplate sending the swift Senator to the plate. If West came up, that meant the Americans had lost their lead. Following the AL outfield shuffle, it was time for Lefty Grove to seal the deal.

Leading off for the National League was first baseman Bill Terry. Terry had played the entire game. He had been reliable in the field, making seven putouts, and he had done his best at the plate, collecting two hits to join Frankie Frisch as the only ones on the NL side to do so. Was it too much to ask for him to add a third hit? He was certainly capable. "Memphis Bill" had hit .401 in 1930, one of the few men immortalized for cracking the .400 average mark. He was on his way to a .322 season in 1933 but could hit even higher in the clutch.

Terry was another product of his environment. He, like many of the early all-stars, grew up poor. He was a full-time laborer by the time he was 15, so he looked at baseball from a serious side, as a way to make a good living and invest for his future. Some may have called baseball a boy's game, but Terry used it as a vehicle to attain manhood. He did not dwell on a romanticized view of the sport, nor did Terry think of baseball as all fun and games. He played hard and did the best he could, but he wanted to win the first All-Star game for himself and the National League, not to give McGraw a pleasant goodbye present.

Because he was playing baseball as much for its financial rewards as any enjoyment it brought him, Terry always drove hard salary bargains with McGraw. Terry wanted to be appropriately compensated, and McGraw always thought it was a special honor for a player to represent the New York Giants. For a period during the 1920s, the two men didn't even speak while inhabiting the same dugout and clubhouse. Once, Terry and a teammate missed night-time curfew in a Chicago hotel by two minutes. McGraw was lobby-sitting, seeking to catch truants. He fined Terry $50 the next day and Terry didn't receive the punishment well. He confronted McGraw and engaged in a shouting match. Refusing to take such insubordination, McGraw benched Terry for that day's game against the Cubs. Angered even more, Terry took his place in the dugout, untied his spikes and removed them and then pretended to go to sleep. McGraw was now rip-roaring mad but didn't say a word.

As the game wore on the two stubborn protagonists shot daggers at one another with narrowed eyes. In the ninth inning, McGraw was in a pickle. The Giants trailed, 2–1, and his best hitter was in the doghouse. What to do? He broke down, sort of, sending a messenger to the other end of the dugout to inform Terry he was being inserted into the game as a pinch-hitter. Terry roused himself, stretched as if waking from a long nap, slowing slipped into his shoes, tied them at a glacial pace, and then walked up to the plate. He then promptly hit the game-winning home run.

Realizing he had been beaten in the contest of wills, McGraw rescinded the fine and according to one account invited Terry to his hotel room to share a beer, though it was during Prohibition. The two men hashed out some of their differences during the meeting. To show there was no lingering ill will, McGraw even gifted Terry with two cases of beer to go. "Depositing the beer in the bathtub in his own room," a reporter later wrote, "Terry summoned several teammates to share in the spoils — after he had phoned room service and ordered $2 worth of ice, which he charged to McGraw."[3]

Still, whenever McGraw grew angry with Terry, he threatened aloud to trade him. When McGraw requested the player's presence in his office in the middle of the 1932 season, Terry believed this was the long-awaited moment of his exile from the Giants. Instead, McGraw shocked him by informing him that he was sick, that he was giving up his job as New York manager, and that he wanted Terry to take over the club reins. No one was more surprised than Terry. For all of their differences, perhaps McGraw recognized that the disagreements stemmed from Terry being a lot like him. If he was going to surrender operation of his baby, he wanted it in Terry's hands. In the end, he trusted Terry's desire to win.

Sure enough, when Terry had time to reflect a year or so later, he expressed warmer emotions about McGraw than one might have suspected. "At times he appeared to be pretty harsh and severe with us," Terry said, "but as I now look back on those days, I realize he was moved in this by only a single purpose, namely to drive us on to do our level best."[4]

Terry was as prickly as Grove and as apt to say "no comment" to sportswriters long before spoiled players decades later took up the refrain and acted like wary politicians every time they were approached with a question. It's possible the pairing of Grove and Terry on the same team would have resulted in an overdose of fireworks, but that was never an issue. They never shared a locker room, even in an All-Star game. At the moment, though, they were on center stage at Comiskey Park, with nearly 48,000 fans taking sides. It was a moment of suspense, with one team holding a slender lead and another within reach on the scoreboard.

This time mighty Bill Terry, who took home a .341 average the final time he hung up his uniform, could not make anything happen. Terry hit a ground ball to second, Charlie Gehringer handled it easily, and tossed without incident to Lou Gehrig at first. The American League had one out.

Wally Berger, who played the entire game in center field and had gone hitless, was the next scheduled batter. Known for his big clouts and proud of his home run hitting, Berger hoped to make some noise and show an American League crowd what he could do. The concept of measuring the distance of home runs had not taken hold in the 1930s, but later in life Berger said he was frequently told his home runs traveled extreme distances. "All I know is I hit 'tape-measure' home run jobs in every major league ballpark I played in," he said. "I never thought of records. I just liked to hit."[5]

Berger would have liked to have hit a home run right then off of Grove, whether it was measured by just slipping over the Comiskey wall or was knocked out of sight. But it didn't happen. If Berger believed he got enough wood on the ball to send Grove's pitch into another time zone,

Carl Hubbell (left) of the Giants and Lefty Grove of the Philadelphia A's shook hands prior to the game. At one point it was expected both men might be the starting pitchers but they ended up facing one another in relief in a game won by Grove's American League team, 4–2. (Photograph courtesy National Baseball Hall of Fame.)

the feeling was brief. He hit a line drive that died in Ben Chapman's glove, the same Chapman who had been moved to center field from right at the start of the inning. There were two outs.

A quick Arch Ward poll of the fans likely would have turned up a result that spectators would have enjoyed more baseball. But under the rules of the game, one more out and the Game of the Century was going to be history. The All-Star exhibition that had fanned the flames of excitement for a few months would be in the books.

There were others who did not want to see the afternoon end. There were those "leftover" players in the American League dugout, from hitters Tony Lazzeri and Jimmie Foxx to pitchers Wes Ferrell and Oral Hildebrand, who might get into the game if a bottom of the ninth or extra innings were played. And surely National League pitcher Hal Schumacher felt that way. He was the last fresh arm left for the NL and McGraw would have eventually had to use him.

Schumacher, nicknamed "Prince Hal," was a McGraw favorite. The 6', 190-pound right-hander broke in with the Giants in 1931, and he was in the middle of a break-out 19-win season in 1933. Schumacher, who won 158 games in a 13-year career, was highly praised by McGraw on his way up. McGraw even referred to Schumacher as "another Christy Mathewson," which was as generous a compliment as McGraw could pay anyone. Schumacher's "out" pitch was his sinker. Batters had trouble zeroing in on the low ball. After he retired as an active player, Schumacher stayed close to the sport by working for Adirondack Bats. Staying close to but not being part of the action was going to be the best he would get out of the first All-Star game if his team didn't rally.

Being Schumacher, one of the anointed, chosen to be on the roster for the Game of the Century, was one thing. Being Pete Pervan was quite another. Pervan never wanted the game to end, either. At the time, Pervan was 11 years old. He was a youngster on the outside of Comiskey Park, not dreaming for a second that he would be looking in. Pervan went to the ballpark that day to sell newspapers to the arriving fans. Much to young Pervan's amazement on the day of the game, as the crowd was streaming in, a well-dressed man in a business suit approached him, and not to buy a newspaper.

The man had an offer that was better than "Keep the change." He told the Chicago newshawk that a friend he expected couldn't come to the game that day, and asked the boy if he wanted to join him in the stands. Pervan raced to return his papers, and then joined the man. Pervan had seen major league baseball games before, but usually when the park was nearly void of fans. He and his friends were always on the prowl for ways to get in free because they couldn't afford tickets. "We used to sneak into the park for lesser games," Pervan said, "climb over the outside gates or walls, to get in free. But this was the All-Star game and I was real thrilled." Pervan said the man treated him to a hot dog and a Coca-Cola as a bonus. "I never saw him again after the game and I don't remember his name. But I told him, 'Thanks a lot. I'll never forget this all my life.'"[6] Given that Pervan was recounting the memory 70 years later, he made good on his word.

For Pervan, the anonymous benefactor was like the Good Fairy, making wishes come true. He would have been pleased if the game lasted 15 innings or continued into the night. But no game, not even baseball without a clock, lasts forever. With two outs and pitcher Carl Hubbell scheduled to bat, it was ten to midnight for the National League. As much as McGraw loved Hubbell, he was not going to leave him in to hit for himself in this circumstance. It was pretty thin pickings on the bench, too, when the manager looked around for someone to wield a bat in this critical situation. In the ninth inning, the NL had just one position player left who had not entered the game. McGraw gave the nod to the only man available, Tony Cuccinello.

Unlike many of the participants in the Game of the Century, Cuccinello was not destined for a Hall of Fame playing career. He was a solid player for whom this All-Star appearance would be his one and only over a 15-year major league run. While compiling a .280 lifetime average — not bad for a second baseman —1933 was not one of Cuccinello's finest years at the plate. He concluded the season with a .252 average. Cuccinello was only the sixth-leading vote-getter at his position in the fan vote but was selected initially as the sole representative of the Brooklyn Dodgers. Lefty O'Doul had been selected as a Dodger but was traded to the Giants before the game. It was determined late in the process by league officials that he could count as a Brooklyn player, but for a short while it seemed unacceptable that Brooklyn would have no player in the game.

There were other years when Cuccinello hit better and probably deserved more All-Star consideration, but since he was never selected at those times, it was just as well that he had his chance in 1933. Born in 1907, Cuccinello stood just 5'7" and played at 160 pounds. He came out of Long Island City, New York, and signed with the St. Louis Cardinals as a 17-year-old, even before graduating from high school. As a major leaguer, Cuccinello was a scrappy fielder and became a long-time coach after he retired.

Decades after his short appearance in the All-Star game, Cuccinello clearly remembered all of the circumstances surrounding the game. He said he was in New York with the Dodgers when the announcement of the team selections was made and he was quite excited to get the news. Max Carey, then coaching for the Dodgers, was set to be a National League coach and they took the train together to Chicago.

Cuccinello was quite fond of the National League team uniforms and caps that touted the league itself rather than the way the American League handled the situation, which had the players wearing their own team uniforms. Manager McGraw, as everyone knew, despised the American League and he conducted an NL team meeting prior to the game. "Let's go out and do a good job," McGraw told the players the way Cuccinello remembered it.[7]

When McGraw called upon Cuccinello he had a chance to be a hero or a goat, or simply turn in an at-bat that faded in memories. Cuccincello had great respect for Lefty Grove and knew what he was up against. Just before he picked up his bat and headed to the batter's box, McGraw called him over to whisper some last-minute instructions. The message? "Young man, take a strike," McGraw said. Cuccinello couldn't believe what he was hearing. "I almost laughed out loud," he recalled years later. "How could I spot a guy like Lefty Grove a strike? He should have given me one!"[8]

Of course, Grove did not know what had been said, but he was obliging anyway. Sure enough, the first pitch from Grove — taken with his bat on his shoulder by Cuccinello — was a called strike. The count was 0–1. Now Cuccinello could think about hitting. Not that it did him much good. Cuccinello got a momentary charge out of the next pitch. Maybe Grove thought the young infielder was going to be a pushover and got careless or simply thought Cuccinello would be easy to overpower. On Grove's second throw, Cuccinello nearly altered the game's dynamics. He smashed a long fly down the left-field line that could have been a home run but curved foul. Two pitches later, Grove had his strikeout, and the American League had its victory.

It was over. American League 4, National League 2. Tony Cuccinello had his what-if All-Star memory. The 48,000 fans could brag about the day they saw the Game of the Century. Connie Mack could smile in quiet satisfaction because his squad defeated that other league. Arch Ward and the *Chicago Tribune* could bask in the glow of a worthy risk taken that succeeded. Major league baseball could be proud of the show that went on under its name and label. The Century of Progress Exposition World's Fair offered up an extra marvel.

And John McGraw, his weakening body failing, could return to retirement, leaving behind the sport he loved so much.

Post Game

The time of the game was two hours and five minutes, a briskly played, low-scoring contest that had just enough action to satisfy the Comiskey Park crowd. The stars from the American League and National League and the pitchers and hitters from each side produced a well-balanced game.

The final score was 4–2, American League, not a rout. There were two home runs, one by that master of rising to the occasion, Babe Ruth, and the other by Frankie Frisch. The National League stroked eight hits, the American League nine. The winning pitcher was the Yankees' Lefty Gomez and the loser was the Cardinals' Bill Hallahan.

Hallahan lasted just two innings and his trademark wildness got him into trouble and cost his team the game. Lon Warneke's four innings of six-hit relief were excellent, though he also allowed a run. Carl Hubbell's two-inning, one-hit relief job for the Nationals was smooth.

Gomez permitted just two hits, neither of which hurt him or his side. Alvin Crowder was the American League pitcher who showed vulnerability, but once Connie Mack went to Lefty Grove it was over for the National League. Grove tossed three innings, surrendered three hits, no runs, and struck out three. It was vintage Lefty.

Only one error was committed — when Lou Gehrig dropped a foul ball.

Although the game was a snapshot of the moment — the players were the best in the sport during the 1933 season — the exhibition answered one of baseball's great theoretical questions: What if? What if the best players in the American League and the best players in the National League met on the field for one day? Well, what if occurred. On this one day the American League was two runs better. Baseball fans love to fantasize about greatest teams of all time. In the absence of time machines, players from one era could not be pitted against players of another. This one game was a substitute.

Arch Ward and the *Chicago Tribune* had tapped into an unspoken desire among fans ... or at least only a whispered desire. F.C. Lane may have propagated the concept of an All-Star game as early as 1915, but there was no general clamor in the baseball universe for the creation of such a game then and there. The confluence of circumstances, the holding of the World's Fair in Chicago at that moment, started the wheels turning on the invention of the All-Star event. Chicago mayor Ed Kelly, Tribune publisher Col. Robert McCormick and sports editor Arch Ward were correct. A special sporting event linked to the Century of Progress Exposition not only made sense, it was a natural, a hugely successful endeavor that fit neatly into the overall show. The All-Star baseball game was indeed just another example of Chicago at its finest.

The players, managers and coaches chosen to represent baseball in the All-Star game knew they were involved in something special. They were proud to fight for their respective leagues in an attempt to prove superiority, but they also recognized the game was an historical event, that there had been nothing else like it before, and they played under the assumption that there would be nothing else like it again in the immediate future.

For a man who made his living with words, Ward was not an especially talented writer. He was a man of big ideas more than tightly phrased sentences. But when he hit upon the phrase "Game of the Century" early in the process to describe this special baseball game, Ward found wording that resonated with people in the game and the public at large. After being uttered a few times in connection with the announcement of a one-time All-Star baseball game being conducted in conjunction with the Fair, everyone knew the topic. The instant labeling did its job and played a tremendous role in promoting the game, the quick sale of tickets, and the engendering buzz. Inside the sport and on the outside looking in as fans, who wouldn't want to be part of or witness to the "Game of the Century?"

The naming of the game was a public relations coup. People did not pick away at the phrase, trying to think of prior games of the century to compete for this title. There was a prompt admission that it was a fitting title. Never had the biggest stars from each league faced off. Game of the Century indeed. Clearly, the application of that phrase contributed magic to the occasion. Fans could go home and forevermore say that they had been on hand at Comiskey Park for the once-in-a-lifetime showdown between the leagues' stars. "We considered it a great honor (to be chosen) simply because we thought it was going to be the only All-Star game," said Joe Cronin.[1]

After Lefty Grove threw the last pitch, striking out Tony Cuccinello, the teams began to wander off the field to the dugouts and then the clubhouses. Fans, satisfied with the show, began shuffling towards the Comiskey Park exits. It was fair to say, though, that everyone had a glow. Major league baseball had never seen a day like this and the game was to be savored and remembered. The American League locker room was a little bit livelier than the National League clubhouse. The AL players were, after all, the victors. It did not take long for thoughts to shift to the immediate future. After showers, trains had to be caught, teams rejoined on the road or at home parks.

One man who had nowhere to go in a hurry was John McGraw. The Giants were no longer his. He had no team with a vested interest in the 1933 pennant race. And since he drew no one's paycheck this season, the only suit he had to pull on was businessman's garb, not one with a team name emblazoned on the front. McGraw had just managed his final game — and lost it. He had been retired before July 6, and he was retired once more from the game he loved.

McGraw's mind was not on his triumphs of the past and it was not on games stretching ahead on the schedule. His mind was focused on the game just played, the experience just shared by his National League club. Uncharacteristically, as he watched his men dress and scatter to the corners of the land to resume playing ball, McGraw went around the room, player to player, shaking their hands. It was a dignified gesture from a man who knew he was leaving the game for good. "Thanks, boys," McGraw said to his team. "Better luck next time."[2]

There was a bit of poignancy in McGraw's message. The great competitor was through competing. Use of the words "Better luck next time" could only have been general. He had no inside knowledge that there would ever be a next time in All-Star game competition. Until completion of the game, the only goal was for this great showdown to come off cleanly.

The All-Star game was conceived as an accompaniment to the World's Fair, not as a permanent fixture on the baseball calendar.

Major league baseball had approached the game with a mixture of enthusiasm and caution but would not have initiated its creation without Arch Ward doing the leg work and his newspaper taking the financial risk of underwriting any difficulties that might arise. The regular-season schedule had been altered to accommodate the plan and newspapers around the country embraced the idea of fans voting and forwarding their ballots.

The choice of the teams and managers was surprisingly free of controversy. Rarely had so much effort been expended in such a short time to produce such a wildly popular hit show without a hitch. The players loved the game and considered it an honor to be part of it. The newspapers lavished free publicity on the game and the sport. Fans stampeded for tickets. What was not to like? And once the game was underway, baseball could not have asked for a more appropriate leading man to step forward. Babe Ruth, who had almost single-handedly rescued the sport with his gargantuan batting feats in the years immediately following the Black Sox Scandal, stepped up on cue. Ruth hit the game-winning home run and made a game-saving catch. And heck, a little bit subtler in the rewards category, it wasn't such a bad thing that the game had been played at Comiskey Park and that the host team was the White Sox. It was the White Sox that had been besmirched as the Black Sox. The team was still desperate to cleanse its soul following the 1919 charges of fixing the World Series.

Although he was kept busy as the ballplayers hustled to dress and go their diverse ways, American League batboy John McBride had just as much fun after the game as he did before and during it. One of McBride's tasks was to gather the bats from the AL dugout and make sure they were returned to their rightful owners. Once the game was a foregone conclusion, baseball administrators realized that the occasion should be marked in certain ways, and they wanted souvenirs, too. McBride was given custody of 60 baseballs that were supposed to be signed by all of the players for the sport's dignitaries.

"Ruth and Gehrig signed the balls," McBride said a half-century later, "but others were so hard-pressed for time they had to beg off. They knew that I could duplicate their signatures (something McBride did not explain), so they asked me to sign their names. I've often wondered if people examining those autographs suspect that some of them may not be genuine."[3]

McBride said that the players "tipped me generously," at least in part as a bonus for forging their names. "When I counted the money, I had somewhere between 12 and 14 dollars, a very good day's income for a 19-year-old kid in those days."[4] And who was the best tipper? Ed Rommel of the Philadelphia A's gave McBride $2 and he was only on hand as the American League's batting practice pitcher.

For the most part, the writers were not shocked that Ruth stood out. They shook their heads in admiration. Knowing he was an old man by baseball standards and not in the best of shape, there was still a feeling that Ruth knew how to crank it up a notch when the lights were brightest. One or more newspapermen even said that if Ruth were plunked down in a stadium with 50,000 fans in it, he was going to provide a show somehow, some way. In the American League clubhouse, Ruth gained the most attention from those newspapermen, and given his role in the game, was full of bonhomie. "Wasn't it swell — an All-Star game?" Ruth said. "Wasn't it a great idea? And we won it, besides."[5]

One sportswriter who had fun writing about the Game of the Century and Ruth's role in it was Joe Williams, a New York columnist who was in attendance in Chicago.

> Maybe, after all, the chief difference between the National League and the American League is an old fat fellow named George Herman Ruth. They tossed all the stars of baseball together here yesterday, chose up sides, and played a ball game for the old players' benefit fund, and when it was all over you had to admit that the old fat fellow was still the king of 'em all. Like King Tut, Prince Mike, and the Silver Dollar, the fat old fellow isn't what he used to be; he wheezes and puffs when he starts to run, and he goes after those sharp liners in the outfield like a tipsy dowager doing the rhumba. But put the old fat fellow in a spot where the pressure is tight and the ball game is at stake and watch him go![6]

More and more, as Ruth said, the All-Star game looked like a swell idea. Those National League naysayers who originally voted to obstruct the game had been quiet for a long time. Even their argument against holding the inaugural game based on how every other city would come up with a charity it wanted to promote evaporated from all discussions.

"The All-Star game, the first of its kind ever played," Williams continued, "was a complete success from every angle."[7] And Williams didn't even write for the *Tribune*.

One of those angles was cash return for the needy players' fund. The gross receipts exceeded $56,000, and the net return for the players' fund was about $45,000.

The sponsoring *Tribune*'s game story was written by Irving Vaughn, not Ward, and the headline read, "Players Prove Stars Can Star With Strangers." The sub-head read, "Pitching Strategy Upsets Hitters." Clearly, the *Tribune* felt the pitchers were ahead of the hitters in this one.[8]

One of the arguments against all-star play in general was that it took time for a team to come together. Decades later, such thoughts are never voiced about baseball all-stars but are still heard about basketball, football and hockey teams. In Vaughn's mind this was a test case and it was proven that baseball players didn't need such long-term interaction to mesh smoothly on the field. "The old theory that it takes practice to perfect team play took a slap between the eyes yesterday," Vaughn wrote. "The ragged work that some of the 49,000 might have expected didn't appear. The spectacle proved that a defensive star in any one position remains a defensive star even when lined up alongside strangers. The players fitted together as well as if they had been pals all summer."[9]

Probably the single most important element in the All-Star game on July 6, 1933, was the elements. The sun came out. If it had been rainy that day and if the rain continued for two days and the Game of the Century became the washout of the century, baseball history might have been changed. Likely, it would have been many years before anyone proposed holding such an all-star shindig again. The *Tribune* would have been out about $10,000 (though there was at least one mention of $25,000) and there was no telling what would have come of Ward's big ideas. If a deluge had drowned the game, Ward said, "The *Tribune* would have been stuck and Ward possibly would have been washed out of journalism."[10]

Anyone who lives in the Chicago area or has visited for any length of time knows the weather can be fickle. In this case it could have been catastrophic. Raindrops falling on the fans' heads probably would have sent Ward out of the press box to pass out thousands of umbrellas on his own. Never mind a century of progress, a rainstorm would have set back baseball all-star games a century.

Even though Ward thought large, he had not really thought about the All-Star game continuing as an annual event. Until the first one was in the books and was deemed a smash, no one did. "What I remember most about All-Star competition," said Ward's son Tom prior to the 1983 game, "is dad's feeling that the All-Star game was to be a one-shot affair. He couldn't envision the millions of fans who'll be watching the golden jubilee event on television. He was overwhelmed when radio made a big thing of the All-Star game."[11]

John P. Carmichael, one-time sports columnist for the *Chicago Daily News*, was a contemporary of Ward's, and said the first game was considered special, but no talk occurred about making it a regular exhibition. "The game was only destined for one year," Carmichael said. "I don't think anyone even thought about (the) next year. And even when the game was played again for the next few years it still wasn't locked in as permanent."[12]

The entire attitude about the All-Star game changed once the first one was in the books. All quarters chimed in about the positive feeling left by the game. Much like a play making its debut on Broadway, the game was reviewed and critiqued and the reviews were all raves. "From the outset, the All-Star game was an unqualified success," noted *The Sporting News*.[13] So why close a hit after one night? From a once-in-a-lifetime event the idea of making the game an annual mid-summer game quickly took hold. Ward had done such a good job of promoting the game and building up the anticipation and suspense for the first one that baseball fans loved the contest at first sight. Do it again, came the cry. It was a universal suggestion, too. No one had anything bad to say about the All-Star game. It was clearly an idea whose time had come. F.C. Lane had been right all along. Mixing play with the stars of the two leagues tickled the public's fancy. Fans wanted to see more.

It seemed as if fans did not root in the same manner for an All-Star team as they did for their own local clubs. Whether they were simply so impressed watching the great array of talent displayed on the Comiskey Park field or not, their personal reactions seemed stifled, one writer noted. Complaints normally recorded in the manner of booing were nominal. *Tribune* writer Harvey Woodruff termed the gathering of about 48,000 fans "the most sportsmanlike crowd ever gathered for such an important event. Those familiar boos and jeers so frequently heard were at a minimum. The crowd of yesterday apparently sensed the occasion as a precursor of more such games to follow in future years and lent its best behavior."[14]

That might have been reading a bit more into the crowd's actions than was warranted. More likely the emotional commitment revolving around winning and losing did not run as deep. And it may be there was a subconscious acknowledgement that these indeed were stars at the pinnacle of the sport and not run-of-the-mill players who should be jeered. Whatever the reason, it is doubtful the crowd was governed by what might or might not take place in the future. Woodruff, though, was thinking ahead and suggested the All-Star game could become "an annual fixture."[15]

Almost immediately, thoughts of others dealing with the notion of the game sticking around made their way into print. Owners of the New York Giants, Boston Braves and St. Louis Cardinals had been among the original protestors of the game but had come around after having their arms twisted. No owner was saying anything against all-star play now. Commissioner Kenesaw Mountain Landis, who ostensibly worked for the owners but enjoyed tremendous power, promptly put his feelings on the record after watching the first All-Star game and surveying the scene at Comiskey Park.

Landis was authoritarian and his idea of what was in the best interests of baseball took on overtones of harshness to some. But he was no dummy, and he saw first-hand how well-received this game was and what a bonanza of free goodwill it had created for his sport. The first thing Landis said when asked for comment about the game was, "That's a grand show and it should be continued."[16] Although some owners still demurred about the need for the game behind the scenes in its early years, Landis, with his shock of white hair and severe frown on his face when crossed, was unyielding. He not only backed the game with words, he attended the first 12 All-Star games played.

When the hoopla died down and the season resumed, the owners conducted one of their regular meetings behind closed doors. A topic on the agenda was approval of continuing the All-Star game and rotating it from city to city. The measure passed and an announcement was made. By December, when the decree was official and the *Chicago Tribune* editorialized on the All-Star game once more, the name in writers' minds had morphed from Game of the Century to "Baseball's Greatest Game."

The editorial in the form of an unusual, unsigned "In the Wake of the News" sports column took pains to slap the paper and Arch Ward on their backs for their wonderful efforts in creating the game but admitted that the time had come for baseball to pick up the torch. The tone of the editorial was smug, indicating now that the *Tribune* had shown the way, it was proper for baseball to oversee the All-Star game, but to make sure it was done in the right way. "In the future, organized baseball will conduct this game itself," the story read. "That is as it should be. Naturally, we of the *Tribune* sports department are gratified to see this game continue, if the same success is maintained. Obviously, however, it can better be conducted under official sanction as a permanent feature than by outside agency."[17] Obviously.

Arch Ward probably wrote the column or at the least supervised its production and appearance in his section. In a way it was a valedictory speech. After being so kind as to create the All-Star game for major league baseball, he went on to other things in other sports.

18

East-West Classic

There were no black players in the first All-Star game. There were no black players in the major leagues at the time — and there wouldn't be until 1947. The Game of the Century was played during baseball's most shameful period, when by "gentleman's agreement" or the sheer force of Commissioner Kenesaw Mountain Landis' will a man with dark skin was unwelcome in the National Pastime.

Until Jackie Robinson broke the color barrier with the Brooklyn Dodgers when general manager Branch Rickey guided his rise to the majors, there were no African American players in the majors during the twentieth century. The most skilled black players operated in a shadow universe representing teams like the Kansas City Monarchs, the Homestead Grays and the Pittsburgh Crawfords in the Negro leagues or on barnstorming clubs that toured the country.

Inhabiting a world of discrimination that consigned them to long bus rides on dusty roads with out-of-the-way eatery stops for their meals and overnighters sitting up on the bus or in low-rent hotels, some of the finest American ballplayers of the era made do. If they wished to make a living playing baseball, this was their tradeoff under the tenets of American society at the time. Prejudice was rampant, worse in the South where there might be lynchings, but often just as insidious, if more subtle, in the North.

As the Depression rotted away the underpinnings of American businesses and family stability, it ate more devastatingly at black citizens who were at the bottom of the economic totem pole. Major league ballplayers took pay cuts and baseball fan attendance declined in even the biggest of cities. The same afflictions assaulted the Negro leagues. Salaries were already lower for black players compared to their white counterparts and they shrunk even more. Attendance was already smaller for Negro leagues games and it shrunk even more. The owners of the black teams suffered from the same financial ills as the white bosses — only more so. Two leagues had gone out of business and black ball was struggling to stay alive in any organized form.

As a result, likely no one eyed the explosive success of the first All-Star game more closely than men like Gus Greenlee, owner of the Crawfords, Alajandro "Alex" Pompez, owner of the New York Cubans, and co-owners Effa and Abe Manley of the Newark Eagles. (Effa was the only woman owner in the sport.) Fan voting, baseball news splashed all over the papers, the biggest stars in the majors brought together, a sellout crowd, all of that was monitored and appraised. It was apparent immediately that such a plan could work equally well for the Negro leagues. The wheels began turning, and quickly. The goal for the team owners was to introduce a similar game featuring their players before the season ended. It was a winning formula. Why not emulate it?

Although Arch Ward was credited with inventing the first All-Star game, it was widely known that F.C. Lane had suggested it long before. In 1932, the year before the majors threw their big party, Roy Sparrow, the Crawfords' club secretary, had the idea for a Negro leagues all-star game to show off the talents of players like Satchel Paige, Josh Gibson and others. Sparrow actually made the suggestion before Ward thought of it for the majors. It was Sparrow's boss, Greenlee, however, who was the spokesperson in league matters and the front man who gave the game a big push.

Greenlee was a passionate baseball man and a firm believer in backing Negro leagues baseball, even when it was most jeopardized by franchise failures during the Depression. But he was always going to have his critics because he operated on the shady side of the law. Greenlee owned nightclubs that served liquor during Prohibition, though some might say that was a public service rather than law-breaking that bothered most citizens. His primary source of income was numbers running. (There were probably some who felt that was a public service, too.) As a result, the straight and narrow folk were always going to be on Greenlee's case. Still, he wanted what was best for black baseball and not only because he made a profit from the sport.

In July 1933, after the majors' big show, Sparrow, who was also a sportswriter for the *Pittsburgh Sun-Telegraph*, and a fellow scribe, Bill Nunn of the *Pittsburgh Courier*, conferred and decided to push for a Negro leagues all-star game. They first met with Cumberland Posey, owner of the Grays. Their idea was to hold an all-star game in conjunction with the New York Milk Fund Day at Yankee Stadium. That idea was quickly dropped, but the all-star idea persisted. They thought New York was the best location and agreed to discuss the plan with Bill "Bojangles" Robinson, the famous dancer who was a part-owner of the New York Black Yankees. Before that happened, though, Sparrow and Nunn ate dinner at Greenlee's Crawford Grill in Pittsburgh and informed him about what was going on. Greenlee immediately jumped on board, introduced the East-West Classic name, and suggested they contact Robert Cole about leasing Comiskey Park in Chicago for such a game.

Much like Ward's idea, this one ignited like a brush fire on dry grass and spread quickly. A meeting was called and representatives of the Crawfords, Cubans, and Eagles, sportswriters, and players like Josh Gibson and Oscar Charleston attended. And much like the condensed time period from announcement to implementation of the All-Star game the majors followed, the Negro Leagues moved lickety-split. The date for the first East-West game was set for September 10, and once again the site was Comiskey Park in Chicago.

Only a small minority of baseball fans watched the happenings of the Negro leagues closely. Aficionados of the game that were not diseased by prejudice attended black ball games and became fans of the best players. The East-West game was not played for white fans, but it did garner more attention in mainstream America than other Negro league contests. More importantly, it became the showcase for black baseball, clearly the single most significant date on the calendar. "It is indisputable that the East-West Classic was the highlight of any season," a history of the event states.[1]

Men and women dressed in their finery, stadiums were sold out, and the fascination with seeing the best against the best never grew old. All of the principles that made the major league All-Star game a success applied to the creation of the East-West Classic. It was never termed the Game of the Century, but the first East-West Classic probably had as much right to the phrase as the white game.

Planning meetings played out off the grid, and it wasn't until mid–August that the official announcement of an East-West black baseball all-

star game was announced to the public at large. Word had come out in
the black press earlier and voting was underway long before white citizens
of Chicago and other baseball communities knew the game was afoot.
Although it did not have the same clout, and the event was not tied to the
Century of Progress Exposition, the *Chicago Defender* served the East-West
Classic in a similar capacity as the *Tribune* had for the majors' game. In
its August 12 edition, the *Defender* carried results of early balloting. The
leaders at the various positions had just topped 1,000 votes apiece. There
was a long way to go, but Satchel Paige was leading the East pitching tabulations.

Soon enough, a sportswriter named Al Monroe was beginning to
sound a lot like Arch Ward when it came to trumpeting the establishment
of this new game. "East versus West baseball supremacy, long a matter of
opinion despite past world's series, is to be tested on the afternoon of Sept.
10," Monroe penned in the *Defender*. "This game — several weeks away at
this time — is already attracting fandom's attention and early indications
are that several thousands will be present when the umpire yells, 'Play
ball!' There is something about this game that makes it stand out as the
peer of all attractions to date and I am not forgetting the American League–
National League loop contest staged at the same park July 6."[2]

The *Chicago Tribune*, at ground zero of this event and the great bull-
horn for the major league game, was not going to be banging the drums
quite so loudly this time around. However, the *Tribune* did not ignore the
game. The paper's first story about the East-West game began this way:
"An outstanding athletic event, insofar as the 300,000 Negroes of Chicago
and the 12,000,000 in the United States are concerned, was announced
yesterday. It is to be an all-star baseball game at Comiskey Park on Sept.
10, enlisting the greatest colored players in the country, to be selected by
popular vote."[3]

It was noted that "the game has the sanction of the Negro National
Association of Professional Baseball Clubs" but that any player could be
voted onto a roster, even if he was not affiliated with a particular team.
Tucked into the short story was a most remarkable line, indicating that
the selection of a few players was a foregone conclusion, such as "Joe Paige,
Pittsburgh pitcher (who) has struck out Bill Terry, Hack Wilson and oth-
ers."[4] This phrase reflected a stunning mixture of ignorance and hubris.
It indicated that this hurler, by virtue of his ability to strike out such big

National League stars, must be good. But a question was raised. Just who was that guy the *Tribune* was talking about? The most famous black player in the land was indeed a pitcher named Paige, who was indeed at that moment affiliated with the Pittsburgh Crawfords. That would be the legendary Satchel Paige, not a mysterious Joe. Oops, nice typographical error.

A mistake like that would have been the equivalent of referring to Carl Hubbell as Charley Hubbell or Lefty Grove as Righty Grove. In any case, when those votes were totaled, Satchel Paige was the leading vote-getter at his position for the East. "Satchel Paige for the East and Willie Foster for the West!" proclaimed the *Defender*. "That is the final pitching selection for the big game to be played at Comiskey Park, Sunday, Sept. 10, under what is termed the greatest baseball attraction ever staged."[5] The phrase Game of the Century was avoided, but this new statement, so deliciously phrased, was being employed to subtly inform fans that this all-star game would be even bigger than the one that had been all the rage all summer.

In a story the day before the game, the *Defender* casually discussed the betting action on the East-West Classic. Given that it was an exhibition with little at stake beyond bragging rights, it should not have been terribly surprising that action was light. It was simply intriguing that betting on the outcome was a fair topic for open discussion. One of the wager options being reported was that bettors were saying Willie Foster would shut out the East during his pitching turn. Excitement was on the agenda, for sure, and fans were in for a treat, the *Defender* opined. "Power at the bat, speed on the base paths and color in the field mark the selections of the fans who have participated in the mammoth poll...."[6]

One of the promising mysteries of the first major league All-Star game in July was that no one seemed to have a strong feeling about what would happen on the field. Indeed, the results, except to managers Connie Mack and John McGraw, and the players seemed almost irrelevant. It was the staging of the glittery contest that was paramount. When *Defender* sportswriter Al Monroe talked up the East-West Classic, however, he played up the idea that an American League victory had been a foregone conclusion.

> In the inter-league contest of several weeks ago there was a bit of feeling on the part of the fans that the American League should and would win just about as it pleased. There was a general belief that the junior loop with its great stars would overpower the parent body

and come through at the asking. And, may we say here, the presence of Al Simmons, Babe Ruth, Lou Gehrig, (Joe) Cronin, (Earl) Averill, and Ben Chapman when the American League took the field to start the last half of the first frame did not lessen the power of that belief at all. The game of Sept. 10, however, presents a different picture.[7]

The manager for the East team was future Hall of Famer John Henry "Pop" Lloyd, a brilliant fielding shortstop with a .343 average in his time in Negro leagues play who also starred in Cuba. The West boss was Joe Green, a one-time second baseman for the Chicago Leland Giants.

Among the stars selected for the East team were Satchel Paige on the mound, catchers Josh Gibson and Biz Mackey, first baseman Oscar Charleston, shortstop Judy Johnson and outfielder Cool Papa Bell. Among the stars voted in for the West team were pitcher Willie Foster, first baseman Mule Suttles, shortstop Willie Wells, and outfielder Turkey Stearnes. Each side had a roster of 17 players, as opposed to the 18 chosen for the major league game, and each manager in theory had four pitchers to work with. However, Paige neither dressed in uniform nor played in the game. This peculiarity was not addressed directly in any of three Paige biographies. Paige was the nation's most recognizable Negro league player and in winter leagues in other countries, as well, so in many ways he was the face of black baseball. But when all the tabulations were in, despite his early lead, Paige came up only third in the voting for the East squad. Perhaps the very prideful man was disappointed in that result and had his feelings hurt enough to sit the game out despite being on site. It's possible he might also have wanted to avoid another in a long line of showdowns with the Chicago American Giants' Willie Foster, a series of which had been taking place during the regular season. Nevertheless, it was not like Paige to back away from either a challenge or the limelight.

Unlike Ward, the *Tribune*, and the majors, the Negro league organizers of the first East-West Classic were not as lucky with the Chicago weather. It rained on the morning of the game, though the field dried enough to start the game. Attendance was 19,568, perhaps held down by the overcast skies. Without Paige's cooperating right arm, the East started Pittsburgh Crawfords hurler Sam Streeter. The diminutive Streeter was a southpaw who stood 5'8", but who over the course of his career threw a half-dozen no-hitters.

The East was the visiting team and the man at the top of the order, and the first man to ever bat in an East-West Classic, was Cool Papa Bell, the center fielder representing the Pittsburgh Crawfords. Bell is regarded as possibly the fastest runner in baseball history. He could dash around the bases from a standing start with Jesse Owens–like speed, timed once in 12 seconds. Bell's signature demoralizing play for opposing pitchers was going from first to third on a bunt. He wrote his name on contracts for professional play in Negro leagues and in Latin American countries from 1922 to 1951, and he was popular wherever he played. Bell hit .437 in Mexico in 1940 and topped the .370 mark at least three times for Negro league teams.

A bit more reticent about self-aggrandizement than his yarn-telling friend Satchel Paige, Bell let Paige do the talking about the outfielder's accomplishments. Most of Paige's Bell stories took the form of informing listeners just how fast that daredevil was. "I saw Bell hit a ground ball," said Paige, "and (he) was declared out because he was hit by his own batted ball while sliding into second base."[8]

The first East-West Classic was not Bell's finest game — he went 0-for-5, though he did score a run.

One black superstar who suffered more than most in obscurity than others was Oscar Charleston. While black stars like Bell, Paige, Gibson and Buck Leonard gradually earned a measure of respect from barnstorming against white teams and being recognized by the more discerning American baseball fan, Charleston came along too soon for all that. He was held in tremendous esteem by those who played with him and against him, and he was the top vote-getter for the first Classic. Charleston was chosen as the East starter at first base.

Charleston was born in 1896 and began playing for Negro clubs in 1915. He was considered a do-everything player, one who batted over .400 twice, and one who would battle fiercely on the field for every advantage, a trait he brought to his subsequent managerial roles. In 1933, he was nearing the end of his best years, and playing in the first Classic was a significant way for one of the all-time greats to be honored before it was too late.

By many accounts, Charleston was tormented that he was an outcast in black baseball when he knew he was as good as any white player in the game. He often played angry and in that sense was compared to Ty Cobb for never giving an inch and being prone to using his fists at the hint of a challenge. "Oscar Charleston loved to play baseball," said Ted Page, who was an all-star teammate of Charleston's in 1933. "There was nothing he liked to do better, unless it was fight. He didn't smoke, he didn't drink, but he enjoyed a good fight — with the opposition."[9]

Charleston excelled before television exposed baseball to the masses. He starred when Negro league games were overlooked by radio, mainstream newspapers and magazines, and when box scores were not meticulously kept. He was, in that sense, an almost invisible superstar, except to those who saw him in the flesh and carried that memory with them for a lifetime. Old-timer Buck O'Neil, the Kansas City Monarchs first baseman and manager who was a walking encyclopedia of Negro league information and knew how to vividly convey his impressions, marveled at Charleston's skill. "To this day," O'Neil wrote in his autobiography years after his retirement, "I always claim that Willie Mays was the greatest major league player I have ever seen ... but then I pause and say that Oscar Charleston was even better. He was like Ty Cobb, Babe Ruth and Tris Speaker rolled into one."[10]

Charleston once said he feared no pitcher of any kind that he had seen, from white stars to black stars. "When I go up there to swing," he said, "it does not matter who is pitching, I'm rough and ready, real rough, on all pitchers, anywhere."[11] Before an exhibition game once, Charleston told Walter Johnson that he was going to hit a home run off of him. Johnson struck out Charleston twice and then Oscar delivered his promised blow. Gashouse Gang Cardinal Dizzy Dean said, "Charleston could hit that ball a mile. He didn't have a weakness. When he came up, we just threw and hoped like hell he wouldn't get ahold of one and send it out of the park."[12]

The hard-hitting first baseman did not get ahold of one in the inaugural East-West Classic, going 0-for-3. He did score two runs.

Josh Gibson, who shared the catching role with Biz Mackey (the player who taught Roy Campanella how to be a slick receiver) for the East, went 1-for-2 that day. Gibson was known as the "black Babe Ruth" for his slugging ability. Records are so sketchy that the number of home runs claimed for him during his career fluctuates wildly, but the figure rises up to 800. Gibson's was the saddest of stories among the great black stars of the mid–twentieth century. Not only was he excluded from the majors despite his terrific talent, he died of a brain tumor in 1947 when he was just 35.

Willie Foster, also called Bill, started for the West and was sharp that day against the East all-stars. Foster's half-brother Rube founded the Negro National League. The bullet-throwing Foster was almost untouchable through the late 1920s and early 1930s, and he and Paige had a great rivalry. "As near as I can remember, we faced each other around 13 or 14 times," Foster said. "I think I got the edge of Satchel when I beat him in a double-header.... I think that put me one ballgame ahead of him in our careers. But I'll tell you something. If Satchel got one run first, he would beat you. If I got one run first, he was beat."[13]

In an unheard-of performance for all-star games of any type, majors or elsewhere, Foster pitched a complete game, nine innings against the best the opposition brought to the plate. He gave up seven runs, but just three of them were earned. He struck out four and walked three. The first five men in the order for the West — Turkey Stearnes in center, Willie Wells at short, Steel Arm Davis in left, Alec Radcliffe at third, and Mule Suttles at first — each stroked two hits. Foster's biggest problem was his infield. Second baseman Leroy Morney of the Cleveland Giants committed three costly errors.

Stearnes was a notable power hitter who said he didn't really care about numbers unless they did the type of damage that won a game. "I hit so many I never counted them, and I'll tell you why," Stearnes said of his homers. "If they didn't win a ball game, they didn't amount to anything. It didn't make any difference if I hit four or five over the grandstand. That's what I wanted, to win the game."[14]

The West broke through on the scoring, 1–0, in the bottom of the third inning. The East took the lead in the top of the fourth with a three-run outburst. But the West retaliated immediately in the bottom of the fourth with three more runs to go up 4–3. In the see-saw game, the East added two runs in the top of the fifth for a 5–4 lead, one that was promptly erased by a three-run West rally in the bottom of the sixth. Back and forth they went. The West took command in the bottom of the seventh with a third three-run explosion and then added a single run in the bottom of the eighth for an 11–5 lead. The East concluded the scoring with two runs in the top of the ninth but could get no closer. The final was West 11, East 7. Foster was the winning pitcher and Streeter was the loser.

In the midst of all that scoring, it was Mule Suttles, whose given name was George, who distinguished himself with a clutch at-bat in the bottom of the fourth with his team behind, 3–1. There were two men on when the West first sacker came to the plate against Streeter. Streeter specialized in keeping the ball low, a tactic that more often than not hindered home run production. Not this time, though. The ball came in low, just above Suttles' shoe-tops, but it didn't matter. He zeroed in on the pitch, connected with the full impact of his swing on the ball and sent it sailing deep out of Comiskey Park in left field. The story goes that the ball cleared the fence and broke the window of a taxi cab parked across the street. The distance from home plate to landing point was estimated at 475, feet and the three-run shot gave the West a 4–3 lead. Suttles' blast was comparable to Babe Ruth's key two-run homer in the major league All-Star game and was the blow that everyone who saw the game remembered best.

Suttles' personal dimensions were listed as 6' 6" and 270 pounds, and the *Chicago Defender* called him "as big as a mountain and that weight is solid bone and muscle. Mule isn't fat, he's just big. He is the greatest hitter this side of Babe Ruth."[15]

Just as the major league All-Star game was proclaimed a success, those who played and organized the East-West Classic quickly realized they were on to something. It was apparent that the game would continue. In 1934, the Classic resumed and this time Paige committed to playing before the voters were polled. He made a vague reference to his absence from the first game, indicating he sort of slept through it. In his autobiography, *Maybe I'll Pitch Forever*, released in 1961, Paige wrote, "I hadn't been in that first game. I was new around the league then and I guess that's why they didn't name me, even if I was one of the top hands around."[16] But Paige, who claimed a record of 31–4 in 1933, had been chosen for the team, even if he had not been the top vote-getter.

A year later, Paige was the leading vote-getter for the second edition of the game. In subsequent years, when he was the biggest name in black baseball and transcended the Negro leagues with coverage in *Life* magazine and elsewhere, Paige sometimes skipped the affair because it didn't pay him enough. No such thought ran through his mind in 1934.

The 1934 game was an epic and attracted 30,000 people to Comiskey Park, to that point the largest crowd ever to witness a Negro league ballgame. Paige was a late arrival to a fantastic pitching duel. Slim Jones started for the East and gave up one hit in three innings. Harry Kincannon followed him, surrendering four hits in two innings. Ted Trent started for the West and gave up two hits in three innings. Chet Brewer followed and allowed two hits in three innings. No runs were allowed by any of those pitchers, setting the stage for a late-game showdown between rivals Willie Foster for the West and Paige for the East.

Paige pitched four innings and allowed two hits while striking out five. Foster went three innings and gave up the game's only run in the top of the eighth inning in a 1–0 loss. The only run came across when Cool Papa Bell walked, stole second, and scored on a looping single by Jud Wilson. Paige, though, was the man of the hour. He replaced Kincannon after that hurler allowed a double. "Three men came up against me and three men died while that runner stayed glued on second," Paige said.[17]

The performance was vintage Paige and it added to his already substantial reputation. The beauty of the 1–0 pitchers duel added to the luster of the Negro leagues' All-Star East-West Classic, too. The game was played from 1933 to 1953, and until the Negro leagues faded out after the long-overdue integration of the majors, the Classic was a cornerstone of the season. Wherever it was played, mostly at Comiskey Park but also at Yankee Stadium and the Polo Grounds in New York and at Griffith Stadium in Washington, D.C., the all-star event was an economic bonanza and a social festival, a reunion among players, and a chance to showcase the best of them.

The East-West Classic was a revered institution in the black community. "People would come from all over the South," said Hall of Famer Monte Irvin, who played in all-star games for the majors and the Negro leagues. "They'd come for that big weekend, Friday, Saturday and Sunday. The nightclubs were filled. The hotels and restaurants were like a picnic. People came to the ballpark early to see guys hit." It was a party for the ballplayers, too, though getting paid just $50 to play didn't cut it. "To come to Chicago for three days with $50 to go see Count Basie or Duke Ellington or Lena Horne, that didn't go very far."[18]

For all of his efforts to promote black baseball across the country, Gus Greenlee deserves more credit for his work establishing the East-West game than anything else, Buck O'Neil believed. "That was the greatest idea Gus ever had," O'Neil said, "because it made black people feel involved in baseball like they'd never been before."[19]

The East-West All-Star game rode the coattails of the major league All-Star game into existence. Once established it was a tremendous point of pride and joy in the black community during the Depression and for

☛ COME SEE ☚

ALL STAR BASEBALL DREAM GAME

ALL STARS ★ ★ ★   ★ ★ ★ ALL STARS
WORLD'S GREATEST NEGRO SPORTING EVENT
INTERLEAGUE CHAMPIONSHIP CONTEST
BETWEEN THE EAST AND WEST

Negro American League All Stars
— VS —
Negro National League All Stars

YANKEE STADIUM
NEW YORK CITY

TUESDAY NITE, AUG. 24, 8:45 P.M.

—— A D M I S S I O N ——

RESERVED BOX SEATS, $3.00 & $2.00

GRAND STAND, $1.25   BLEACHERS, 60c

Advance Sale at Yankee Stadium, 84 Lenox Ave. — and
New York Black Yankees, 127 W. 135th Street

—— L I N E U P S ——

(EAST) NEGRO NATIONAL LEAGUE		(WEST) NEGRO AMERICAN LEAGUE
BUCK LEONARD, Homestead Grays	1st Base	PIPER DAVIS, Birmingham Barons
JAMES GILLAM, Baltimore	2nd Base	RAY NEIL, Indianapolis Clowns
THOMAS BUTTS, Baltimore	SS	ART WILSON, Birmingham Barons
ORESTE MINOSO, N. Y. Cubans	3rd Base	HERB SOUELL, Kansas City Monarchs
ROBERT HARVEY, Newark	RF	JOSEPH COLAS, Memphis Red Sox
LUIS MARQUEZ, Homestead Grays	CF	WILLARD BROWN, Kan. City Monarchs
LUCIOUS EASTER, Homestead Grays	LF	CLYDE NELSON, Cleveland Buckeyes
LOUIS LOUDEN, N. Y. Cubans	C	QUINCY TROUPE, Chicago
WILLIAM CASH, Phildelphia Stars	C	SAM HAIRSTON, Indianapolis Clowns
MAXWELL MANNING, Newark	P	CHET BREWER, Cleveland
ROBERT ROMBY, Baltimore	P	BILL POWELL, Birmingham
DAVID BARNHILL, N. Y. Cubans	P	GENTRY JESSOP, Chicago
JOSEPH BLACK, Baltimore	P	BOB LA MARQUE, Kansas City
PAT SCANTLEBURY, N. Y. Cubans	P	LEFTY VERDELL MATHIS, Memphis
	P	JOHNNY WILLIAMS, Clowns
		KING TUT, COACH

— SEE —

LUCIOUS EASTER

who hit a 490-ft. homer into
the centerfield bleachers at the
Polo Grounds this summer, and
other great stars!

Almost as soon as the major league baseball All-Star game was completed,
administrators of the Negro leagues started their own All-Star contest, called
the East-West Classic. The first East-West game also took place at Comiskey
Park, later in 1933, and became a popular institution. This was an ad for the
1948 East-West game played at Yankee Stadium. The player featured was powerful Luke Easter. (Photograph courtesy National Baseball Hall of Fame.)

years beyond the worst of America's economically challenging times and World War II.

The "other" all-star game followed the "Game of the Century" with the "greatest baseball attraction ever staged." Neither claim was really accurate, but they were both good selling points, and certainly any serious baseball fan given the chance to go back to 1933 in a time machine would revel in the opportunity to see either, or both, games.

19

Here to Stay

Once the first All-Star game proved to be a tremendous hit, there was sure to be a second one. With the full backing of major league baseball, a supportive public on board, and players throwing their enthusiasm ever more strongly behind the idea, the All-Star game took another step towards becoming a baseball institution.

The All-Star game was never meant to be more than a one-night stand, linked to the Century of Progress Exposition in Chicago in 1933. The game served its purpose, becoming a shiny showpiece, if only a shooting star compared to the grounded World's Fair that continued on a daily basis and was even revived for a second run in 1934. The Depression lingered longer, but by the middle of the decade new President Franklin Delano Roosevelt's New Deal policies were taking hold and the American economy was beginning to perk up.

Baseball itself had a new toy, and while Commissioner Kenesaw Mountain Landis was grateful to Arch Ward and the *Chicago Tribune* for their unflagging efforts to promote the Game of the Century, the All-Star game belonged to the sport now. True to Landis' inclination, the event found a new home for 1934. The second All-Star game was scheduled for the Polo Grounds in New York on July 10, 1934.

Leading up to the game, similar voting procedures were followed, enlisting the fans' participation to choose the players. In a sad aside, the weakening John McGraw had passed away since the first game was played and new managers assumed the role of guiding the teams. Young Joe Cronin of the Senators was assigned to lead the American League and veteran Bill Terry of the Giants led the National League squad.

Comiskey Park was a sellout for the first All-Star game and the second game was even more popular. It attracted 48,363 fans, but thousands more lined up outside the Polo Grounds seeking admission before the game. Officials locked the park's gates 15 minutes before the first pitch as the mob milled around outside.

Although much less publicized and remembered, the second All-Star game had a specific local historical tie-in, too. The game commemorated 300 years of New York area sport, dating to 1634 when a bowling alley area was established. More emotionally, a memorial to the late McGraw was revealed at the field with his wife Blanche looking on.

Once again the fans did the voting, but the managers sought to exercise their power with the final roster, only to meet with an outcry of protest. The fans wanted the managers to follow their dictates to the letter. This prompted polls by some sportswriters asking around to see what people thought about who should be in charge of the rosters and lineups. Former heavyweight champion Jack Dempsey weighed in on the fans' side: "With the fans, first, last and all the time. Let them manage a ball club one day officially. They do it the other 154 days, anyway." Not terribly surprisingly given that the same people might make the choice to vote for or against him, Mayor Fiorello LaGuardia was a people's champ, too. "I would like to see the fans get a break. Their opinions should be respected."[1]

Many of the same stars who were on the AL and NL rosters for the first All-Star game were also chosen for the second game. On the American League side that included Lefty Gomez, Bill Dickey (healthy this time), Lou Gehrig, Charlie Gehringer, Jimmie Foxx, Joe Cronin, Babe Ruth, Al Simmons, Earl Averill, Ben Chapman, Jimmy Dykes, Rick Ferrell and Sam West. The National League side featured Carl Hubbell, Gabby Hartnett, Bill Terry, Frankie Frisch, Pie Traynor, Wally Berger, Chuck Klein, Pepper Martin, Paul Waner, and Lon Warneke.

The American League won this game, 9–7, using a six-run fifth inning to take control. Ruth was not as bombastic a figure, with two walks his biggest offensive contribution. Simmons, top vote-getter in the first All-Star game, collected three hits in this one and Gehringer reached base five times. But almost none of those details, except by the protagonists themselves, were remembered for long. This game belonged to Hubbell, who recorded a performance for the ages, one that three-quarters of a century later remains one of the stellar milestones in All-Star play.

Hubbell, who had relieved so ably at Comiskey Park, was playing in his home park this time and his choice was well received by Polo Grounds fans. Soon, they would be standing on their feet shouting his name. Hubbell had pitched a no-hitter. He won two games in the 1933 World Series. He won a National League Most Valuable Player award. And he compiled a 16-game regular-season winning streak at one point. But he is perhaps best remembered so many years following his departure from the game for a short stretch of mound work during the second All-Star game in New York.

For the second year in a row, the American League looked like the favorite in the match-up of the best players in the sport. The starting lineup for the AL consisted entirely of future Hall of Famers. Gehringer was at second, Heinie Manush in left, Ruth in right, Gehrig at first, Foxx at third, Simmons in center, Cronin at short, Dickey at catcher, and Gomez pitching. Nine men in a row whose plaques would one day adorn the wall of the National Baseball Hall of Fame in Cooperstown, New York. The NL was nearly as star-studded, but Hubbell did not have to face those batters.

"No question, but it had the best sluggers," Hubbell said of the AL. "When I looked over that batting order of American League hitters, I feared them all. There were a lot of guys in it with power. The only one who didn't scare me was their starting pitcher, Lefty Gomez."[2] Of course, Gomez actually had a critical hit in the first All-Star game.

Hubbell was 31 years old, in his seventh big league season, had been a winner in the World Series, and was in the midst of a run of five consecutive 20-plus-win seasons. There was little that could rattle him. Still, the atmosphere at the Polo Grounds brought as much glitz, sound and fury to a ballpark as he could recall experiencing. "To me this game had all the roar and noise and flavor of a World Series contest," Hubbell said. "The park was filled and I had the feeling I was fighting for my own underdog league against a superior lineup. I felt my pride was at stake and I wanted to be on the winning side."[3]

Screwball as his secret weapon or not, Hubbell did not start very well. Gehringer led off the game with a single to center and Wally Berger bobbled the ball, allowing the Tigers' infielder to take second. Hubbell immediately faced a situation with a man in scoring position. Manush, then playing for the Senators and on his way to a .349 season, walked. And that's when it began, a streak of pitching that is among the most legendary stretches in baseball history, and not incidentally, one that provided a special cache to the All-Star game when it was only a toddler.

There were men on first and second with nobody out in Hubbell's shaky first inning when everything clicked. Babe Ruth was at the plate in a situation he loved. All eyes were on him. He had a chance to be a hero, just as he became one the summer before in the first All-Star game. The situation was perfect for adding to the Babe's legend. Only a fresh legend was about to be established. This was a pivotal moment in Hubbell's legacy, as well as that of the All-Star game.

Hubbell worked Ruth as carefully as he ever had any batter and it paid off. Ruth struck out for the first out on a called strike. Lou Gehrig stepped in, and although Gehringer and Manush pulled off a double steal, they were tangential to the story unfolding. Gehrig struck out, too, swinging. Later, Gehrig said, "That screwball of his looked like the easiest pitch in the world to hit. Every time I swung, I was sure I was going to rip it good, but the ball just disappeared."[4]

Foxx was up next. Foxx, who would slug 534 home runs in his career, liked to show off his huge biceps as an intimidating tool against pitchers. The year before Foxx was selected for the first All-Star game but didn't play. This was his first All-Star action. Hubbell smoked him, as well. With the American League threatening, Hubbell fanned Ruth, Gehrig and Foxx in order to get out of the inning and earn the applause of his hometown fans. But he wasn't done yet. Leading off the second for the American League was Al Simmons. He, too, went down on strikes. Player-manager Joe Cronin had kept a close eye on the proceedings and was amazed to see his men meekly sent back to the dugout one after another. Sure enough, he joined them, the fifth straight strikeout victim. "He had the greatest screwball I ever looked at," Cronin said. "He'd drop one in for a strike, then really explode one when you thought sure you had him."[5]

Bill Dickey broke the hex with a single. Gomez, a terrible hitter, teased Dickey that he had robbed him of fame because he wanted the chance to interrupt Hubbell's string. Regardless, Hubbell had notched a remarkable feat. He struck out five straight future Hall of Famers in an All-Star game.

The next day there was discussion about who won the game, but the result was nearly overshadowed by Hubbell's brilliance. Decades later, few could tell you who won the game or what the score was, but everyone recalls Hubbell's singular accomplishment. As the achievement took on luster, it eclipsed many of Hubbell's other feats. Years later he said, "I reckon the biggest thrill I got in baseball was in the All-Star game in 1934."[6]

Eyewitnesses to the occasion might have said the same. Hubbell's eye-opener was a bonus boost to the All-Star game in its infancy. No other setting would have provided the opportunity for a pitcher to work his magic against such an array of batsmen. Hubbell made the game the talk of the town and the talk of the baseball world. At a time when the All-Star game still needed momentum to progress beyond a year-to-year event and truly take hold as a regular exhibition, Hubbell did more than his share to aid its image.

In the ensuing years, the All-Star game went on tour, much as Landis had prophesied. In 1935, it was played in Municipal Stadium in Cleveland before a record 69,831 fans. In 1936, it took place at Braves Field in Boston. In 1937, the game was contested at Griffith Stadium in Washington, D.C. The first return engagement was in 1942 when the game was held at the Polo Grounds. The All-Star game did not return to Comiskey Park until 1950. The fact that it was still around was a milestone. Conceived as a one-time event, the All-Star game gained strength the more it was played. It was always talked about as if it would be played the next year, but it took some time before it was truly established as a locked-in part of the schedule. It was almost as if some owners were hoping things might go wrong so they wouldn't have to be bothered with it.

In a 1939 column, Joe Williams, one of the sportswriters who had attended the first All-Star game in 1933, reported a question-and-answer session with AL president Will Harridge. In the middle of the column was a sub-headline reading, "All-Star Game Here to Stay." Six years after its debut, it was still necessary to make that point. Harridge, however, emphasized how the game had become solidified as a regular aspect of the sport. "Speaking for our league," he said, "and I think the National League feels the same way about it, the All-Star game will continue to be just as much a part of baseball as the foul lines and home plate. As a matter of truth, we took on the All-Star game as an experiment and with certain misgivings.

"That's why we tied it up with the Century of Progress. This was to be our out. If we didn't like it, we'd discontinue it promptly. Well, you know what happened.... I'll admit frankly that even if we did want to discontinue it, which we certainly do not, we couldn't. Its hold on the fans of the nation is too great."[7]

Candid stuff and an intriguing look into the minds of the moguls who were skittish about backing Arch Ward's original proposition. Harridge was right that there was no going back, only forward. The All-Star game grew in popularity. After the first one was played, there was no more mention of the Game of the Century. One couldn't exactly promote a Game of the Century every year. Eventually, the All-Star game was termed "The Midsummer Classic." The phrase is occasionally used in newspaper accounts and by broadcasters, but by no means slips easily off the tongue of every fan.

Over time the names of the stars changed. Older players retired or their skills dropped off. New faces appeared. New stars came along to dominate play. Over the course of decades records were eclipsed. By the 1970s, Hank Aaron, Stan Musial and Willie Mays had each played in 24 All-Star games. Mays, the five-tool baseball genius employed primarily by the Giants of New York and then San Francisco, was in some quarters seen as the star of stars, the greatest player of all time. In an annual game where the spotlight shone on the best players, Mays always seemed to do something that attracted applause. Ted Williams, the Hall of Fame left fielder for the Boston Red Sox, once said, "They invented the All-Star game for Willie Mays."[8] Not literally true, as Arch Ward would have told Williams, but the sentiment was clear.

Although he never met Mays, John McGraw, that old American League hater, would have reveled in the spirit that the player brought to the inter-league confrontations and would have guffawed louder than a bear's growl if he heard the star's comment about the NL–AL games during his time. "I loved the All-Star game," Mays said. "I just loved to play in it even though we thought the guys in the American League were Little Leaguers."[9]

For a long time the tangible rewards of being voted onto an All-Star game roster were negligible. Players earned lovely parting gifts. Among the choices at various times were pewter beer mugs, grandfather clocks and silverware. Over time, as players accrued more power and were paid higher salaries, some of the biggest stars negotiated provisions in their contracts that called for bonuses of many thousands of dollars if they were selected to play in the All-Star game. Frank Robinson, a star for both leagues, played in 12 All-Star games. "I got a bonus all right," Robinson said once, "a ticket to get there. There was no bonus. It was just an honor to be voted onto the All-Star team. You selected a gift and that was it."[10]

Although the All-Star game has always been used as a measuring stick of American League–National League superiority, the intensity brought to proving that point has seemingly ebbed and flowed over the decades. Outshining the opposition was a point to be made from the start, but long-term meaning was difficult to glean. In the first two years the All-Star game was played, the AL won the contest but National League teams won the World Series. There were ebbs and flows involving long-term winning streaks that were supposed to reinforce supremacy, but by 2009, after the 80th All-Star game was played in St. Louis, the all-time record was 41 wins for the National League, 37 wins for the American League, and two ties.

Due to travel restrictions during World War II, no All-Star game was played in 1945. But as an experiment, two All-Star games were played each year between 1959 and 1962.

Eventually, baseball adopted inter-league play during the regular season. No longer were the All-Star game and World Series match-ups the only times players from each league would go up against one another and no longer were those occasions the only times fans could see players from the other league in person. By the 2000s (further blurring the identities of the AL and NL), no longer were they separate administrative entities. Both operated under the umbrella of the commissioner's office.

Consistent with its role as the National Pastime, baseball often attracted sitting presidents to throw out the first pitch on Opening Day for Washington Senators or Baltimore Orioles games. Only four presidents, with John F. Kennedy, Richard Nixon, Gerald Ford (twice) and Barack Obama doing the tossing, have thrown out a first pitch at an All-Star game. Obama, a Chicagoan and a White Sox fan, wore his White Sox shirt and cap on the field in 2009.

Most players have viewed selection to play in the All-Star game as an honor. Minnesota Twin Gary Gaetti, chosen once in a 20-year career, said, "It's right up there with lobster." But some players and managers at times seemed to prefer having a mid-season vacation rather than going to the game. "The only bad thing about winning the pennant is that you have to manage the All-Star game the next year," said Hall of Fame manager Whitey Herzog. "I'd rather go fishing for three days."[11]

Herzog's comment reflected one change in All-Star game procedure over time. Rather than the commissioner's office picking the managers, the exhibition's field bosses were selected on merit based on the previous season's league champions.

There were periods of time when the vote to choose the All-Star rosters was taken away from the fans and given to the players. But in one form or another, the power (with some veto authority by those running the sport) was always returned to fans and they were encouraged to vote. By the 2000s, the number of ballots returned on site at ballparks or tallied via the Internet jumped to the millions and millions. The All-Star game has been tweaked in other ways, as well. Following an unsatisfactory 7–7 tie game in 2002, Commissioner Bud Selig ruled that ties would be unacceptable in the future. It was also decreed that the league that won the All-Star game would receive the home-field advantage for that fall's World Series, the possibly crucial seventh game.

In 2003, major league baseball expanded NL and AL all-star rosters to 32 players a side each year. Over time, fanfare surrounding the All-Star game also expanded. A wildly popular home run derby was added in 1985 the day before the game, and a "futures" all-star game featuring young professional players was added to the agenda, as well. The imagination runs riot wondering what a home run derby would have been like involving Babe Ruth, Lou Gehrig, Jimmie Foxx and others from the initial All-Star generation and so many other great sluggers, from Hank Aaron and Willie Mays to Mickey Mantle. In 1971, National League manager Sparky Anderson ruminated on what kind of impact Pittsburgh's Willie Stargell might have on the game to be played in Tiger Stadium. "He's such a big, strong guy he should love that porch. He's got power enough to hit home runs in any park, including Yellowstone."[12] Yellowstone National Park remains one place that hasn't hosted the All-Star game.

Still going strong in 1973, some 40 years after the playing of the first All-Star game, surviving players from that Comiskey Park encounter were invited to a celebration party in Kansas City hosted by Royals owner Ewing Kaufman. The players from that first game who attended the bash wore red carnations on their sport coats. Among those who came to party and watch the game were pitchers Lefty Gomez, Lefty Grove, Lon Warneke, Bill Hallahan, and Hal Schumacher, plus Tony Cuccinello, the man who made the last out in 1933. There were 22 players still living from the first game and 20 of them showed up in Kansas City for the fun.

Hallahan and Grove shared the honor of throwing out the first pitch at Royals Stadium and Hallahan received a level of national attention that he hadn't experienced in a while. When he returned home to Binghamton, New York, Hallahan was a rekindled celebrity. "One of the kids across the street came over the next day," Hallahan said. "He said, 'Why didn't you tell me you were a baseball player?'"[13]

In 1973, Commissioner Bowie Kuhn, with an eye on the improvement in the quality of play in Japan, predicted the likelihood of an international All-Star game being contested within a decade. Kuhn's thinking was not far off, but he wasn't completely on-target either. A few decades later, major league baseball is densely populated with the best players from Japan, the Dominican Republic, Venezuela and other countries. Day-to-day, baseball, not merely as a once-a-year All-Star game, has gone international.

While the 1973 gathering of 1933 stars in Kansas City was a pleasant reunion, far more effort, backed by major league baseball in a more formal way, was thrown into marking the 50th anniversary of the first All-Star game. The game was once again scheduled for Comiskey Park, at that point probably the sturdiest survivor of July 6, 1933. There were 15 living players invited to the festivities for the July 6, 1983 game.

In activities surrounding the 13–3 American League victory at the 73-year-old ballpark, an Old-Timers All-Star game was played, with stars from several generations in the majors on the field. Also, the U.S. Postal Service issued a 20-cent stamp that featured Babe Ruth. Ruth was long deceased, but his influence was duly marked in a special way.

Lefty Gomez had been the American League starting pitcher in 1933, and in the days leading up to the 1983 game he made it sound as if he was prepared to throw a few more innings. Then he backed down a little bit. "Whoever catches my first pitch this time better wear a sponge because I don't want to bruise his hand," Gomez said. "On second thought, the ball probably will reach the plate on the second bounce. I understand there's a rule now that you can't roll the ball to the plate."[14]

American League catcher Rick Ferrell revealed that years after the first All-Star game, the National League's Frankie Frisch asked him for a favor. Frisch hit a solo home run and had come by a photograph of himself in the game at Comiskey with Ferrell in the background. "Since I was also in the picture he asked me to inscribe it," Ferrell said. "I wrote on it: 'To a great hitter from a fellow who called the wrong pitch.'"[15]

Hal Schumacher, the old Giants pitcher, was the only hurler left available to throw for the National League if his team had tied the score in the first All-Star game and forced a bottom of the ninth inning or extra innings. Instead, the American League held on to its 4–2 lead to prevail. Schumacher's memories of the Game of the Century were not made playing in the game, but during warm-ups and by watching it unfold up close. "I was awestruck when I walked on the field and saw all those superstars I'd idolized for many years."[16]

Schumacher was one of the stars, one of players honored by being chosen to represent his league in the first major league baseball All-Star game ever played. But he spoke like a genuine fan. Schumacher's words surely echoed what many of the 48,000 fans in Comiskey Park felt on July 6, 1933, while gazing out at the many baseball greats arrayed across the field. Babe Ruth, Lou Gehrig, Bill Terry, John McGraw and their brethren were all idols in flannels.

20

Arch's Brain Keeps Whirring

Arch Ward did not have to give his salary back, as he had promised if the first All-Star game fizzled. The *Chicago Tribune* did not have to cash in its rain insurance policy.

Decades after the brainstorm that introduced the baseball world to what became the mid-summer classic, Ward is regarded as an innovator credited with the foresight and energy to establish one of the most beloved events on the nation's sports calendar. For those with only a rudimentary knowledge of how the All-Star game began, Ward is an admired figure.

Ward took pride in his accomplishment and he had certainly built up credibility in his office and community through his efforts. He now had a track record of success that stretched beyond words on the sports page. Ward's official position was sports editor, a man with a pen who could wield it as he saw fit. However, he was far more than a writer. Throwing the full force of his office behind the All-Star game made it a reality. Now that he entered the realm of inventing events as well as covering them, Ward decided he liked the role of promoter. Not that he was about to surrender his sports editor title — he realized his job was his power base — but Ward searched for other ways to expand his involvement in the sports world.

"Ward's identification with the beginnings of the (baseball) all-star games impressed a great many very important people," his biography states. "At the *Tribune*, in Chicago, and throughout the sports establishment Arch had become someone to be reckoned with. Here was a newspaperman who could make things happen." It was noted that for years, each time mention was made of the All-Star game, Ward received credit in print for starting it, which helped spread his fame.[1]

Not often remarked upon outside of Chicago was Ward's connection to promoting the Golden Gloves amateur boxing championships that were deeply ingrained in Chicago and as popular a sporting event as the city had. The *Chicago Tribune* was a key supporter even before Ward began his tenure as sports editor, but Ward cut his teeth promoting the heck out of the massive boxing tournament before he turned his attention to the All-Star game. The Golden Gloves was already in place in its Chicago home, but Ward worked ceaselessly to grow it any way he could to expand the local event beyond prior boundaries. He pushed for international show-downs between Chicago boxers and teams from other countries. He was the key go-between in arranging matches between Chicago fighters and France in an event held at Soldier Field alongside Lake Michigan. The matches attracted 40,000 ticket buyers.

Thomas B. Littlewood, Ward's biographer, saw a man unharnessed by the types of ethical restraints that govern journalistic patterns in the 2000s. Today, sportswriters shun involvement or connections that could be deemed too close to promoters or event organizers. They are on the opposite side of the fence. Ward wore both hats simultaneously, as pro-moter introducing the public to an event and as a journalist writing about his own event.

"Arch wanted the power to force sports leaders to do what he wanted them to do," Littlewood wrote. "Ward wanted to put on gala events that would attract throngs of spectators. That would be the real test of a news-paper promotion. How many spectators would buy tickets to participate in the excitement of the event?"[2]

Baseball's All-Star game was both a critical success and a box office hit, the perfect combination. No one could ask for more than that. Although he was a natural at coming up with ideas and promoting them to a wide audience, Ward's original assignment from Colonel Robert McCormick was to dream up one sporting event that would fit in with the Century of Progress Exposition. He had done his job and done it well. But the task was completed, over, done. The World's Fair would continue into the fall, as planned, but the sporting event was a one-hit wonder, and no one was looking for a sequel.

The circumstances changed later. The Fair was so popular that city fathers decided to extend it. The original scheduled closing date was November 12, 1933. However, business was so good (a rarity in the Depres-sion) that after a break for the winter, the Exposition re-opened on May

26, 1934, and ran until October 31. By the time it closed, the Fair had attracted 48.7 million customers and became the first international Fair to pay for itself.

Ward had made a flashy contribution to this happy success story for the Windy City. His All-Star game was both a moneymaker and a publicity generator. But once the game was played and the powers-that-be in the sport witnessed its popularity, they took control of most aspects of it. The second All-Star game was definitely not coming back to Comiskey Park, or to Chicago. That was out of Ward's hands now. Instead, he began pushing a new concept, another new sporting event that could be held in conjunction with the World's Fair during the second segment of its run. One could almost hear the wheels turning in Ward's brain. "You want progress, I'll show you progress," he may have been thinking. And now that baseball had been covered, it was time to show the world something fresh in another sport.

Football. That was the ticket, Ward decided. In 1934, professional football was just emerging from its infancy. The National Football League was founded in 1920 and one of the flagship franchises was the Chicago Bears. There had been a shakedown period during the 1920s, with clubs coming and going, but by the early 1930s the league had stabilized. What had not changed in the minds of many fans was its credibility. College football, where the lads played the game for free and the glory of their universities, was believed in many quarters to be a purer form of the game. It was difficult in many instances to convince fans weaned on Red Grange's exploits at the University of Illinois that the pros were better than the amateurs.

This argument monumentally annoyed Bears founder George Halas. He knew his pros were rougher, tougher, and better all-around players than the collegians. When discussions began about the prospect of pitting the championship NFL team against a college all-star crew for charity, Halas was easily enticed. The entire concept appealed to him, but more so since his Bears happened to be the reigning pro champions. On July 6, 1934, exactly one year after the playing of the first major league baseball All-Star game, Arch Ward informed the world about yet another new all-star contest. "This is an announcement of the most unusual football game ever scheduled," he wrote. "It will bring together the Chicago Bears, champions of the National Professional Football League, and the strongest team of last year's college seniors that can be recruited."[3]

Halas, who remained owner of the Bears until his death in 1983, suggested that the football all-star game's creation was more of a collaborative effort than simply Ward sitting around doing all of the thinking himself. Whether Halas remembered the sequence of events clearly decades after their occurrence or not, he said that Chicago mayor Ed Kelly was on the prowl for another sporting event to add to the Fair. Halas could have been confusing the original approach by Kelly in 1933, or Kelly may have sought out a second suggestion given the success of the baseball game. "At about the same time I asked Ward about the possibility of bringing together the Bears and a college all-star team," Halas wrote in his autobiography.[4] There were many occasions when the pros clobbered the collegians, but there also were some surprising results posted by the young players. By the time the game was discontinued in 1976, the pros had won 31 games, the collegians nine, and there were two ties.

The game was scheduled for August 31, a night game with temporary lighting fixtures erected at Soldier Field. Following the formula Ward had introduced a year earlier for the baseball game, fans across the land were invited to vote through their newspapers for a team of 27 freshly ex-collegians to line up against the Bears. Once again in his prose Ward invoked the *Chicago Tribune*'s support, and informed his readers that the proceeds would go to charity.

Ward's acumen did help promote the contest. As he had already proven, Ward was quite capable of spending someone else's supply of ink in pouring forth words for the masses. And as he had also already shown, Ward paid attention to detail and made sure the visiting players were housed, that halftime entertainment would be provided for, and that the bills would be paid, leaving no ill will behind.

By the time the game rolled around, Ward had termed it "the outstanding sports event of 1934" and "football's greatest show." The team was selected from the votes collected by 30 newspapers and was dubbed "the people's team." Votes exceeded 617,000.[5] The game attracted 79,432 fans, and most surprising was the final score: 0–0. The result, in its own way, served as promotion for the continuation of the game. The question of who was better, the pros or the college stars, went unresolved, meaning the game virtually begged for a re-match.

After expenses, with Ward once again steering his employer clear of the financial risk, the proceeds divided by different charities totaled

$21,000. All together, over the years the game was played, some $4 million was raised for charity.

The praise that accompanied the donation of those checks from recipients and the compliments that gushed from Colonel McCormick were not sufficient strokes for Ward's ego. Once in a while, in a less direct manner, he praised his work in his column. "Regardless of the outcome," Ward wrote before the second all-star football game, "this game has set a new standard for football promotion."[6] For those in the know, Ward's comment was self-aggrandizing. He might as well have written, "If I do say so myself."

Ward's genius for promotion, essentially manufacturing new events that were popular treats immediately while producing financial dividends for those involved, caught the eye of pro football's power brokers. In the late 1930s, pro football ranked behind major league baseball, horse racing, boxing, and college football in popularity among the American sports fan. True prosperity lay two decades in the future, but the men whose passion and pocketbooks were tied up in their teams needed help in raising the profile of their game. When commissioner Joe Carr died in 1939, a trio of NFL leaders — Halas, Charles Bidwell of the Chicago Cardinals, and Curly Lambeau of the Green Bay Packers — approached Ward about taking over league affairs. According to an account by Ward's biographer, he was offered a 10-year contract worth $25,000 a year to become commissioner. He nearly took it but was talked out of the move by his daughter who told him he would be happier if he stayed in his current job.

Although Ward declined to make the switch, a handful of years later he tried to make an even bigger impact on pro football. While retaining his position as sports editor of the *Tribune*, Ward conjured up an entire new pro football league, the All-America Football Conference. Ward organized a meeting on June 4, 1944, that brought together wealthy football proponents who were seeking their own franchises. The eight-team league began play for the 1946 season. The AAFC lasted four years and was a vigorous competitor to the NFL for players and fans. Ward originally envisioned that the AAFC would grow into a serious enough rival to challenge the NFL in an annual championship game, but that did not happen. Seen more as an economic threat than any type of partner, the NFL eventually absorbed the strongest AAFC teams and put the upstart league out of business. The Cleveland Browns and the San Francisco 49ers owe their existence to Arch Ward's ingenuity.

While only the most knowledgeable fans of football history remember the All-America Football Conference and only those with long memories recall the college all-star teams playing against the pros, Ward's true lasting legacy is the major league baseball All-Star game. The reading public and the baseball world are reminded of this on periodic anniversaries of the game when special celebrations are planned. Ward receives his props whenever a newspaper, *Baseball Digest*, or *The Sporting News* revisit the game's origins. There is Ward, at ground zero of the behind-the-scenes negotiations, taking his instructions from *Tribune* publisher Robert McCormick, whispering in secret with the American League's Will Harridge, negotiating with other influential figures of the game, all to make the first All-Star game a reality. No one writes about the All-Star game's creation or the Game of the Century of 1933 without mentioning Ward's name and contributions.

Jerome Holtzman, the long-time Chicago sportswriter who became major league baseball's official historian before he passed away in 2008, said that if someone called a Hollywood producer and tried to convince him to do a movie on Arch Ward's life, the mogul would hang up the phone on the grounds that the story was not believable. "That's the problem writing about Archibald Burdette Ward," Holtzman wrote. "Nobody believes it. Ward was the most influential newspaperman in the history of American sports. The baseball All-Star game launched Ward's career as a promoter/entrepreneur without compare."[7]

Ward was in the right place, in the right position, at the right newspaper, with the right boss, at the right time to pull off the stunts he orchestrated. He was a promoter par excellence when most newspapers were simply looking for their sports editor to write and edit copy. The *Chicago Tribune* under McCormick wielded enormous influence and waved a big stick. Most newspapers wanted merely to write about the news. The *Tribune* was not shy about making the news. In Chicago, Ward had major league baseball's headquarters at his doorstep. He had the down-the-street Century of Progress Exposition trolling for an event. In George Halas, Ward had a ready-made partner for his charitable football game. And Ward came along during an era when he was not given the ultimatum that other sports editors in the future trying to do the same things would have been given. It's either us or them, they would have been told by superiors with no tolerance for a sports editor moonlighting as a sports event promoter.

In the 1930s and 1940s, no one blinked at the notion that Ward could be involved on both sides of the line. At the time there was no line to cross.

In November of 1952, Ward suffered a heart attack, and in an era before the sophistication of treatment available now, he spent a month in bed recuperating. Gradually, Ward returned to his full-throttle pace of life, but in 1954 he had a second heart attack. In April of 1955, Ward, who had experienced some family crises and was not in chipper health, lost his patron. Colonel McCormick passed away. By this stage of his career, Ward had been employed by the *Tribune* for 30 years and had been sports editor for 25. He was his own institution.

The 1955 baseball All-Star game was scheduled to be played in Milwaukee in July. On July 9, three days before the game, Ward suffered another heart attack and died in his sleep at his Chicago home. Ward would have been attending his 22nd straight All-Star game. It was fitting that his final "In the Wake of the News" column, which appeared after his death, was about the Game of the Century. In it he recounted the story of the game's beginnings, again tooting his own horn as he informed readers how the All-Star game came about "on a suggestion to big league owners from this department."[8]

Ward's death was unexpected. He was still on the job, still working full-time running one of the largest newspaper sports departments in the country. There was no indication that he had a new sporting event up his sleeve about to spring on the world, but no one would have been surprised if he had blurted out the news of the next basketball game of the century in a future column. Ward was not an old man. When he died he was less than six months shy of turning 59.

In its sports department news story about Ward passing away, the *Tribune* referred to him as the paper's "famous sports editor." It noted that telephone calls and telegrams "began pouring into the *Tribune* within an hour" after news of Ward's death spread. The story called Ward's professional rise a meteoric one and acknowledged him as one of the linear successors writing the famed "In the Wake of the News" column, but called him "a sports promoter without peer" who would be "best remembered" for creating or supporting the baseball All-Star game, the college football-pro football all-star game, and the Golden Gloves tournament.[9]

It was also noted that Ward wrote books about subjects like Notre Dame football coach Frank Leahy (his ties to the school where he worked as a publicist were life-long), was granted the first interview with Pope Pius XII in Rome, worked as an executive for Chicago Tribune Charities, broadcast a syndicated radio show, and appeared on WGN-TV. "Ward always worked at top speed and not even a series of heart attacks in the last three years could slow him down," the story said. Ward left behind one already-filmed segment of his TV show that ran posthumously. Again, appropriately enough the sit-down was with AL president Will Harridge, the man who had so critically aided Ward in getting the baseball All-Star game started more than two decades earlier.[10]

"Baseball and all sports have lost a great champion," Harridge said. "To me Arch Ward's passing comes as a sad and personal loss, for we were closely associated for many years, even before he conceived, and then made possible by his many talents, that first All-Star baseball game in 1933."[11]

Tributes to Ward from sports world leaders and others swiftly arrived at the Tribune Tower. "Sports, amateur and professional, have lost their best friend and staunchest defender," wrote Curly Lambeau, the Packers' long-time coach. The Rev. Edmund Joyce, vice president of Notre Dame, said, "The field of sports has lost one of its outstanding leaders of the century."[12]

Ward's own paper wrote about his life in an editorial, getting to the heart of his success as a promoter of new sporting events in a brief synopsis: "His precept that made all of these ventures so successful was simple. It was that people will always throng to see the best — the champions — in any sport. His organizing talent assured that they saw the best."[13]

Arch Ward was buried in Chicago on July 12, 1955. The scheduled start of the 22nd annual major league baseball All-Star game was delayed for 30 minutes so baseball dignitaries in mourning could attend his funeral in Chicago before attending the game in Milwaukee.

Not long after Ward's death, the new sports department administration of the *Tribune* informed major league baseball it no longer wanted to be responsible for counting the ballots fans used to select the annual All-Star game rosters.

21

What Happened to Everyone

What started as a one-time-only Game of the Century quickly morphed into an annual event that became a highlight of the baseball season. The major league All-Star game was highly anticipated, a huge fan favorite, and players selected to compete in it considered it a first-rate accolade. As the game grew in stature, those who participated in the first one became a fraternity of sorts. Their appearance took on a special cache, and as time passed the significance of their place on the initial All-Star rosters grew.

When a newspaperman wrote about their baseball feats, playing in the first All-Star game was often mentioned. When they retired, playing in the first All-Star game was sure to be noted. When they died, their obituary was certain to tell the reader that they were one of the lucky and proud players to be chosen for the first All-Star game.

As the years passed, the popularity of the All-Star game increased, but the members of the club who had been present at the creation began to shrink. The All-Star game itself has long outlasted the men who founded it and played in the debut game on the sunny afternoon of July 6, 1933, at Comiskey Park. All of the key figures, from the organizers to the players, have passed away, the last more than a decade ago.

Administrators

Baseball commissioner **Kenesaw Mountain Landis** died on November 25, 1944, while still holding office. The first major league commissioner, Landis spent nearly 25 years in the job. Selected to be a strong leader who could enforce discipline, Landis' primary task when hired by the owners was to restore the credibility of the game following the Black Sox Scandal of 1919. Initially, Landis was a lukewarm supporter of the All-

Star game and like others felt it was certain to be a one-shot deal in conjunction with the World's Fair. But when he saw what a tremendous success the game was, he quickly endorsed the notion of playing more All-Star games. A hard-nosed, strict leader, the chief blemish on Landis' term in office was his failure to even admit that major league baseball discriminated against African Americans by keeping them out of the majors. Landis had it within his power to be a hero and enforce social justice but looked the other way and embarrassed himself by saying that there was no color barrier in the game.

National League president **John Heydler** died on April 18, 1956. Heydler had to drag some of his recalcitrant owners kicking and screaming into cooperating with the plan for the first All-Star game. Heydler was NL president from 1918 to 1934 after being an umpire, a sportswriter, and secretary-treasurer of the league. Ironically, given that his league has never embraced the concept, Heydler was the first baseball official to suggest a designated hitter to bat in place of weak-hitting pitchers.

American League president **Will Harridge** died on April 19, 1971. Harridge was one of the first baseball confidantes that *Chicago Tribune* sports editor Arch Ward approached with the idea to hold the All-Star game in connection with the Century of Progress Exposition. He backed the proposal and worked hard to convince doubters that it was a good idea. Harridge was president of the AL from 1931 to 1958. The American League championship trophy is named after him.

Managers

Running the National League team in the first All-Star game was indeed the final role as a field manager of **John McGraw**'s life. After 30 years at the helm of the New York Giants, McGraw retired in 1932. Already ill, McGraw came out of retirement for the game between the all-star squads. He died on February 25, 1934, before the next season began. McGraw was the first of those involved in the first All-Star game to pass away.

Connie Mack set records for baseball longevity that are unlikely to be approached. Born Cornelius McGillicuddy, Sr., in 1862, Mack died February 8, 1956, in Philadelphia, where he had managed the American League club for 7,755 games. Mack, who always wore street clothes on the bench rather than a baseball uniform, set the records for most wins and most losses by a manager. His Athletics won five World Series and nine pennants.

Place

Comiskey Park, the marvelous baseball palace constructed as a state-of-the-art stadium by Chicago White Sox owner Charles Comiskey in 1910, remained the home field of the American League club through the 1990 season. A new Comiskey Park was built across the street on Chicago's South Side and opened in 1991. The park's name was later changed to U.S. Cellular Field. The site of home plate from the original Comiskey Park is preserved in a parking lot.

Players

The great shock that rippled through major league baseball in 1939 was that the "Iron Horse," **Lou Gehrig**, was taking himself out of the New York Yankees' lineup after playing in a record 2,130 straight games. Gehrig felt weak, out of sorts, and could no longer hit the way he had for 17 seasons while compiling a .340 lifetime batting average as a stellar first baseman. That was only the beginning of one of baseball's saddest stories. One of its greatest players of all time was brought low by an insidious disease that steadily eroded his entire body and killed him on June 2, 1941, at the age of 37.

Gehrig was felled by the creeping paralysis stemming from amyotrophic lateral sclerosis, an incurable illness that later became known simply as "Lou Gehrig's Disease." Before he became too weak to stand or talk, on July 4, 1939, on a special day recognizing his contributions to his team, Gehrig addressed a packed Yankee Stadium with one of the most moving speeches of modern times. In it, he called himself "the luckiest man on the face of the earth" and said he would beat the disease ravaging his body. That was one obstacle he could not overcome, however.

Tony Lazzeri, like Gehrig a member of the 1927 New York Yankee "Murderers' Row" team that is considered one of the greatest assemblages of talent in baseball history, was chosen for the American League side in the first All-Star game but did not get into the contest. Lazzeri, a .292-

hitting second baseman in 14 seasons, died on August 6, 1946. He was
found at the foot of a staircase in his San Francisco area home. Lazzeri was
elected to the Hall of Fame 52 years after he retired.

National League starting catcher **Jimmy Wilson** died on May 31,
1947. Wilson played in four World Series and another All-Star game in
1935. After managing the Philadelphia Phillies and Chicago Cubs for a
combined nine years, he went into the fruit and produce business. He was
growing oranges on 500 acres of land after trying to grow young players
into pennant-winning veterans. Wilson died after collapsing on a golf
course in Florida.

It was no secret that **Babe Ruth** was becoming debilitated by illness
in the late 1940s. Losing weight and energy, Ruth limited his public schedule. Like his old partner Gehrig, Ruth made one more honorary appearance
at Yankee Stadium. Dressing out in his old No. 3 Yankee uniform, the
Bambino thanked the fans that had applauded him while he compiled his
record 714 home runs and a .342 batting average. The fans sat in the seats
of the House That Ruth Built when early in the 1920s the stadium was
constructed because of the demand to watch his prodigious feats. Ruth
died on August 16, 1948, only 53 years old. The diagnosis was throat can-
cer, though Ruth was never told about the disease that caused his death.

When Ruth died, long-time baseball correspondent Frederick Lieb
wrote his lengthy obituary for *The Sporting News*, the first sentence reading,
"Baseball's most renowned of all stars, the inimitable George Herman
(Babe) Ruth, the idol of millions, is dead." Added Lieb, "A shocked nation
heard the verdict, 'You're out,' with the sense of personal loss one feels
when advised of the passing of one's kin or a dear personal friend."[1] Less
than a month earlier, rising from his hospital bed, Ruth had attended the
premiere of the movie, *The Babe Ruth Story*, with his wife Claire. The
American flag flew at half-mast at Yankee Stadium after Ruth's death and
his body lay in state at the ballpark for fans by the thousands to pay last
respects. Ruth's performance in the first All-Star game was only a tiny
accomplishment compared to his many other achievements in regular-season and World Series play. But when the lights were at their brightest in
the Game of the Century, Ruth was the one who smashed the biggest hit.

Rarely has any player started his major league career with such consistency as **Al Simmons**, the slugging Philadelphia A's outfielder who drove
in 102 runs and batted .308 as rookie in 1924. He kept surpassing those

milestones for another decade with Simmons knocking in as many as 157 runs and batting as high as .390 in a 20-year career. Yet fans still shouted at Simmons because of his fundamentally unsound stance that meant he hit with one foot "in the bucket." Manager Connie Mack refused to tamper with success following Simmons' .398 minor-league season. "I don't care if he stands on his head," Mack said.[2] Elected to the Hall of Fame in 1953, Simmons, nicknamed "the Duke of Milwaukee," his place of birth, did not have much chance to enjoy it. He was only 53 when he died of a heart attack on May 26, 1956, in his hometown.

Chuck Klein did not live to see his election to the Baseball Hall of Fame. Klein made his mark with the Philadelphia Phillies in the late 1920s and early 1930s, putting up a string of overwhelming hitting performances. Three times he led the National League in runs scored, twice in hits, twice in doubles, four times in home runs, four times in RBIs, and won the 1933 batting title with a .368 average. Klein died on March 28, 1958, at the age of 53, and was selected for the Baseball Hall of Fame in 1980. Because he played before Phillies players wore numbers on their jerseys, the team later used an old-style English "P" to represent Klein on its wall of stars at Veterans Stadium.

Pepper Martin was selected to represent the National League in the first three All-Star games. Martin led the NL in stolen bases three times and in runs scored once while recording a .298 batting average. He was a daring runner who specialized in driving pitchers cuckoo and was the spiritual leader of the St. Louis Cardinals' Gashouse Gang. Among his other activities, Martin was the co-manager of a heavyweight boxer and played basketball for a bearded House of David touring team. Martin served as a deputy sheriff and in 1948 was a kicker for the Brooklyn Dodgers of the All-America Football Conference. In retirement, Martin operated a ranch in Oklahoma. He died from a heart attack at the ranch on March 5, 1965.

The 1933 game, when **Paul Waner** made his brief appearance in the late going in the field, was the first of four All-Star games for the Pittsburgh Pirates' terrific hitter. Waner collected his 3,152 hits over 20 seasons and earned his nickname of "Big Poison." He was just a little better player than younger brother Lloyd, known as "Little Poison." Waner was a longtime coach after he finished playing in 1945 and died of emphysema, complicated by pneumonia.

Jimmie Foxx was a spectator for the first All-Star game, stuck on the

American League bench, but he was one of the most impressive players of his time. He was selected to eight All-Star squads. Nicknamed "Double X" and sometimes called "the Beast," Foxx was a three-time Most Valuable Player award winner for the Philadelphia A's and Boston Red Sox whose power and strength were highly publicized and documented by his 534 career home runs and phenomenal 1,922 RBIs. Foxx spent parts of 20 years in the big leagues, and in 1951, six years after his retirement, he was elected to the Baseball Hall of Fame. He managed the Fort Wayne Daisies of the All-American Girls Professional Baseball League and coached the University of Miami baseball team. Foxx died on July 21, 1967, at age 59 with the cause of death attributed to choking on a bone.

His finest years were behind him when **Lefty O'Doul** was chosen for the first All-Star game. O'Doul started late, and his major league career ended after parts of 11 seasons. At a time when the Pacific Coast League was considered an equally respectable way to make a living, he spent considerable time competing in the warm weather league. O'Doul at his best was a phenomenal hitter, winning two batting titles, with a high mark of .398. If anything, O'Doul was a better manager than player, though he concentrated on the PCL rather than the majors. The Tokyo Giants of the Japan League were named after O'Doul as thanks for his work in helping to develop baseball in that country. There is also a restaurant-bar bearing his name in San Francisco. O'Doul died December 7, 1969.

One of the greatest hitting third baseman of all time, **Pie Traynor** had a cameo appearance in the first All-Star game, but the Pirates' star was selected to play again the next year. Traynor ended his 17-season career in 1937 and also served the Pirates as manager. In other baseball work, Traynor was a scout and a broadcaster. In Pittsburgh, as the headline read in the *Pittsburgh Press* when he died on March 16, 1972, Traynor was "a living legend."

Alvin Crowder did not have the longevity at the peak of his game as many of the other 1933 All-Stars did, but he won more than 20 games three times. "The General" won as many as 26 games in a season. A well-traveled former tobacco factory worker and soldier who was a late bloomer on the diamond, Crowder won 15 games in a row one season for the Washington Senators. He died April 3, 1972, in Winston-Salem, North Carolina, where he was born.

The old chatterbox **Gabby Hartnett**'s most legendary moment on the field was swatting the so-called "homer in the gloamin,'" a late-game home run as dusk fell that propelled his Chicago Cubs to the 1938 National League pennant over the Pirates. Chosen for six NL All-Star teams, Hartnett compiled a .297 average and managed the Cubs for three seasons. Hartnett, whose real name was Charles Leo, won one Most Valuable Player award and was selected for the Baseball Hall of Fame in 1955. He died on December 20, 1972.

Frankie Frisch truly earned his nickname "The Fordham Flash" during his undergraduate days at the New York university. He won letters in four sports in addition to earning his college degree. A switch-hitter, Frisch joined the New York Giants in 1919 right out of school without minor-league seasoning. A fixture for the Giants at third base and a regular .300 hitter, Frisch and manager John McGraw were very close. They had an abrupt falling out after Frisch missed a sign, McGraw yelled at him front of the other players, and Frisch jumped the team. The suddenly poor relationship with McGraw resulted in Frisch being traded to the St. Louis Cardinals, just in time to become an integral part of the Gashouse Gang. A 19-year big leaguer, Frisch was selected for the first three National League All-Star teams, and he batted .316 overall. Frisch died March 12, 1973.

The 1933 appearance of **Chick Hafey** in the All-Star game was a one-time experience for the hard-luck outfielder who had to overcome many physical ailments en route to his .317 lifetime average over 13 major league seasons. During the 1929 season, Hafey, whose given name was Charles James, collected 10 straight hits. Hafey won one batting title and was elected to the Baseball Hall of Fame in 1971. Hafey was selected by the Veterans Committee and barely lived long enough to receive the award in person. He died July 2, 1973.

Lefty Grove may have been in a bad mood throughout his pitching career with the Philadelphia Athletics and Boston Red Sox, leaving enemies fed up with his attitude in his wake, but he was a fabulous pitcher, which no one ever denied. Grove's record was 300–141, won four World Series games, and was the MVP of the American League in 1931. Once able to depend almost solely on his fastball, in the closing days of his 17-year career a sore arm meant that Grove had to resort to a more crafty approach to fooling hitters. An eight-time 20-game winner, Grove won more than two-thirds of his career decisions. He surrendered less than one hit per inning pitched and nearly kept his lifetime earned run average under 3.00.

Near the end of his career, in recognition of the satisfaction he derived from his 300th victory, Grove spoke a little bit more graciously to the press. He said he had been taciturn for most of his career because he was misquoted in the 1920s when he was just starting out. Grove died on May 22, 1975, in Newark, Ohio.

A witty man, quick with a quip, **Jimmy Dykes** was one of the best friends baseball writers ever had. Dykes, the third baseman for the American League in the first All-Star game, was selected for the roster in 1934, as well. Dykes had a solid 22-year-old career as a player and followed it up with a respected career as a manager. It fell to Dykes to restore the Black Sox Scandal–tainted White Sox to respectability. He attained his dream job when he took over the A's in 1951, succeeding his mentor, Connie Mack. Dykes led American League third basemen in fielding in 1932 and was renowned for his hard play. Culminating his life in baseball, as a manager Dykes won 1,407 games as boss of the White Sox, A's, Baltimore Orioles, Cincinnati Reds, Detroit Tigers and Cleveland Indians. He joked that trying to win the pennant without good players was like trying to steal first base. Dykes died on June 15, 1976.

Chicago Cubs pitcher **Lon Warneke** played a prominent role in the first All-Star game. He pitched four innings, and his triple led to Warneke scoring the first National League run in All-Star history. The only thing that would have made his day better would have been getting the victory. Warneke played in two more All-Star games. After his playing days were done and his 192 wins were in the bank, Warneke became an umpire and worked his way back to the majors. He had the unique distinction of playing and umpiring in All-Star and World Series games. Warneke died on June 23, 1976, in Hot Springs, Arkansas, not far from where he grew up.

He would rather have gotten into the game, but **Wes Ferrell** was able to share the experience of being part of the American League roster for the first All-Star game with his catching brother Rick. Four of Wes' six 20-game winning seasons were recorded before the All-Star game, but he was selected for the AL squad once more, in 1937, even as the speed was diminishing on his fastball. At his best, Ferrell was considered one of the top guns in the AL, and he won 25 games in 1935. Ferrell was also known for being temperamental — he was in Lefty Grove's league when it came to blowing his top. When they shared the same battery, the eternally cocky Wes Ferrell sometimes argued with Rick over what to throw. During one infamous outing, after being criticized, Rick decided not to call any other pitches the rest of the game. Wes tossed a three-hit shutout and taunted Rick about it. Rick retorted that if he had called the pitches it would have been a no-hitter. Wes Ferrell played 15 seasons, though only about 10 of them with a healthy right arm. He died December 9, 1976.

At the time of the 1933 All-Star game, **Oral Hildebrand** was a Cleveland teammate of Wes Ferrell's, and like that Indians hurler Hildebrand rode the bench the entire game, uncalled upon by Connie Mack. Hildebrand's 16–11 record that season was the best of his 10-year career and getting in free to the first All-Star game was as close as he came to playing in one. Hildebrand grew up on an Indiana farm milking cows and was a late comer to baseball. He picked up the game in high school when he was a teammate of future Hall of Famer Chuck Klein. Hildebrand picked up experience pitching for Butler University before turning pro. Hildebrand's lifetime record was 83–78 and he died on September 8, 1977.

"Wild Bill" Hallahan of the St. Louis Cardinals was the starting and losing pitcher for the National League in the first All-Star game, done in by his nemesis — too many walked batters. In a 12-year career, the 1933 Game of the Century was Hallahan's only All-Star appearance. He won a league-leading 19 games that season but never topped 20 wins in a career that included 102 wins and 94 losses. Hallahan, who famously intoned that everyone in baseball wanted to see Babe Ruth in the game, gave up the Bambino's game-winning homer at Comiskey Park. Hallahan retired in 1938 and he died on July 8, 1981.

When major league baseball invited all of the surviving players from the first All-Star game to attend the 50th anniversary event at Comiskey Park in 1983, there were 15 living players. The only one among them who could not make the trip was **Earl Averill**. Averill, residing in Snohomish, Washington, was not strong enough to travel. Averill's son, also named Earl, was a catcher who had a seven-year major league career between 1956 and 1963. The first Earl batted .318 and was inducted into the Baseball Hall of Fame in 1975, 34 years after he retired. Averill, used briefly in the first All-Star game, was selected five more times in his 13-year career. Averill, who was married for 61 years, died from pneumonia at the end of a long illness on August 16, 1983, at the age of 81. It was barely more than a month after the anniversary All-Star game took place.

During his 20-year playing career, shortstop **Joe Cronin** was a seven-time All-Star. He was also a player-manager for the Washington Senators, married the boss' daughter in D.C., was general manager of the Boston Red Sox, and ultimately became president of the American League. Cronin advanced from leading a team with his play in the field, to leading a team on the field, to leading an entire league. Supposedly a weak-hitting middle infielder, Cronin batted .300 or better in 10 full seasons and in parts of three others. He slugged as many as 51 doubles in a season and seven times reached double figures in home runs with a high of 24. The Red Sox retired Cronin's uniform number — 4 — and he was inducted into the Baseball Hall of Fame in 1956. Cronin died on September 7, 1984.

An outstanding flyhawk who twice led American League outfielders in fielding, **Sam West** was an up-and-coming player when chosen as a representative of the St. Louis Browns for the first All-Star game. In a 16-year career, West was voted to three additional All-Star rosters. Never a power hitter, West was always on the lookout to take the extra base when he connected. He had a knack for running his way into triples, five times in a season reaching double figures in that statistic. West was a lifetime .299 hitter while reaching or exceeding .300 nine times. A Texan by birth and upbringing, he returned to the Lone Star state after retiring and died in Lubbock on November 23, 1985, at age 81.

While his two-inning All-Star debut in relief was efficient, though not good enough to help his National League team to overcome its deficit, **Carl Hubbell**'s 1934 consecutive strikeouts of five Hall of Famers is perhaps the most memorable of All-Star moments. Hubbell, who made the screw-ball his trademark, did not lose a regular-season game for his New York Giants for nearly a year at one point in his career. Starting on July 17, 1936, and concluding on May 27, 1937, Hubbell won an amazing 24 straight decisions. He went home for the winter with a 16-game winning streak and then won another eight in a row to start the 1937 campaign. Hubbell earned the nickname "Meal Ticket" because all Giants managers had to do was punch his ticket and he paid off. Hubbell was the Most Valuable Player of the National League in 1933, leading the Giants to the world title, as well as making his mark in the first All-Star game. He also was voted the most outstanding performer in the world of sports — the year before his big moment fanning the superstars. In 16 seasons, Hubbell finished 253–154. Later a scout for the Giants, Hubbell was chosen for the Hall of Fame in 1947. He died November 21, 1988.

A home run hitter when the weapon was just coming into its own, **Wally Berger**'s rookie record of 38 homers in 1930 lasted for 57 years. Berger played the entire first All-Star game for the National League but did not get a hit. He was selected to the next three contests, as well. In 1933, when Berger smacked 27 home runs, that was half the total his entire Boston Braves team recorded. Berger's 34 homers and 130 runs batted in led the NL in 1935. An injured shoulder led to Berger being traded from the Braves to the New York Giants and eventually cut short his 11-year career. Although he was born in Chicago, Berger grew up in San Francisco and in high school shared the infield with Joe Cronin. After retiring, Berger scouted for the New York Yankees and served as a minor league manager. He died of a stroke on November 30, 1988.

Hitter extraordinaire, **Bill Terry**'s lifetime average of .341 produced just one batting title, though it was a doozy. The mainstay first baseman of the New York Giants and later the club's manager hit .401 in 1930. That made Terry the last National League player to hit .400 in a season. The Giants later retired Terry's uniform number — 3. As manager of the Giants for 10 seasons, Terry won three pennants and one World Series title. Terry was elected to the Baseball Hall of Fame in 1954, and near the end of the twentieth century was featured on lists choosing the 100 greatest ballplayers of all time. After retiring as a manager, Terry became a successful businessman. He was living in Jacksonville, Florida, when he died on January 9, 1989, at the age of 90.

Next to Babe Ruth, the biggest hero of the first All-Star game was American League starting pitcher **Lefty Gomez**. The Yankees hurler was the winning pitcher and knocked in a run with a hit, a rarity that Gomez was the first to acknowledge was not a likely occurrence. Gomez was selected for four more All-Star contests. The southpaw won 189 games in his career, topping 20 in four seasons, and probably had a humorous story for each victory. A natural talker, Gomez, who worked for Wilson Sporting Goods, was in constant demand as a sports banquet speaker for decades. He got verbal mileage out of every move he made on the field. The 1934 season was Gomez's greatest. He went 26–5 while leading the American League in shutouts, strikeouts, complete games and innings pitched. Gomez also won six World Series games without a loss. The 1972 Baseball Hall of Fame inductee died at age 80 on February 17, 1989.

Charlie Gehringer, the 19-year second baseman for the Detroit Tigers, left baseball in 1942 and became a lieutenant in the navy in time to serve his country in World War II. The starter for the AL at second base in the 1933 All-Star game preferred to sign autographs "Chas. Gehringer" rather than spelling out his name. Long after he retired from any type of work, he dressed in a suit when being interviewed by sportswriters. The left-handed-swinging Gehringer was selected for six All-Star teams and posted a lifetime .320 average. The 1937 American League Most Valuable Player was inducted into the Baseball Hall of Fame in 1949. Gehringer was considered as graceful in the infield as Joe DiMaggio was in the outfield because he rarely made mistakes. Gehringer died on January 21, 1993, at age 89 after suffering a stroke.

Hal Schumacher's view of the first All-Star game was limited to the sidelines as the last pitcher available for the National League when the team sought to make its late-inning comeback. That was the only All-Star game selection for the New York Giants twirler who played 13 seasons and won 158 games. Long after he left the big leagues Schumacher became an executive with Little League in Williamsport, Pennsylvania, seeking to expand baseball opportunities for young people. Schumacher was nick-named "Prince Hal" with the Giants because he teamed with Carl Hubbell, known as "the King." Schumacher was 82 when he died on April 21, 1993.

The fine on-field career of **Ben Chapman**, leadoff man for the American League in the first All-Star game, was overshadowed by his managerial tenure when he was admonished for racist remarks made by his Phillies when Jackie Robinson broke the color barrier for the Brooklyn Dodgers in 1947. Chapman was forced by league officials to apologize. Chapman played 15 years in the big leagues and owned a .302 average and earned four All-Star selections. He died on July 7, 1993.

Regarded as one of the greatest catchers in baseball history, **Bill Dickey** would have started the inaugural All-Star game if not for an injury and was forced to watch like the 48,000 other spectators at Comiskey Park. Even without Dickey, the New York Yankees had four players in the starting lineup. Dickey made up for missing the first stars contest by being selected to compete 11 times in his 17-year career. The slick receiver, who was born in Louisiana but called Arkansas home, batted .313 lifetime. In his final season as a player, Dickey managed the Yankees for part of 1946. After his playing days concluded, Dickey stayed with the Yankees as a coach and tutored future Yankee stars Yogi Berra and Elston Howard in the finer points of the position. Between playing and coaching, Dickey was in pinstripes for 14 World Series champions. Dickey was elected to the Baseball Hall of Fame in 1954. He died on November 12, 1993, in Little Rock.

After sitting next to Connie Mack in the Game of the Century in order to absorb the old master's knowledge of the game, **Rick Ferrell** was picked for the All-Star team five additional times. Considered a savvy handler of pitchers (except for perhaps his brother Wes), Ferrell enjoyed an 18-year playing career before becoming a front office man for the Detroit Tigers, culminating with the rank of vice president. Ferrell batted .281, but his field work was paramount in his selection for the Baseball Hall of Fame in 1984.

National League shortstop **Dick Bartell** was an above-average hitter for his position during an 18-year big league career, during which he batted .284. In addition to his starting role for the NL in the first All-Star game, Bartell was also selected to compete in 1937. Bartell was viewed as an expert bunter, and he was a contact hitter who was difficult to strike out. After retiring, Bartell shifted to coaching and represented the Tigers and Reds. Before going into private business with a dairy products company, Bartell managed teams in the high minors. He died on August 4, 1995.

The man who made the last out in the first All-Star game had a 15-year major league career primarily as a .280-hitting second baseman. **Tony Cuccinello** made three All-Star teams and surprised pitchers who thought of him as a light hitter with four seasons of 10 or more home runs. Sometimes called "Chick," Cuccinello finished his big league career with the Chicago White Sox after thriving with the Brooklyn Dodgers and Boston Braves. He was a coach with the White Sox when in 1959 the AL club won its first pennant in 40 years. It was managing friend Al Lopez who brought Cuccinello into the coaching ranks in the minors and kept him aboard throughout the 1950s with the Indians and White Sox. Cuccinello retired to Florida and died September 21, 1995, at age 87.

The last surviving player from the first All-Star game was Cubs shortstop **Woody English**. The 1933 Game of the Century was English's only All-Star appearance in a 12-season career that produced a .286 batting average. English was a member of the Cubs for their pennant-winning 1929, 1932 and 1935 seasons. English retired in 1938, but he managed the Grand Rapids Chicks of the All-American Girls Professional Baseball

League for five seasons. "I'm not famous," English said when he was 89, "but I'm proud to say that I played in the first All-Star game. And to this day I still root for the National League."[3] English was 90 when he died on September 26, 1997, in Newark, Ohio.

The Founder

When Arch Ward died at home on July 9, 1955, he was 58 years old and had good reason to believe he had plenty of time to unveil another grand scheme before he reached retirement age. His Associated Press obituary mentioned his role as *Chicago Tribune* sports editor first in summing up his life, but "originator" of the All-Star baseball game and College Football All-Star game was noted in the first paragraph.[4] Ward's son, Thomas, told the wire service that the fire department had sent a rescue team to the house but could not revive his father.

In 1991, the *Tribune* authorized a writer to put together a directory of past employees. The entry on Ward read, in part, "He was one of the most influential persons ever to work for the *Tribune*, exerting far-reaching influence, not only in the world of sports, but in the broader reaches of American society." It also noted "Ward's genius raised millions of dollars for Tribune Charities" and that Ward was "described by one newspaper at 'The Cecil B. de Mille of sports.'"[5]

In 1962, *The Sporting News* organized a campaign to get major league baseball to recognize Ward's efforts in establishing the All-Star game. That year, the Most Valuable Player award given out at the end of the All-Star game was called the "Arch Ward Memorial Award." Ward's name stayed on the trophy until 1970, but then was replaced by the name "Commissioner's Trophy." It reverted back to the Arch Ward award in 1985, but in 2002 it became the Ted Williams Most Valuable Player Award.

What would Ward have thought about all this waffling between honoring and ignoring him? "He didn't brag about it," said Ward's son, Tom, "but I know my dad considered the All-Star game one of his biggest achievements."[6]

In 2003, when major league baseball decided to give the All-Star game more specific meaning than just a measuring-stick war between the leagues and award the side that won the game home-field advantage in the World Series, Commissioner Bud Selig invoked Ward's name in his reasoning. "The objective is to energize the All-Star game because Arch Ward had it right," Selig said. "It should be the Midseason Classic."[7]

Seventy years after the first All-Star game, the contest returned to Comiskey Park — the new Comiskey Park. One of Ward's newspaper descendents, a sportswriter named Rick Morrissey, who had inherited the "In the Wake of the News" column at the *Tribune*, paid a visit to Tom Ward, then 79, who was still living in the Lake Shore Drive apartment his family inhabited since the late 1930s. Morrissey noted the door knocker still had Arch Ward's name on it.

The younger Ward recalled a father who was close friends with champion fighters like Jack Dempsey and Rocky Marciano, Bears owner George Halas, Notre Dame coach Frank Leahy and others, and who sometimes brought them over to the house. Tom Ward was a retired public relations executive and college journalism instructor. "I just adored my father," the younger Ward said. "I thought he was the finest man I have ever known. He would be astonished to know that it (the All-Star game) is still going after all these years and that it's still popular after all these years."[8]

Morrissey wrote about a caller who constantly complained about his stories and signed off by repeating "Arch Ward must be spinning in his grave." After visiting with Tom Ward, Morrissey concluded that would not be true. The headstone above Arch Ward's Illinois grave is a simple one. It bears a large cross and the name "Ward." At the base of the stone is Arch Ward's date of birth and death and his wife Helen's date of birth and death.

Looking at the gravestone and site there was no evidence that Ward was rolling over. His All-Star game baby, birthed so long ago as a one-time Game of the Century, is alive and thriving and very much a cornerstone of the major league baseball schedule.

Appendix 1:
1933 All-Star Box Score

July 6, 1933
Comiskey Park Attendance: 47,595

	1	2	3	4	5	6	7	8	9	Total
NL All-Stars	0	0	0	0	0	2	0	0	0	2
AL All-Stars	0	1	2	0	0	1	0	0	X	4

	R	H	E
NL All-Stars	2	8	0
AL All-Stars	4	9	1

W: Lefty Gomez (1–0), **L:** Bill Hallahan (0–1), **S:** Lefty Grove (1)

NL All-Stars

NL All-Stars	AB	R	H	RBI	BB	SO	BA	OPS	Pit	Str	PO	A	Details
P Martin 3B	4	0	0	1	0	1	.000	.000			0	3	
F Frisch 2B	4	1	2	1	0	0	.500	1.750			5	3	HR
C Klein RF	4	0	1	0	0	0	.250	.500			3	0	
P Waner RF	0	0	0	0	0	0					0	0	
C Hafey LF	4	0	1	0	0	0	.250	.500			1	0	
B Terry 1B	4	0	2	0	0	0	.500	1.000			7	2	
W Berger CF	4	0	0	0	0	0	.000	.000			3	0	GDP
D Bartell SS	2	0	0	0	0	1	.000	.000			0	3	
P Traynor PH	1	0	1	0	0	0	1.000	3.000			0	0	2B
C Hubbell P	0	0	0	0	0	0					0	0	
T Cuccinello PH	1	0	0	0	0	1	.000	.000			0	0	
J Wilson C	1	0	0	0	0	0	.000	.000			2	0	
L O'Doul PH	1	0	0	0	0	0	.000	.000			0	0	
G Hartnett C	1	0	0	0	0	1	.000	.000			2	0	
B Hallahan P	1	0	0	0	0	0	.000	.000			1	0	
L Warneke P	1	1	1	0	0	0	1.000	4.000			0	0	3B
W English PH-SS	1	0	0	0	0	0	.000	.000			0	0	
Totals	34	2	8	2	0	4					24	11	

195

Batting Events

2B: P Traynor (1, off L Grove).
3B: L Warneke (1, off A Crowder).
HR: F Frisch (1, off A Crowder; 6th inn, 0 on, 2 outs to Deep RF).
TB: F Frisch 5; L Warneke 3; P Traynor 2; B Terry 2; C Klein; C Hafey.
GIDP: W Berger (1).
RBI: P Martin (1); F Frisch (1).
2-out RBI: F Frisch.
Team LOB: 5.
With RISP: 0 for 5.

Fielding Events

DP: 1. D Bartell-F Frisch-B Terry.

AL All-Stars

AL All-Stars	AB	R	H	RBI	BB	SO	BA	OPS	Pit	Str	PO	A	Details
B Chapman LF-RF	5	0	1	0	0	1	.200	.400			1	0	
C Gehringer 2B	3	1	0	0	2	0	.000	.400			1	3	SB
B Ruth RF	4	1	2	2	0	2	.500	1.750			1	0	HR
S West CF	0	0	0	0	0	0					0	0	
L Gehrig 1B	2	0	0	0	2	1	.000	.500			12	0	
A Simmons CF-LF	4	0	1	0	0	0	.250	.500			4	0	GDP
J Dykes 3B	3	1	2	0	1	0	.667	1.417	4		2	4	
J Cronin SS	3	1	1	0	1	0	.333	.833			2	4	
R Ferrell C	3	0	0	0	0	0	.000	.000			4	0	SH
L Gomez P	1	0	1	1	0	0	1.000	2.000			0	0	
A Crowder P	1	0	0	0	0	0	.000	.000			0	0	
E Averill PH	1	0	1	1	0	0	1.000	2.000			0	0	
L Grove P	1	0	0	0	0	0	.000	.000			0	0	
Totals	31	4	9	4	6	4			4		27	11	

Batting Events

HR: B Ruth (1, off B Hallahan; 3rd inn, 1 on, 0 outs to Deep RF).
SH: R Ferrell (1, off L Warneke).
TB: B Ruth 5; J Dykes 2; J Cronin; B Chapman; L Gomez; A Simmons; E Averill.
GIDP: A Simmons (1).
RBI: B Ruth 2 (2); E Averill (1); L Gomez (1).
2-out RBI: L Gomez.
Team LOB: 10.
With RISP: 2 for 10.

Fielding Events

DP: 1. J Dykes-L Gehrig.
E: L Gehrig (1).

Baserunning Events

SB: C Gehringer (1, 2nd base off B Hallahan/J Wilson).

Pitching

NL All-Stars	IP	H	R	ER	BB	SO	HR	ERA
B Hallahan, L (0–1)	2	2	3	3	5	1	1	13.50
L Warneke	4	6	1	1	0	2	0	2.25
C Hubbell	2	1	0	0	1	1	0	0.00
Totals	**8**	**9**	**4**	**4**	**6**	**4**	**1**	

B Hallahan faced 3 batters in the 3rd inning.

AL All-Stars	IP	H	R	ER	BB	SO	HR	ERA
L Gomez, W (1–0)	3	2	0	0	0	1	0	0.00
A Crowder	3	3	2	2	0	0	1	6.00
L Grove, S (1)	3	3	0	0	0	3	0	0.00
Totals	**9**	**8**	**2**	**2**	**0**	**4**	**1**	

Balks: None.
WP: None.
HBP: None.
IBB: None.
Pickoffs: None.

Umpires: HP — Bill Dinneen, 1B — Bill Klem, 2B — Bill McGowan, 3B — Cy Rigler.
Time of Game: 2:05.
Attendance: 47,595.

Appendix 2: Player Voting for the First All-Star Game

National League

First Base

Terry	New York	278,545
Bottomley	Cincinnati	81,525
Grimm	Chicago	37,094
Hurst	Philadelphia	29,832
Suhr	Pittsburgh	24,597
Leslie	Brooklyn	19,355
Collins	St. Louis	7,599
Jordan	Boston	1,688

Second Base

Frisch	St. Louis	276,802
Herman	Chicago	71,184
Critz	New York	47,524
Piet	Pittsburgh	29,842
Maranville	Boston	25,636
Cuccinello	Brooklyn	12,555
Grantham	Cincinnati	6,658
Hornsby	St. Louis	5,022

Third Base

Traynor	Pittsburgh	304,101
Martin	St. Louis	88,462
English	Chicago	67,335
Whitney	Boston	33,719
Vergez	New York	11,465
Stripp	Brooklyn	6,932
Adams	Cincinnati	4,404

Shortstop

Bartell	Philadelphia	231,639
Vaughan	Pittsburgh	104,607
Durocher	St. Louis	31,789
Jurges	Chicago	22,224
Koeing	Chicago	10,952
Jackson	New York	8,305
Wright	Brooklyn	5,661

Catcher

Hartnett	Chicago	338,653
Wilson	St. Louis	137,937
Grace	Pittsburgh	47,834
Davis	Philadelphia	15,318
Mancuso	New York	14,222
Lombardi	Cincinnati	11,901
Lopez	Brooklyn	6,820
Hogan	Boston	2,464

Outfielders

Klein	Philadelphia	342,282
P. Waner	Pittsburgh	269,291
O'Doul	New York	230,058
Berger	Boston	136,856
Lindstrom	Pittsburgh	85,695
L. Waner	Pittsburgh	84,617
Hafey	Cincinnati	52,549
Ott	New York	40,791
Frederick	Brooklyn	24,974
Cuyler	Chicago	12,316

Martin	St. Louis	11,929
Stephenson	Chicago	9,003
F. Herman	Chicago	7,610
Wilson	Brooklyn	2,194
Taylor	Brooklyn	1,654
Douthit	Chicago	1,309
Watkins	St. Louis	1,074

Pitchers

Warneke	Chicago	312,960
Hubbell	New York	299,099
Lucas	Cincinnati	142,669
Hallahan	St. Louis	82,583
Dean	St. Louis	35,050
Brandt	Boston	34,744
Si. Johnston	Cincinnati	31,942
Meine	Pittsburgh	24,284
Swift	Pittsburgh	15,395
French	Pittsburgh	13,613
Swetonic	Pittsburgh	12,601
Carleton	St. Louis	10,164
Schumacher	New York	4,417
Clark	Brooklyn	4,064
Bush	Chicago	2,235
Carroll	Brooklyn	1,447
Fitzsimmons	New York	1,324

American League

First Base

Gehrig	New York	312,680
Foxx	Philadelphia	127,104
Kuhel	Washington	4,834
Alexander	Boston	3,566
Davis	Detroit	1,451

Second Base

Gehringer	Detroit	239,756
Lazzeri	New York	164,830
Melillo	St. Louis	32,457
Hodapp	Boston	32,194
Cissell	Cleveland	15,826
Bishop	Philadelphia	11,617

Myer	Washington	8,003
Hayes	Chicago	4,935
Foxx	Philadelphia	891

Third Base

Dykes	Philadelphia	207,992
Foxx	Philadelphia	142,418
Kamm	Cleveland	67,295
J. Sewell	New York	41,232
McManus	Boston	11,521
Higgins	Philadelphia	2,604

Shortstop

Cronin	Washington	337,766
Crosetti	New York	34,289
Appling	Chicago	27,755
Kress	Chicago	2,883
Burnett	Cleveland	2,661
Rogell	Detroit	1,740
Levey	St. Louis	1,643

Catcher

Dickey	New York	297,382
Cochrane	Philadelphia	174,530
R. Ferrell	Boston	29,431
Hayworth	Detroit	7,034
L. Sewell	Washington	3,096
Spencer	Cleveland	1,845
Berry	Chicago	981
Grube	Chicago	938

Outfielders

Simmons	Chicago	346,291
Ruth	New York	320,518
Averill	Cleveland	246,913
Chapman	New York	108,645
West	St. Louis	59,670
Goslin	Washington	40,590
Combs	New York	32,890
Schulte	Washington	30,674
Manush	Washington	24,179
Haas	Chicago	7,135
Vosmik	Cleveland	7,132

Stone	Detroit	4,318	W. Ferrell	Cleveland	191,120
Swanson	Chicago	3,770	Hildebrand	Cleveland	86,232
Cramer	Philadelphia	3,144	Lyons	Chicago	49,956
Porter	Cleveland	3,114	Crowder	Washington	31,605
Reynolds	St. Louis	2,416	Bridges	Detroit	26,195
G. Walker	Detroit	2,240	Ruffing	New York	19,563
R. Johnson	Boston	2,237	Marberry	Detroit	6,163
Oliver	Boston	2,094	Earnshaw	Philadelphia	4,857
Foxx	Philadelphia	1,095	Allen	New York	4,526
Fox	Detroit	1,062	Blaeholder	St. Louis	2,694
Coleman	Philadelphia	964	Rowe	Detroit	1,626
White	Detroit	703	Pipgras	Boston	1,575
Rice	Washington	580	Weaver	Washington	1,537
			Whitehill	Washington	1,283
Pitchers			Hadley	St. Louis	864
Grove	Philadelphia	327,242	Brennan	New York	472
Gomez	New York	253,000	Jones	Chicago	442

Appendix 3: All-Star Game Scores, 1933–2010

The Midsummer Classics

Game	Ballpark City, State	Date	A.L.	N.L.
1	Comiskey Park Chicago, Illinois	07–06–1933	4	2
2	Polo Grounds New York, New York	07–10–1934	9	7
3	Municipal Stadium Cleveland, Ohio	07–08–1935	4	1
4	Braves Field Boston, Massachusetts	07–07–1936	3	4
5	Griffith Stadium Washington, D.C.	07–07–1937	8	3
6	Crosley Field Cincinnati, Ohio	07–06–1938	1	4
7	Yankee Stadium New York, New York	07–11–1939	3	1
8	Sportsman's Park St. Louis, Missouri	07–09–1940	0	4
9	Briggs Stadium Detroit, Michigan	07–08–1941	7	5
10	Polo Grounds New York, New York	07–06–1942	3	1
11	Shibe Park Philadelphia, Pennsylvania	07–13–1943	5	3
12	Forbes Field Pittsburgh, Pennsylvania	07–11–1944	1	7
n/a	Fenway Park Boston, Massachusetts	07–10–1945	n/a	n/a

Game	Ballpark City, State	Date	A.L.	N.L.
13	Fenway Park Boston, Massachusetts	07–09–1946	12	0
14	Wrigley Field Chicago, Illinois	07–08–1947	2	1
15	Sportsman's Park St. Louis, Missouri	07–13–1948	5	2
16	Ebbets Field Brooklyn, New York	07–12–1949	11	7
17	Comiskey Park Chicago, Illinois	07–11–1950	3	4
18	Briggs Stadium Detroit, Michigan	07–10–1951	3	8
19	Shibe Park Philadelphia, Pennsylvania	07–08–1952	2	3
20	Crosley Field Cincinnati, Ohio	07–14–1953	1	5
21	Municipal Stadium Cleveland, Ohio	07–13–1954	11	9
22	County Stadium Milwaukee, Wisconsin	07–12–1955	5	6
23	Griffith Stadium Washington, D.C.	07–10–1956	3	7
24	Sportsman's Park St. Louis, Missouri	07–09–1957	6	5
25	Memorial Stadium Baltimore, Maryland	07–08–1958	4	3
26	Forbes Field Pittsburgh, Pennsylvania	07–07–1959	4	5
27	Memorial Coliseum Los Angeles, California	08–03–1959	5	3
28	Municipal Stadium Kansas City, Missouri	07–11–1960	3	5
29	Yankee Stadium New York, New York	07–13–1960	0	6
30	Candlestick Park San Francisco, California	07–11–1961	4	5
31	Fenway Park Boston, Massachusetts	07–31–1961	1	1
32	D.C. Stadium Washington, D.C.	07–10–1962	1	3

Game	Ballpark City, State	Date	A.L.	N.L.
33	Wrigley Field Chicago, Illinois	07–30–1962	9	4
34	Municipal Stadium Cleveland, Ohio	07–09–1963	3	5
35	Shea Stadium New York, New York	07–07–1964	4	7
36	Metropolitan Stadium Bloomington, Minnesota	07–13–1965	5	6
37	Busch Memorial Stadium St. Louis, Missouri	07–12–1966	1	2
38	Anaheim Stadium Anaheim, California	07–11–1967	1	2
39	Astrodome Houston, Texas	07–09–1968	0	1
40	R.F.K. Memorial Stadium Washington, D.C.	07–23–1969	3	9
41	Riverfront Stadium Cincinnati, Ohio	07–14–1970	4	5
42	Tiger Stadium Detroit, Michigan	07–13–1971	6	4
43	Atlanta-Fulton County Stadium Atlanta, Georgia	07–25–1972	3	4
44	Royals Stadium Kansas City, Missouri	07–24–1973	1	7
45	Three Rivers Stadium Pittsburgh, Pennsylvania	07–23–1974	2	7
46	County Stadium Milwaukee, Wisconsin	07–15–1975	3	6
47	Veterans Stadium Philadelphia, Pennsylvania	07–13–1976	1	7
48	Yankee Stadium New York, New York	07–19–1977	5	7
49	San Diego Stadium San Diego, California	07–11–1978	3	7
50	Kingdome Seattle, Washington	07–17–1979	6	7
51	Dodger Stadium Los Angeles, California	07–08–1980	2	4
52	Municipal Stadium Cleveland, Ohio	08–09–1981	4	5

Game	Ballpark City, State	Date	A.L.	N.L.
53	Olympic Stadium Montreal, Quebec	07–13–1982	1	4
54	Comiskey Park Chicago, Illinois	07–06–1983	13	3
55	Candlestick Park San Francisco, California	07–10–1984	1	3
56	H. Humphrey Metrodome Minneapolis, Minnesota	07–16–1985	1	6
57	Astrodome Houston, Texas	07–15–1986	3	2
58	Oakland-Alameda County Coliseum Oakland, California	07–14–1987	0	2
59	Riverfront Stadium Cincinnati, Ohio	07–12–1988	2	1
60	Anaheim Stadium Anaheim, California	07–11–1989	5	3
61	Wrigley Field Chicago, Illinois	07–10–1990	2	0
62	SkyDome Toronto, Ontario	07–09–1991	4	2
63	Jack Murphy Stadium San Diego, California	07–14–1992	13	6
64	Oriole Park at Camden Yards Baltimore, Maryland	07–13–1993	9	3
65	Three Rivers Stadium Pittsburgh, Pennsylvania	07–12–1994	7	8
66	The Ballpark at Arlington Arlington, Texas	07–11–1995	2	3
67	Veterans Stadium Philadelphia, Pennsylvania	07–09–1996	0	6
68	Jacobs Field Cleveland, Ohio	07–08–1997	3	1
69	Coors Field Denver, Colorado	07–07–1998	13	8
70	Fenway Park Boston, Massachusetts	07–13–1999	4	1
71	Turner Field Atlanta, Georgia	07–11–2000	6	3
72	Safeco Field Seattle, Washington	07–10–2001	4	1

Game	Ballpark City, State	Date	A.L.	N.L.
73	Miller Park Milwaukee, Wisconsin	07–09–2002	7	7
74	U.S. Cellular Field Chicago, Illinois	07–15–2003	7	6
75	Minute Maid Park Houston, Texas	07–13–2004	9	4
76	Comerica Park Detroit, Michigan	07–12–2005	7	5
77	PNC Park Pittsburgh, Pennsylvania	07–11–2006	3	2
78	AT&T Park San Francisco, California	07–10–2007	5	4
79	Yankee Stadium New York, New York	07–15–2008	4	3
80	Busch Stadium St. Louis, Missouri	07–14–2009	4	3
81	Angel Stadium Anaheim, California	07–13–2010	1	3

Chapter Notes

Introduction

1. Thomas B. Littlewood, *Arch: A Promoter, Not A Poet* (Ames: Iowa State University Press, 1990), p. 39.

Chapter 1

1. *El Paso Herald*, "The All Stars And National Baseball Men," November 3, 1902.
2. *Sporting Life*, "Mercer's Luck: The Treasurer of the Base Ball Tourists Narrowly Escapes Being Mulcted of All the Velvet," December 20, 1902.
3. *Boston Globe*, "Mercer's Suicide," January 14, 1903.
4. *Chicago Tribune*, "Pitcher Mercer Ends His Life," January 14, 1903.
5. *Oakland Tribune*, "Baseball Pitcher Takes His Life," January 13, 1903.
6. *Sporting Life*, "Was Mercer Murdered?" January 18, 1903.
7. Ibid.
8. Ibid.
9. W.A. Calhoun, "Vale, Winnie Mercer," *Sporting Life*, January 31, 1903.
10. Brendan Macgranachan, "Addie Joss' Benefit Game," Seamheads.com, July 25, 2009.
11. Ibid.
12. Ibid.
13. F.C. Lane, "An All-Star Baseball Contest for a Greater Championship," *Baseball Magazine*, July 1915.
14. Ibid.
15. Ibid.

Chapter 2

1. Littlewood, *Arch*, p. 67.
2. Ibid., p. 71.

Chapter 3

1. Arch Ward, "Picked Stars of Big Leagues to Play July 6," *Chicago Tribune*, May 19, 1933.
2. Ibid.
3. Ibid.
4. Ibid.
5. Ibid.
6. Arch Ward, "$500 in Prizes for Naming Inter-League Lineups," *Chicago Tribune*, May 20, 1933.
7. Ibid.
8. Ibid.
9. Ibid.
10. Arch Ward, "Votes Pour in on Baseball's Biggest Game," *Chicago Tribune*, May 21, 1933.
11. Arch Ward, "47 Newspapers Join Tribune to Pick Best Teams," *Chicago Tribune*, May 22, 1933.
12. Arch Ward, "White Sox to Accept Ticket Orders June 1," *Chicago Tribune*, May 27, 1933.
13. Arch Ward, "Simmons Leads Ruth In American League Poll," *Chicago Tribune*, May 24, 1933.
14. Arch Ward, "Leagues Spar for Advantage in Big Game," *Chicago Tribune*, June 9, 1933.
15. Ibid.
16. Ibid.
17. Arch Ward, "Open Bleacher Seat

Sale at 10 a.m. Tomorrow," *Chicago Tribune*, July 2, 1933.

Chapter 4

1. Arch Ward, "Gehrig and Cronin Appear Certain of All-Star Berths," *Chicago Tribune*, June 5, 1933.
2. Ibid.
3. Arch Ward, "Babe Ruth Eager To Play in Game of Century," *Chicago Tribune*, May 28, 1933.
4. Ibid.
5. Arch Ward, "Hubbell Gains on Lon Warneke in Baseball Poll," *Chicago Tribune*, May 29, 1933.
6. *Chicago Tribune*, "The Game of the Century," May 23, 1933.
7. Ward, "Gehrig and Cronin Appear...".
8. Arch Ward, "O'Doul, Averill May Lose Out in All-Star Game," *Chicago Tribune*, June 11, 1933.
9. Ibid.
10. Ibid.
11. *Sporting News*, "It's Last Inning in the Big Contest for Free Trip to All-Star Game!" June 22, 1933.
12. Arch Ward, "Al Leads Ruth, Klein in Total for Star Game," *Chicago Tribune*, June 25, 1933.
13. Arch Ward, "Every Player Chosen By Fans Gets A Place," *Chicago Tribune*, June 27, 1933.
14. Arch Ward, "Heydler Picks Men According To Fans' Vote," *Chicago Tribune*, June 23, 1933.
15. *Chicago Tribune*, "Elson At Mike For Ball Game Of A Century," July 2, 1933.
16. Ward, "O'Doul, Averill May...".

Chapter 5

1. Westbrook Pegler, "All-Star Game Just What Doctor Ordered For Baseball," *Chicago Tribune*, June 20, 1933.
2. Ibid.
3. Littlewood, *Arch*, p. 73.
4. *Sporting News*, "McGraw and Mack to Match Wits Fourth Time in All-Star Game," June 8, 1933.

5. Hal Bodley, "Economic State May Affect Spending," MLB.com, October 17, 2008.

Chapter 6

1. Alan Ross, *White Sox Glory* (Nashville: Cumberland House, 2006), p. 20.
2. Edgar Munzel, "Harridge Dead; President of A.L. for 27 Years," *Sporting News*, April 24, 1971.
3. Ibid.

Chapter 7

1. *www.baseballalmanac.com*.
2. Dave Nightengale, "Comiskey: Still a Pitchers' Haven," *Sporting News All-Star Special*, July 1983.
3. Ibid.
4. Lowell Reidenbaugh, "Memories... The 15 Surviving Members of the First All-Star Game Remember The Big Event," *Sporting News All-Star Special*, July 1983.
5. Ibid.
6. Ibid.
7. Ibid.
8. Ibid.
9. Ward, "Gehrig and Cronin Appear...".

Chapter 8

1. John Kuenster, "Warmup Tosses," *Baseball Digest*, July 1973.
2. Joseph Durso, "Vernon Lefty Gomez, 80, Dies; Starred as a Pitcher for Yankees," *New York Times*, February 18, 1989.
3. Ibid.
4. Jerry D. Lewis, "Gomez Crusade Against Gloom Strong As Ever," *Sporting News*, February 25, 1978.
5. Ibid.
6. Ibid.
7. Thomas Barthel, *Pepper Martin: A Baseball Biography* (Jefferson, North Carolina: McFarland, 2003), p. 124.
8. *Sporting News*, "Wild Bill Hallahan," July 25, 1981.
9. Jim Collins, "By Gashouse Stan-

dards, 'Mild Bill,'" *Binghamton Press-Bulletin*, April 9, 1978.

10. William Wallace, "Ben Chapman, 84, All-Star Outfielder With Yanks in 30's," *New York Times*, July 8, 1993.

11. Dan Albaugh, "Ben Chapman: Jackie Robinson's Worst Nightmare," *Sports Collectors Digest*, September 26, 1997.

12. Wayne Martin, "'Sure, We Rode Jackie,' Says Chapman," *Sporting News*, March 24, 1973.

Chapter 9

1. F.C. Lane, "A Great Player's Heavy Handicap," *Baseball Magazine*, March 1933.

2. Ibid.

3. L.H. Addington, "Chick Hafey, Wearing Glasses, Goes After Slugging Laurels," National Baseball Hall of Fame Library archives, May 2, 1929.

4. Thomas J. Connery, "Glimpse of Chick Hafey's Life Shows Baseball's Uncertainties," *Providence Visitor*, August 25, 1933.

5. Bob Broeg, "Terry Recalls First Star Game," *St. Louis Post-Dispatch*, June 26, 1983.

6. Neil Singelais, "After 57 years, Berger's Mark About to Fall," *Boston Globe*, National Baseball Hall of Fame Library archives.

7. Wells Twombly, "First All-Star Shocker — Gomez Got Hit and RBI," *Sporting News*, July 26, 1973.

8. Ibid.

9. Ibid.

10. Ibid.

11. Ibid.

Chapter 10

1. Francis J. Powers, "The Score Card — McGraw Hated American League," *Chicago Daily American*, January 20, 1944.

2. Hugh Bradley, "Jimmy Wilson Has Theory of His Own For Making Hurlers," *New York Post*, July 8, 1938.

3. J.G. Taylor Spink, "Hall of Game Gehringer Called 'Perfect Player,'" *Sporting News*, May 11, 1949.

4. Ibid.

5. John McBride, "The Thrill of A Lifetime For a Kid," *Sporting News All-Star Special*, July 1983.

6. Ibid.

7. Fred Lieb, "There Were Stories About Babe Ruth That Were Never Written," *St. Petersburg Times*, January 30, 1975.

8. Ibid.

9. McBride, "The Thrill…".

Chapter 11

1. *Baseball Magazine*, "He Learned His Trade in the Philippines," January 1929.

2. Joe Williams, "Al Crowder, Symphony in Tattooing, Adds Picturesque Touch to Conflict," *New York World-Telegram*, October 4, 1933.

3. Quentin Reynolds, "McGraw's Boy," *Collier's Magazine*, June 29, 1935.

4. Harvey Woodruff, "American Stars with Game of Century," *Chicago Tribune*, July 7, 1933.

5. George DeGregorio, "All-Stars of 1933 Recall Scene of Glory," *New York Times*, July 5, 1983.

6. Ibid.

7. Dan Daniel, "Chapman Seen Super-Star," *New York World-Telegram*, July 17, 1933.

8. Wallace, "Ben Chapman, 84…".

Chapter 12

1. Joe Cronin, "Original All-Star Recalls the Early Games," *New York Times*, National Baseball Hall of Fame Library archives.

2. Ibid.

3. Pat Robinson, "Baseball World Mourns — Lou Gehrig Is Dead at 37," International News Service, June 2, 1941.

4. Jonathan Eig, *Luckiest Man: The Life and Death of Lou Gehrig* (New York: Simon & Schuster, 2005), p. 224.

5. *http://www.lougehrig.com/about/quotes.htm*.

6. Ibid.

7. Dick Bray, "Baseball Biographies: Inside Dope on Two Stars of the National

League By One Who Knows," *St. Anthony Messenger*, September 1938.

8. Joe King, "His First American League Hit Pleased Bartell Most," *New York World-Telegram*, 1942, National Baseball Hall of Fame Library archives.

9. William C. Duncan, "Simmons Will Knock Home Run for White Sox on Opening Day If Tradition Runs True to Form," *Philadelphia Ledger*, April 1, 1933.

10. Ibid.

11. United Press International, "Al Simmons, Ball Player, Dead; Noted Hitter Was in Hall of Fame," May 27, 1956.

Chapter 13

1. Richard Leutzinger, "Historical Perspective: Lefty O'Doul," National Baseball Hall of Fame Library archives.

2. Dave Hoekstra, "Lefty O'Doul's, the Last Great Sports Bar," *Chicago Sun-Times*, August 31, 2003.

3. Ogden Nash, "Lineup For Yesterday," *Sport*, January 1949.

4. Thomas J. Connery, "Leo Hartnett, R.I. Player, Is Majors' Noisiest Catcher," *Providence Visitor*, July 28, 1933.

5. Ibid.

6. Chicago Cubs press release, National Baseball Hall of Fame Library archives.

7. Gabby Hartnett file, National Baseball Hall of Fame Library archives.

8. Harry T. Brundidge, "Earl Averill Is Ball Player by Public Subscription of His Home Town," *St. Louis Star*, August 11, 1931.

9. Ibid.

10. Bob Dolgan, "A Man of Talent, Consistency, Class," *Cleveland Plain Dealer*, August 7, 1996.

11. Ibid.

12. Ibid.

Chapter 14

1. *Sporting News*, "Hall of Famer Lefty Grove Leaves Record of 300 Pitching Victories," June 14, 1975.

2. Ibid.

3. Pat Livingston, "Traynor Dies...

The End Of A Living Legend," *Pittsburgh Press*, March 17, 1972.

4. Luther W. Spoehr, "Harold Joseph 'Pie' Traynor," *The Biographical Dictionary of American Sports*, National Baseball Hall of Fame Library archives.

5. Brent Kelley, "Former Cubs Shortstop Woody English Interviewed," *Sports Collectors Digest*, July 27, 1990.

6. John Hulkenberg, "Baseball Is a Little More Rich with Woody English," *Reynoldsburg News*, July 24, 1996.

7. Sam Carchidi, "A 1933 All-Star, He's Glowing Still," *Philadelphia Inquirer*, July 1, 1996.

8. "Hubbell Was King on July 2, 1933," National Baseball Hall of Fame Library archives.

9. Quentin Reynolds, "I Can Hit Pretty Good," *Collier's Magazine*, July 1937.

10. Tom Meany, "Cronin Proves Real Hero," *New York World-Telegram*, October 3, 1933.

11. Gene Kessler, "Joe Cronin's Funniest Story," *Chicago Daily Times*, November 16, 1933.

Chapter 15

1. *Sporting News*, "Pepper Martin — Firebrand of Gashouse Gang," March 26, 1965.

2. Jim Kaplan, *Lefty Grove: American Original* (Cleveland: Society for American Baseball Research, 2000), p. 158.

3. Ed Rumill, "Grove Looks Back: Developed Speed Throwing Rocks," *Christian Science Monitor*, National Baseball Hall of Fame Library archives.

4. *Sporting News*, "Hall of Famer Lefty Grove Leaves Record of 300 Pitching Victories," June 14, 1975.

5. Kaplan, *Lefty Grove*, p. 132.

6. Ibid., p. 141.

7. *Sporting News*, "Hall of Famer Lefty Grove...".

8. Ibid.

9. *www.baseball-alamanc.com*.

10. Lane, "A Great Player's Heavy Handicap."

11. Jeff Lenberg, *Baseball's All-Star Game: A Game by Game Guide* (Jefferson,

North Carolina: McFarland, 1987), p. 22–23.

12. Frederick G. Lieb, "Paul Waner, 3,000-Hit Hall of Famer, Dead," *Sporting News*, September 11, 1965.

Chapter 16

1. *Washington Post*, "Sam West's Whip," 1929, National Baseball Hall of Fame Library archives.
2. Ibid.
3. Ben Henkey, "Giant Great Terry Is Dead at 90," *Sporting News*, January 23, 1989.
4. John Drebinger, "Baseball World Mourns Passing of McGraw, 'The Greatest Manager of Them All,'" *New York Times*, February 26, 1934.
5. Neil Singlelais, "After 57 Years, Berger's Mark About to Fall," *Boston Globe*, National Baseball Hall of Fame Library archives.
6. Michael Hirsley, "11-Year-Old Newsboy Pete Pervan Was Stunned When He Was Invited to Watch 1st All-Star Game," *Chicago Tribune*, July 11, 2003.
7. Steve Calhoun, "Where Are They Now? Tony Cuccinello," *Sports Collectors Digest*, October 30, 1983.
8. Ibid.

Chapter 17

1. Chris DeLuca, "The Game of the Century," *Chicago Sun-Times*, July 15, 2003.
2. John Kuenster, "Warm Up Tosses," *Baseball Digest*, 1973, National Baseball Hall of Fame Library archives.
3. John McBride, "The Thrill of a Lifetime For a Kid," *Sporting News All-Star Special*, July 1983.
4. Ibid.
5. Lenberg, *Baseball's All-Star Game*, p. 23.
6. Joe Williams, "That Inter-League Scrap Shows 'Em the Difference; It's 'The Old Fat Fellow,'" *New York World-Telegram*, July 7, 1933.
7. Ibid.
8. Irving Vaughn, "Players Prove Stars Can Star With Strangers," *Chicago Tribune*, July 7, 1933.
9. Ibid.
10. C. Johnson Spink, "We Believe... Birth of All-Star Game," *Sporting News*, July 15, 1978.
11. Major League Baseball press release, June 24, 1983.
12. Ibid.
13. Spink, "We Believe...".
14. Littlewood, *Arch*, p. 75.
15. Ibid.
16. J.G. Taylor Spink, *Judge Landis And 25 Years of Baseball* (New York: Thomas Y. Crowell Company, 1947), p. 212.
17. *Chicago Tribune*, "In the Wake of the News: Baseball's Greatest Game," December 15, 1933.

Chapter 18

1. Larry Lester, *Black Baseball's National Showcase* (Lincoln: University of Nebraska Press, 2001), p. 22.
2. Al Monroe, "Speaking of Sports," *Chicago Defender*, August 19, 1933.
3. *Chicago Tribune*, "Negroes Meet in All-Star Game Sept. 10," August 15, 1933.
4. Ibid.
5. *Chicago Defender*, "Votes Show Bill Is West's Ace Pitcher," September 9, 1933.
6. *Chicago Defender*, "Betting Even on Big Game if Foster and Page Start," September 9, 1933.
7. Monroe, "Speaking of Sports."
8. Major League Baseball press release, "James 'Cool Papa' Bell Named to Hall of Fame," February 13, 1974.
9. Thom Loverro, *The Encyclopedia of Negro League Baseball* (New York: Checkmark Books, 2003), p. 51.
10. Buck O'Neil, Steve Wulf, and David Conrads, *I Was Right on Time* (New York: Simon & Schuster, 1996), p. 25.
11. Ric Roberts, "Now in Baseball's Hall of Fame," *Pittsburgh Courier*, National Baseball Hall of Fame Library archives.
12. *Black Sports Magazine*, "Historically Speaking: Oscar Charleston," March 1976.
13. Loverro, p. 100.
14. Ibid., p. 277.

15. Ibid., p. 283.
16. Satchel Paige and David Lipman, *Maybe I'll Pitch Forever* (New York: Grove Press, 1962), p. 71.
17. Mark Ribowsky, *Don't Look Back: Satchel Paige In The Shadows Of Baseball* (New York: Simon & Schuster, 1994), p. 106.
18. Chuck Finder, "Off in a Galaxy Long, Long Ago...," *Pittsburgh Post-Gazette*, July 9, 2006.
19. Ibid.

Chapter 19

1. *New York World-Telegram*, "Baseball Fans Demand Terry and Cronin Follow Their Vote on All-Star Players," July 7, 1934.
2. Jack McDonald, "King Carl Crown Prince of All-Stars," *Sporting News*, July 11, 1964.
3. Ibid.
4. Ibid.
5. Ibid.
6. Bill McCullough, "The Meal Ticket," *Baseball Magazine*, National Baseball Hall of Fame Library archives.
7. Joe Williams, "League Prospers Because of Yanks, Says Harridge," *New York World-Telegram*, 1939, National Baseball Hall of Fame Library archives.
8. *www.baseball-almanac.com*.
9. Associated Press, "Old Pros Help All-Star Promotion," May 7, 1987.
10. Chris Baker, "All-Star Game: They're Working on Incentive Plan," *Los Angeles Times*, July 9, 1997.
11. *www.baseball-almanac.com*.
12. Ibid.
13. Paul White, "Gashouser 72 Today and Still A Hero," *Binghamton Press*, August 4, 1974.
14. Reidenbaugh, "Memories."
15. Ibid.

Chapter 20

1. Littlewood, *Arch*, p. 76.
2. Ibid., pp. 53, 55.

3. Ibid., p. 89.
4. George S. Halas, Gwen Morgan, and Arthur Veysey, *Halas: An Autobiography* (Chicago: Bonus Books, 1979), p. 178.
5. Littlewood, *Arch*, pp. 92–93.
6. Ibid., p. 96.
7. Jerome Holtzman, "Arch Ward: The Father of the All-Star Game Was an Enterprising Sportswriter," National Baseball Hall of Fame Library archives.
8. Littlewood, *Arch*, p. 198.
9. *Chicago Tribune*, "Arch Ward, Tribune Sports Editor, Dies," July 10, 1955.
10. Ibid.
11. *Chicago Tribune*, "Sports World Mourns Arch Ward; Rites Tuesday," July 10, 1955.
12. *Chicago Tribune*, "More Tributes to Ward From Nation Leaders," July 11, 1955.
13. *Chicago Tribune*, "Arch Ward," July 10, 1955.

Chapter 21

1. Frederick G. Lieb, "Nation Mourns Ruth: Game's Most Famous Star Dies at 53," *Sporting News*, August 25, 1948.
2. United Press International, "Al Simmons, Ball Player, Dead; Noted Hitter Was in Hall of Fame," May 27, 1956.
3. Sam Carchidi, "A 1933 All-Star, He's Glowing Still," *Philadelphia Inquirer*, July 1, 1996.
4. Associated Press, "Arch Ward, the Originator of All-Star Games, Is Dead," July 9, 1955.
5. Rudolph M. Unger, *The Chicago Tribune News Staff 1920s–1960s*, 1991.
6. Mark Purdy, "Thanks, Arch, For Being A Sportswriter," *San Jose Mercury News*, July 14, 1987.
7. Phil Rogers, "A 'Classic' Shake-up," *Chicago Tribune*, January 11, 2003.
8. Rick Morrissey, "Arch Would Approve," *Chicago Tribune*, July 13, 2003.

Bibliography

Books

Barthel, Thomas. *Pepper Martin: A Baseball Biography*. Jefferson, North Carolina: McFarland, 2003.

Eig, Jonathan. *Luckiest Man: The Life and Death of Lou Gehrig*. New York: Simon & Schuster, 2005.

Halas, George S., Gwen Morgan, and Arthur Veysey. *Halas: An Autobiography*. Chicago: Bonus Books, 1979.

Kaplan, Jim. *Lefty Grove: American Original*. Cleveland: Society for American Baseball Research, 2000.

Lenberg, Jeff. *Baseball's All-Star Game: A Game by Game Guide*. Jefferson, North Carolina: McFarland, 1987.

Lester, Larry. *Black Baseball's National Showcase*. Lincoln: University of Nebraska Press, 2001.

Littlewood, Thomas B. *Arch: A Promoter, Not A Poet*. Ames: Iowa State University Press, 1990.

Loverro, Thom. *The Encyclopedia of Negro League Baseball*. New York: Checkmark Books, 2003.

O'Neil, Buck, Steve Wulf, and David Conrads. *I Was Right on Time*. New York: Simon & Schuster, 1996.

Paige, Satchel, and David Lipman. *Maybe I'll Pitch Forever*. New York: Grove Press, 1962.

Ribowsky, Mark. *Don't Look Back: Satchel Paige in the Shadows of Baseball*. New York: Simon & Schuster, 1994.

Ross, Alan. *White Sox Glory*. Nashville: Cumberland House, 2006.

Spink, J.G. Taylor. *Judge Landis and 25 Years of Baseball*. New York: Thomas Y. Crowell, 1947.

Newspaper Articles

Addington, L.H. "Chick Hafey, Wearing Glasses, Goes After Slugging Laurels." National Baseball Hall of Fame Library archives, May 2, 1929.

"The All Stars and National Baseball Men." *El Paso Herald*, November 3, 1902.

"Arch Ward." *Chicago Tribune*, July 10, 1955.

"Arch Ward, Tribune Sports Editor, Dies." *Chicago Tribune*, July 10, 1955.

Baker, Chris. "All-Star Game: They're Working on Incentive Plan." *Los Angeles Times*, July 9, 1997.

"Baseball Fans Demand Terry and Cronin Follow Their Vote on All-Star Players." *New York World-Telegram*, July 7, 1934.

"Baseball Pitcher Takes His Life." *Oakland Tribune*, January 13, 1903.

Bradley, Hugh. "Jimmy Wilson Has Theory of His Own For Making Hurlers." *New York Post*, July 8, 1938.

Bray, Dick. "Baseball Biographies: Inside Dope on Two Stars of the National League by One Who Knows." *St. Anthony Messenger*, September 1938.

Broeg, Bob. "Terry Recalls First Star Game." *St. Louis Post-Dispatch*, June 26, 1983.

Brundidge, Harry T. "Earl Averill Is Ball Player by Public Subscription of His Home Town." *St. Louis Star*, August 11, 1931.

Carchidi, Sam. "A 1933 All-Star, He's

Glowing Still." *Philadelphia Inquirer*, July 1, 1996.

Collins, Jim. "By Gashouse Gang Standards, 'Mild Bill.'" *Binghamton Press-Bulletin*, April 9, 1978.

Connery, Thomas J. "Glimpse of Chick Hafey's Life Shows Baseball's Uncertainties." *Providence Visitor*, August 25, 1933.

_____. "Leo Hartnett, R.I. Player, Is Majors' Noisiest Catcher." *Providence Visitor*, July 28, 1933.

Cronin, Joe. "Original All-Star Recalls the Early Games." *New York Times*, date missing, National Baseball Hall of Fame Library archives.

Daniel, Dan. "Chapman Seen Super-Star." *New York World-Telegram*, July 17, 1933.

DeGregorio, George. "All-Stars of 1933 Recall Scene of Glory." *New York Times*, July 5, 1983.

DeLuca, Chris. "The Game of the Century." *Chicago Sun-Times*, July 15, 2003.

Dolgan, Bob. "A Man of Talent, Consistency, Class." *Cleveland Plain Dealer*, August 7, 1996.

Durso, Joseph. "Vernon Lefty Gomez, 80, Dies; Starred as a Pitcher for Yankees." *New York Times*, February 18, 1989.

Duncan, C. William. "Simmons Will Knock Home Runs for White Sox on Opening Day If Tradition Runs True to Form." *Philadelphia Ledger*, April 1, 1933.

"Elson At Mike For Ball Game Of A Century." *Chicago Tribune*, July 2, 1933.

Finder, Chuck. "Off in a Galaxy Long, Long Ago...." *Pittsburgh Post-Gazette*, July 9, 2006.

"The Game of the Century." *Chicago Tribune*, May 23, 1933.

Hoekstra, Dave. "Lefty O'Doul's, the Last Great Sports Bar." *Chicago Sun-Times*, August 31, 2003.

Holtzman, Jerome. "Arch Ward: The Father of the All-Star Game Was an Enterprising Sportswriter." Publication and date missing, National Baseball Hall of Fame Library archives.

"Hubbell Was King on July 2, 1933." Publication and date missing, National Baseball Hall of Fame Library archives.

Hulkenberg, John. "Baseball Is a Little More Rich with Woody English." *Reynoldsburg News*, July 24, 1996.

"In the Wake of the News." *Chicago Tribune*, December 15, 1933.

Kessler, Gene. "Joe Cronin's Funniest Story." *Chicago Daily Times*, November 16, 1933.

King, Joe. "His First American League Hit Pleased Bartell Most." *New York World-Telegram*, 1942, National Baseball Hall of Fame Library archives.

Lieb, Fred. "There Were Stories about Babe Ruth That Were Never Written." *St. Petersburg Times*, January 30, 1975.

Livingston, Pat. "Traynor Dies ... The End Of A Living Legend." *Pittsburgh Press*, March 17, 1972.

Meany, Tom. "Cronin Proves Real Hero." *New York World-Telegram*, October 3, 1933.

"Mercer's Suicide." *Boston Globe*, January 14, 1903.

Monroe, Al. "Speaking of Sports." *Chicago Defender*, August 19, 1933.

"More Tributes to Ward From Nation Leaders." *Chicago Tribune*, July 11, 1955.

Morrissey, Rick. "Arch Would Approve." *Chicago Tribune*, July 13, 2003.

"Negroes Meet in All-Star Game Sept. 10. *Chicago Tribune*, August 15, 1993.

Pegler, Westbrook. "All-Star Game Just What Doctor Ordered For Baseball." *Chicago Tribune*, June 20, 1933.

"Pitcher Mercer Ends His Life." *Chicago Tribune*, January 14, 1903.

Powers, Francis J. "The Score Card — McGraw Hated American League." *Chicago Daily American*, January 20, 1944.

Purdy, Mark. "Thanks, Arch, For Being A Sportswriter." *San Jose Mercury News*, July 14, 1987.

Roberts, Ric. "Now in Baseball's Hall of Fame." *Pittsburgh Courier*, date missing, National Baseball Hall of Fame Library archives.

Rogers, Phil. "A 'Classic' Shake-up." *Chicago Tribune*, January 11, 2003.

Rumill, Ed. "Grove Looks Back: Developed Speed Throwing Rocks." *Christian Science Monitor*, date missing, National Baseball Hall of Fame Library archives.

"Sam West's Whip." *Washington Post*, 1929, National Baseball Hall of Fame Library archives.

Singelais, Neil. "After 57 Years, Berger's Mark About to Fall." *Boston Globe*, date missing, National Baseball Hall of Fame Library archives.

"Sports World Mourns Arch Ward; Rites Tuesday." *Chicago Tribune*, July 10, 1955.

Vaughn, Irving. "Players Prove Stars Can Star With Strangers." *Chicago Tribune*, July 7, 1933.

"Votes Show Bill Is West's Ace Pitcher." *Chicago Tribune*, September 9, 1933.

Wallace, William. "Ben Chapman, 84, All-Star Outfielder With Yanks in '30s." *New York Times*, July 8, 1993.

Ward, Arch. "Picked Stars of Big Leagues To Play July 6." *Chicago Tribune*, May 19, 1933.

_____. "$500 In Prizes for Naming Inter-League Lineups." *Chicago Tribune*, May 20, 1933.

_____. "Votes Pour In On Baseball's Biggest Game." *Chicago Tribune*, May 21, 1933.

_____. "47 Newspapers Join Tribune To Pick Best Teams." *Chicago Tribune*, May 22, 1933.

_____. "Simmons Leads Ruth In American League Poll." *Chicago Tribune*, May 24, 1933.

_____. "White Sox To Accept Ticket Orders June 1." *Chicago Tribune*, May 27, 1933.

_____. "Babe Ruth Eager To Play in Game of Century." *Chicago Tribune*, May 28, 1933.

_____. "Hubbell Gains on Lon Warneke in Baseball Poll." *Chicago Tribune*, May 29, 1933.

_____. "Gehrig and Cronin Appear Certain of All-Star Berths." *Chicago Tribune*, June 5, 1933.

_____. "Leagues Spar for Advantage in Big Game." *Chicago Tribune*, June 9, 1933.

_____. "O'Doul, Averill May Lose Out In All-Star Game." *Chicago Tribune*, June 11, 1933.

_____. "Heydler Picks Men According To Fans' Vote." *Chicago Tribune*, June 23, 1933.

_____. "Al Leads Ruth, Klein In Total For Star Game." *Chicago Tribune*, June 25, 1933.

_____. "Every Player Chosen By Fans Gets A Place." *Chicago Tribune*, June 27, 1933.

_____. "Open Bleacher Seat Sale at 10 a.m. Tomorrow." *Chicago Tribune*, July 2, 1933.

White, Paul. "Gashouser 72 Today and Still A Hero," *Binghamton Press*, August 4, 1974.

Williams, Joe. "That Inter-League Scrap Shows 'Em the Difference; It's 'The Old Fat Fellow.'" *New York World-Telegram*, July 7, 1933.

_____. "Al Crowder, Symphony in Tattooing, Adds Picturesque Touch to Conflict." *New York World-Telegram*, October 4, 1933.

_____. "League Prospers Because of Yanks, Says Harridge." *New York World-Telegram*, 1939, National Baseball Hall of Fame Library archives.

Woodruff, Harvey. "American Stars With Game of Century." *Chicago Tribune*, July 7, 1933.

Periodical Articles

Albaugh, Dan. "Ben Chapman: Jackie Robinson's Worst Nightmare," *Sports Collectors Digest*, September 26, 1997.

Calhoun, Steve. "Where Are They Now? Tony Cuccinello." *Sports Collectors Digest*, October 30, 1983.

Calhoun, W.A. "Vale, Winnie Mercer." *Sporting Life*, January 31, 1903.

Drebinger, John. "Baseball World Mourns Passing of McGraw, 'The Greatest Manager of Them All." *New York Times*, February 26, 1934.

"Hall of Famer Lefty Grove Leaves Record of 300 Pitching Victories." *Sporting News*, June 14, 1975.

"He Learned His Trade in the Phillippines." *Baseball Magazine*, January 1929.

Henkey, Ben. "Giant Great Terry Is Dead at 90." *Sporting News*, January 23, 1989.

Hirsley, Michael. "11-Year-Old Newsboy Pete Pervan Was Stunned When He Was Invited to Watch 1st All-Star Game." *Chicago Tribune*, July 11, 2003.

"Historically Speaking: Oscar Charleston." *Black Sports Magazine*, March 1976.

"It's Last Inning in the Big Contest for Free Trip to All-Star Game." *Sporting News*, June 22, 1933.

Kelley, Brent. "Former Cubs Shortstop Woody English Interviewed." *Sports Collectors Digest*, July 27, 1990.

Kuenster, John. "Warmup Tosses." *Baseball Digest*, July 1973.

Lane, F.C. "An All-Star Baseball Contest for a Greater Championship." *Baseball Magazine*, July 1915.

_____. "A Great Player's Heavy Handicap." *Baseball Magazine*, March 1933.

Leutzinger, Richard. "Historical Perspective: Lefty O'Doul." Publication and date missing, National Baseball Hall of Fame Library archives.

Lewis, Jerry D. "Gomez Crusades Against Gloom Strong As Ever." *Sporting News*, February 25, 1978.

Lieb, Frederick G. "Nation Mourns Ruth: Game's Most Famous Star Dies at 53." *Sporting News*, August 25, 1948.

_____. "Paul Waner, 3,000-Hit Hall of Famer, Dead." *Sporting News*, September 11, 1965.

Martin, Wayne. "'Sure, We Rode Jackie,' Says Chapman." *Sporting News*, March 24, 1973.

McBride, John. "The Thrill of a Lifetime for a Kid." *Sporting News*, 1983 All-Star Special, July 1983.

McCullough, Bill. "The Meal Ticket." *Baseball Magazine*, date missing, National Baseball Hall of Fame Library archives.

McDonald, Jack. "King Carl Crown Price of All-Stars." *Sporting News*, July 11, 1964.

"McGraw and Mack to Match Wits Fourth Time in All-Star Game." *Sporting News*, June 8, 1993.

"Mercer's Luck: The Treasurer of the Base Ball Tourists Narrowly Escapes Being Mulcted of All the Velvet." *Sporting Life*, December 20, 1902.

Munzel, Edgar. "Harridge Dead; President of A.L. for 27 Years." *Sporting News*, April 24, 1971.

Nash, Ogden. "Lineup For Yesterday." *Sport*, January 1949.

Nightengale, Dave. "Comiskey: Still a Pitchers' Haven." *Sporting News*, 1983 All-Star Special, July 1983.

"Pepper Martin — Firebrand of Gashouse Gang." *Sporting News*, March 26, 1965.

Reidenbaugh, Lowell. "Memories…The 15 Surviving Members of the First All-Star Game Remember The Big Event." *Sporting News*, 1983 All-Star Special, July 1983.

Reynolds, Quentin. "McGraw's Boy," *Collier's Magazine*, June 29, 1935.

_____. "I Can Hit Pretty Good." *Collier's Magazine*, July 1937.

Spink, C. Johnson. "We Believe…Birth of All-Star Game." *Sporting News*, July 15, 1978.

_____. "Hall of Famer Gehringer Called 'Perfect Player.'" *Sporting News*, May 11, 1949.

Twombley, Wells. "First All-Star Game Shocker — Gomez Got Hit and RBI." *Sporting News*, July 26, 1973.

Unger, Rudolph. "The Chicago Tribune News Staff 1920s-1960s," 1991.

"Was Mercer Murdered?" *Sporting Life*, January 18, 1903.

"Wild Bill Hallahan." *Sporting News*, July 25, 1981.

Websites

Baseball Alamanc, *www.baseballalmanac.com*.

Bodley, Hal. "Economic State May Affect Spending." MLB.com, October 17, 2008.

Macgranachan, Brendan. "Addie Joss' Benefit Game." Seamheads.com, July 25, 2009.

Official Web Site of Lou Gehrig, *http://www.lougehrig.com/about/quotes/htm*.

Wire Services

Associated Press. "Arch Ward, the Originator of All-Star Games, Is Dead." July 9, 1955.

_____. "Old Pros Help All-Star Promotion." May 7, 1987.

Robinson, Pat. "Baseball World Mourns — Lou Gehrig Is Dead at 37." International News Service, June 2, 1941.

United Press International. "Al Simmons, Ball Player, Dead; Noted Hitter Was in Hall of Fame." May 27, 1956.

Press Releases

Chicago Cubs (undated).
Major League Baseball, June 24, 1983.
Major League Baseball, February 13, 1974.

Index